World Economy
Book Series
Volume 7

The European Crisis

Titles produced by the World Economics Association & College Publications

Volume 3
Developing an economics for the post-crisis world
Steve Keen

Volume 4
On the use and misuse of theories and models in mainstream economics
Lars Pålsson Syll

Volume 5
Green Capitalism. The God that Failed
Richard Smith

Volume 6
40 Critical Pointers for Students of Economics
Stuart Birks

Volume 7
The European Crisis
Victor Beker and Beniamino Moro, eds.

The **World Economics Association (WEA)** was launched on May 16, 2011. Already over 13,000 economists and related scholars have joined. This phenomenal success has come about because the WEA fills a huge gap in the international community of economists – the absence of a professional organization which is truly international and pluralist.

The World Economics Association seeks to increase the relevance, breadth and depth of economic thought. Its key qualities are worldwide membership and governance, and inclusiveness with respect to: (a) the variety of theoretical perspectives; (b) the range of human activities and issues which fall within the broad domain of economics; and (c) the study of the world's diverse economies.

The Association's activities centre on the development, promotion and diffusion of economic research and knowledge and on illuminating their social character.

The WEA publishes 20+ books a year, three open-access journals (*Economic Thought, World Economic Review* and *Real-World Economics Review*), a bi-monthly newsletter, blogs, holds global online conferences, runs a textbook commentaries project and an eBook library.

www.worldeconomicassociation.org

The European Crisis

Edited by

Victor Beker

and

Beniamino Moro

© Individual authors, WEA and College Publications 2016.
All rights reserved.

ISBN 978-1-84890-208-4 print
ISBN 978-1-911156-32-1 eBook-PDF

Published by College Publications (London) on behalf of the World Economics Association (Bristol)

http://www.worldeconomicsassociation.org
http://www.collegepublications.co.uk

Cover photo by Kyla Rushman
Cover design by Laraine Welch
Printed by Lightning Source, Milton Keynes, UK

All rights reserved. No part of this publication may be reproduced, stored in a retrieval system or transmitted in any form, or by any means, electronic, mechanical, photocopying, recording or otherwise without prior permission, in writing, from the publisher.

Contents

Foreword from the WEA Conference Books Series editor   1
Maria Alejandra Madi

Acknowledgements   5

Introduction   7
Victor A. Beker and Beniamino Moro

Chapter 1   15
The euro, long-run convergence and the impact of the crises
Enrico Marelli and Marcello Signorelli

Chapter 2   47
A euro area government – A dream come true?
Tom Vleeschhouwer and Tara Koning

Chapter 3   83
Parallel currencies, Varoufakis' plan B and the ongoing debate on euro
Jacques Sapir

Chapter 4   113
The euro area's experience with unconventional monetary policy
Cristiano Boaventura Duarte and André de Melo Modenesi

Chapter 5   145
Greece: conditions and strategies for economic recovery
Dimitri B. Papadimitriou, Michalis Nikiforos and Gennaro Zezza

Chapter 6   177
Economic policy and political power in European crises
Gerson P. Lima

Chapter 7 201
**At the root of economic fluctuations: expectations,
preferences and innovation. Theoretical framework and
empirical evidences**
Carmelo Ferlito

Chapter 8 251
Unemployment around the North Atlantic, 1948-2014
Merijn Knibbe

Conclusions 272
Victor A. Beker and Beniamino Moro

About the editors and the authors 281

Foreword from the WEA Books Conference Series editor

The book *The economics curriculum: towards a radical reformation* is, appropriately, the first in our series and it is an outcome of the WEA Online Conference that took place in May–June 2013. The first book was written within the spirit of global effort at fundamental change in economics education. One of the main ideas underlined throughout the book, that was designed by Grazia Ietto-Gillies, is that "being an economist" in the 21st century requires a radical change in the training of economists.

Openness and flexibility are major trends in contemporary education, research, and business, influencing the whole spectrum of institutions and corporations across the globe. Indeed, technological innovations are bringing about a paradigm shift in contemporary livelihoods. Modes of interaction are becoming more open and flexible in terms of time, space, organization, infrastructure and requirements. With this background, the World Economics Association organizes conferences which are held online. The WEA practice of holding digital conferences on special topics followed by books, especially topics of current importance, aims to support the development of research and to enhance its social nature in an inclusive and pluralistic context.

This WEA book *The European Crisis* addresses monetary, financial and debt issues, alongside the questions of social stabilization, strategies for structural reform and economic growth that may be re-considered to frame new economic perspectives for Europe. Indeed, the problems and issues around the future of the European Union are among the most pressing ones of our times since the current European economic, social and political challenges are intricately related to the process of financial globalization.

The European crisis

From 1971 to 2008, there was the expansion of the age of high finance where the U.S. deficits have been at the center of the global economic order. In the system of international economic flows built after the 1970s, the whole world surpluses aimed to finance the unsustainable expansion of a double deficit on which the U.S. built its political and economic hegemony. The American trade surplus turned into a large and increasing deficit that joined the government deficit to form the twin deficits. However, without the Wall Street institutions recycling the global surpluses, the U.S. had not been able to hold its twin deficits. Indeed, the new global order after the 1970s was supported thanks to the close collaboration of the expansion of high finance overwhelmed by the political power of economic neo-liberalism. Besides, the global expansion of corporations and supply chains enhanced business models based on increasingly lower wages. As a result, the global surplus recycling mechanism reversed the flow of global trade and capital flows: the United States provided sufficient demand for manufacturing in foreign countries – mainly China – in return for capital inflows. As a matter of fact, between 1971 and 2008, the era of high finance, supported the expansion of global trade at the cost of financial bubbles, corporate mega-profits and increasing social inequalities. In this scenario, mainstream economics supported the free market efficiency discourse.

Looking back, the launch of the last phase of the European Monetary Union, in 1999, constituted a major step aiming at a higher level of convergence in national economic policies. According to the European Central Bank, the macroeconomic stability would rely on the financial integration of the euro-area economy. In order to qualify to be a member, a country needed to satisfy the Maastricht's requirements to achieve the targets relative to inflation, long-term interest rates, government deficits and exchange rates.
The immediate impacts of the 2008 global crisis provoked a fall in the levels of production, investment and employment in addition to liquidity constraints in credit and capital markets. Soon after the crisis, the responses put in place by both European Union officials and national member states mainly aimed to prevent the financial markets from collapsing.

According to the International Monetary Fund (IMF), the financial crisis revealed the economic unbalances inside the Euro area between different productive structures and unit labour costs. Under the pressure of the

Foreword

sovereign debt crisis and the Troika recommendations, Greece, as well as Portugal and Spain, among other countries, have undergone painful adjustments, mainly through deflationary policies and further market flexibilization.

In truth, the social and political costs of the austerity policies bear the seeds for rethinking the European economic and social sustainability. These policies have proved to be devastating, not only socially and politically, but economically as well, as they quickly affected the evolution of effective demand and the possibilities of economic growth. Fiscal austerity has been a risky strategy as tight fiscal policies mainly result in even weaker economic growth and a higher debt/GDP rate. In addition, the migration crisis has put pressure on the European Union's commitment to human rights and open borders.

As the fundamental structural flaws in the European Union have still not been addressed, one decisive challenge is certainly the asymmetry of power between "creditor" and "debtor" countries. The result of the recent British European Union referendum certainly added new risks for the region as the Brexit may lead to a decisive shift in the balance of power within the euro-zone.

The current volume is one of the outcomes from a conference on *The European Crisis*. It was led by Victor A. Beker and Beniamino Moro and took place in October–December 2015. We hope that the volume will make a contribution to the debate towards the search for new economic policy solutions to promote positive effects on economic activity and reduce social inequalities. We are very grateful to Victor and Beniamino for developing this volume.

Maria Alejandra Madi
Chair, WEA Conferences and Editor of the WEA Books Conference Series
July 2016

The European crisis

Acknowledgements

We are grateful to the World Economics Association (WEA) for giving us the opportunity to organize and lead an online conference on *The European Crisis*, and to develop this e-book from it
http://europeancrisis2015.weaconferences.net/

We benefitted from many of the open comments that the conference attracted and we would like to thank the following contributors to the debate: Ayoub, Bob Williams, M. C. Morley, M. M. van Wijck, Pasbaxo, Henk Vrooman, Mstislav Afanasiev, Renaud Bouchard, Panayotis Econmopoulos, Garrett Connelly, Laszlo Kulin, and Rudolf T. Z. Sche.

A special thanks to Maria Alejandra Madi, the Chair of the WEA Conference Programme. She has given us encouragement and support throughout the conference and the edition of this e-book. Also a special thanks to Jake McMurchie and Malgorzata Dereniowska for all their support during the Conference organization and through the Discussion Forum.

The European crisis

Introduction
Victor A. Beker and Beniamino Moro

The origins of the European debt crisis can be directly traced back to the global financial crisis of 2007–2009, which spilled over into a sovereign debt crisis in several euro area countries in early 2010. To offset sharp falls in output, euro area governments (as governments in the rest of the world) responded with counter-cyclical fiscal policies that increased fiscal deficits. Moreover, fiscal positions worsened as tax revenues declined and transfer payments grew larger due to rising unemployment during the crisis. In many countries, government bailouts of banking systems also contributed to an increase in public debt. Private debt became public debt, be it through banking crises or the burst of housing bubbles, leading to sovereign crisis.

The debt crisis in several member states of the euro area has raised doubts about the viability of the European Economic and Monetary Union (EMU) and the future of the euro. The crisis has highlighted the problems and tensions that will inevitably arise within a monetary union when imbalances build up and become unsustainable.

The European crisis has shown that crises can spread quickly among closely integrated economies. The implementation of austerity policies, prompted by the Troika (European Commission, European Central Bank and the IMF) have reinforced a spiral of economic contractions, and provoked a rising political rebellion against austerity, inspired in part (and especially in Spain, but also to a certain degree in Greece) by the successful exit from crisis of the South American countries in the past decade.

As far as banking crises are concerned, it had been understood that they could occur also within the EMU. But what was not understood was that the combination of strong interdependence between banks and sovereigns and the absence of a lender of last resort for sovereigns made euro area countries particularly prone to such crises.

The potential severity of what would become known as the 'doom loop' was not foreseen. Furthermore, the EU relied on a rather loose framework of cooperation between national authorities, and lacked a comprehensive template for dealing with cross-border issues. The generally prevailing view was that sovereign debt crises – also because of the prohibition of monetary financing – could occur. A substantial body of literature had emphasized that sovereign solvency would be a concern in a monetary union and that crises had to be prevented through fiscal surveillance. But no framework existed for such an eventuality and its potentially serious consequences.

In setting up the EU policy framework, the focus was on crisis prevention mainly through the Stability and Growth Pact (SGP) and other surveillance mechanisms. No thought was given to crisis management. In addition, until 2010, interpretations of the meaning of Article 125 of the EU Treaty (the no-bail out clause) differed in different countries and institutions, but these interpretations were not discussed, let alone reconciled.

Finally, balances of payments (BOP) crises were deemed impossible since solvent agents within a country would always retain access to private funding. BOP crises were in fact ruled out by most authors.

An important element that much contributed to the European crisis was the mispricing of sovereign risk by capital markets and an ensuing misallocation of capital in the decade before the outbreak of the crisis. This had the effect of giving wrong incentives to policymakers. In fact, during the boom years, when financial markets were blind to the sovereign risks, no incentives were given to policy makers to reduce their debts, as the latter were priced so favorably. Since the start of the financial crisis, financial markets driven by panic overpriced risks and gave incentives to policymakers to introduce excessive austerity programmes.

A high level of public debt is not a problem *per se*, as long as the government is able to refinance itself and roll over its debt. This requires public debt and the interest burden to grow more slowly than the economy

Introduction

and the tax base. This is not the case in many peripheral European countries. Therefore, today's debt crisis is not merely a debt crisis; it is first and foremost a competitiveness and growth crisis that has led to structural imbalances within the euro area. In fact, below the surface of the sovereign public debt and banking crises lies a balance of payments crisis, caused by a misalignment of internal real exchange rates.

Since the European Monetary Union (EMU) has been built as a union of sovereign states, each state has retained its own national central bank, which has become a member of the so-called Eurosystem with the European Central Bank (ECB) at the top. National interbank payment systems have been merged into a euro area interbank payment system (TARGET2), where national central banks have assumed the role of the links between countries.

So, TARGET2 plays a key role in ensuring the smooth conduct of monetary policy, the correct functioning of financial markets, and banking and financial stability in the euro area, by substantially reducing systemic risk. The settlement of cross-border payments between participants in TARGET2 results in intra-Eurosystem balances – that is, positions on the balance sheets of the respective central banks that reflect claims/liabilities on/to the Eurosystem. They are reported on the National Central Banks' (NCB) balance sheets as TARGET2 claims, if positive, or TARGET2 liabilities, if negative, *vis-à-vis* the ECB as the central counterpart. TARGET2 balances reflect funding stress in the banking systems of crisis-hit countries, which must be interpreted with caution as they also reflect transactions among multi-country banking groups.

The tensions in sovereign debt markets and within the banking sector have fed each other, creating severe funding problems for many borrowers. These developments have also led to the fragmentation of the financial system along national borders, with a retrenchment of financial activities to national domestic markets. The resulting limited or costly access to funding for many businesses and households wishing to invest has been a major obstacle to recovery across Europe.

The European crisis

At the same time, high levels of indebtedness mean that many economic actors need to reduce their financial exposure or increase their savings. Such "deleveraging" can also hamper recovery in the short term. The problems are particularly acute in the vulnerable euro area member states.

Currently, the unconventional monetary policies implemented by the ECB (LTROs, TLTROs and quantitative easing policies) succeeded in overcoming the European financial Great Crisis. Anyway, the rate of growth in the Eurozone still remains a half than that in the US. Therefore, one possibility to definitely overcome also the economic crisis is to launch a new phase of growth and promote a substantial increase in European employment.

In the medium term, there is a widespread consent that a successful policy will need to include at least the following four components: 1) a fiscal union, i.e. a mechanism that ensures that fiscal policies in the Eurozone are partly centralized; 2) a banking union, i.e. a framework for banking policy and banking supervision at the European level; 3) an overhaul of EU/Eurozone institutions that would enable fiscal and banking unions to be sustainable; and, finally, 4) short-term arrangements that chart a path towards the completion of the previous three programs.

Anyway, in the short term, there exists a safe policy to promote growth in the European Union that can be implemented without interfering in the fiscal consolidation needs of the austerity-hit southern countries. This aim may be pursued if Germany does not maintain its public budget in balance for next few years and commits itself to promote an expansionary fiscal policy. In fact, Germany is the only country in the EU that can expand its aggregate demand without paying a substantial increase in domestic inflation.

In order to expand European aggregate demand in the measure necessary to promote growth, Germany could also let domestic wages increase. The combined effects of the two policies (budget deficit plus wage increases) and the ensuing moderate increase in domestic inflation could be sufficient to appreciate the real exchange rate in Germany, permitting the austerity-hit EMU countries to regain their external competitiveness vis-à-vis surplus countries.

Introduction

The WEA online conference

Between October 1st and December 1st, 2015, the World Economics Association (WEA) organized an online Conference to analyze the current crisis in the countries of the Eurozone. This volume contains the papers presented and discussed at the Conference.

Enrico Marelli and Marcello Signorelli analyze two different issues concerning economic performances and policies in Europe after the introduction of euro: the long-run real economic convergence (or divergence) across Eurozone countries and the impact of the recent crisis. Regarding the first issue, the results show that the role of the monetary union in favoring real convergence is disputable. As regards the second issue, their opinion is that the austerity measures undertaken in the area, especially in the peripheral countries, have caused a prolonged recession, stagnation and persistent unemployment. They conclude that radical reforms are needed in the EU institutions and governance – in particular to guarantee a viable monetary union and favor real convergence of its economies – as well as changes in the current macroeconomic policies.

Tom Vleeschhouwer and *Tara Koning* study three important problems that have led to or have aggravated the euro crisis: moral hazard in accumulating debt by sovereigns, lack of macroeconomic policy coordination and stabilization, and macroeconomic imbalances. They use both theoretical and empirical evidence to argue that these problems were largely caused by coordination problems. They then investigate whether a supranational government, a layer of government above all euro member countries, can alleviate these problems. They find that macroeconomic stabilization and macroeconomic imbalances can be improved by such a government, though moral hazard cannot be solved. The only, but certainly not insignificant, obstacle seems to be that politicians and voters may not be willing to transfer their authority to this government.

Jacques Sapir argues that the last round of the Greek crisis has put on the forefront the issue of the Euro. According to him, the European Monetary Union has turned into an instrument of enforcement of austerity and deflation all over the Eurozone. The crisis ended temporarily with an agreement that was forced upon the Greek government but it will have enduring consequences, he warns. However, he understands that in the process of this crisis the possibility of another way has emerged. What has been called "Yanis Varoufakis' plan B" was an attempt to create a parallel payment system, and possibly a parallel currency. It was not intended to be a short road for Greece to return to the Drachma, but it could have been so. Sapir's paper studies the process of this so-called "plan B" in the light of previous experiments with parallel currencies.

Cristiano Boaventura Duarte and *André de Melo Modenesi* discuss the role of monetary policies implemented by the European Central Bank (ECB) after the 2008 financial crisis, with a special focus on unconventional measures, analyzing to what extent they influenced Euro area's macroeconomic performance in the period. For the authors, the ECB stimulus programs conveyed a strong commitment to fight deflation, and led to positive effects on several macroeconomic indicators (sovereign yields, euro exchange rate, credit, output, inflation), although with some volatility on yields and the euro. Nevertheless, serious problems remain for households (high levels of indebtedness and unemployment), enterprises (challenges for investment, financial volatility) and governments (fiscal, political and institutional constraints). It is argued that the path for a sustained growth recovery in the Euro area not only goes through unconventional monetary policies. According to the authors, they should also be complemented by a coordinated fiscal policy, more flexible (and countercyclical) in periods of economic downturns, coupled with adequate institutional reforms that foster credit markets, encourage private and public investments in the long term and reduce regional asymmetries. Additionally, they believe that a more robust and integrated financial supervisory framework (not only on banking but also on capital, insurance and pension markets) would contribute to reduce negative spillovers from financial volatility episodes, break the sovereign-bank "doom loop" and bring more financial stability to the zone.

Dimitri B. Papadimitriou, Michalis Nikiforos and *Gennaro Zezza* focus on the Greek crisis. They argue that access to alternative financing sources such as zero-coupon bonds ("Geuros") and fiscal credit certificates could provide the impetus and liquidity needed to push economic growth and create jobs. They discuss two proposals to fund a programme of direct job creation;

Introduction

neither proposal requires access to liquidity in euro, and both are compatible with the EU treaties and the current rules regulating monetary issues. But there are preconditions - they warn -: the existing government debt must be rolled over and austerity policies put aside, restoring trust in the country's economic future and setting the stage for sustainable income growth, which will eventually enable Greece to repay its debt.

Gerson P. Lima analyses the European Union crisis assuming that the economy is commanded by a veiled political power linked to the financial market. He argues that a financial crisis is the consequence of financial capital supply excess, especially money supply excess, leading to risky operations and financial capital losses internally and abroad. An experiment with US data done by the author is quoted to support the idea that the origin of the past and future American financial crises is the money printed to pay interest on the US public debt. It is also observed that fiscal policy does not cause inflation for it is not always expansive and higher prices in this case are indication that people's wealth increased. The European Union is said to have two crises: the general one affecting almost all countries, where monetary policy prevails, and its particular crisis, where the risk of dismantling is due to potential state members' bankrupts. Lima's conclusion is that there are evidences to support Hellinger's proposal for a parallel currency issued by state-members to make local fiscal policy possible. It is finally stated that even if this proposal is attractive to decision makers it must be, as any other economic policy, interesting to the political power and preserve democracy.

Carmelo Ferlito's paper aims to develop the Austrian Theory of Business Cycle in order to conclude that economic fluctuations are unavoidable. The conventional version of Austrian business cycle theory focuses on a temporary imbalance between natural and monetary rates of interest. When, because of the role of monetary authorities in defining the monetary rate, the two values are in a situation of imbalance, the resulting expansion stage is followed by a recession. On the other hand, if the expansive phase arises without any interference by monetary authorities but through re-adaptation of the productive structure to a modified structure of temporal preferences, a period of sustainable growth begins that will not be followed by a crisis. The purpose of this essay is to demonstrate, however, that because of profit-expectations and the combined action of Schumpeterian elements (imitations-speculations and the 'creation of money' by banks), even a so-called 'sustainable' boom will be affected by a liquidation and settling crisis. What distinguishes the latter situation from the conventional case of imbalance between monetary and natural interest rates is not the onset or otherwise of a crisis, but rather its intensity and duration.

Merijn Knibbe argues that flow data on the labor market show that during crises there is a temporary and relatively small increase of inflows into unemployment and a decrease of outflows out of unemployment, which, however, combine into a fast increase in the stock of unemployment. This evidence shows that major crises tend to shift countries to a semi-permanent situation of higher unemployment. Instead of countering this situation, after 2008 public policies aimed at increased levels of 'discipline' led by EU institutions. At the same time, government transfers to banks increased, leading to a deterioration of government balances and leaving less room for government spending. For the author, the solution proposed by Mitchell and Muysken – a job guarantee financed by money printing and shredding – might still be a good idea but has to be accompanied by a central bank buying bad debts from banks; while, considering the high levels of unemployment, allocation of unemployed over the guaranteed jobs might have to be enhanced by using the same kind of planning algorithms which are, at the moment, used to match donor kidneys with patients.

Chapter 1
The euro, long-run convergence and the impact of the crises
Enrico Marelli and Marcello Signorelli

1. Introduction

More than fifteen years have passed since euro's birth. In the first ten years (1999-2008) the European monetary union (EMU) was characterized by an overall macroeconomic stability, low inflation and calmness in financial markets. The Global financial crisis (2007-08) with the Great Recession (2008-09) and the following sovereign debt crisis (2010-14) have not only caused a "double-dip" recession in many Eurozone countries, but also produced a long-lasting impact on real economies, especially because of the rising and persistent unemployment.

In this chapter, we analyse two different issues concerning economic performance and policies in Europe after the introduction of euro: the long-run real economic convergence (or divergence) across Eurozone countries and the impact of the mentioned crises. Regarding the first issue, we briefly review the relevant economic theories – with particular reference to "Optimal currency area" (OCA) theories; then we accomplish some empirical analyses to assess the extent of long-run economic convergence, the similarity of economic cycles and trade integration within the euro area. Our work partly integrates some recent research on ex-post assessments of developments in the EMU based on OCA's and related theories. Our results show that the role of the EMU in favouring real convergence is disputable.

Moreover, this union has proved to be fragile after the recent economic shocks: this is the second issue dealt with in the paper. In particular, the austerity measures undertaken to face the sovereign debt crisis, especially in the peripheral countries, have caused a prolonged recession, stagnation and persistent unemployment.

The structure of the chapter is as follows. In section 2 we review the original features and weaknesses of EMU and we emphasize how such construction fails to match the well-known requisites of the "optimum currency areas". In section 3 we present our empirical analyses on real convergence, by focusing on beta convergence (absolute and extended), on the similarity of business cycles and on trade integration. In section 4 we discuss the events following the crises in the Eurozone and we critically evaluate the macroeconomic policies that have been followed at the EU and national levels. The concluding section emphasizes the radical reforms required at the European level for a viable "economic and monetary union" and the needed changes in current macroeconomic policies.

2. EMU, "Optimal Currency Area" conditions and real convergence

As well known, the Maastricht Treaty fixed the steps required to realize an Economic and Monetary Union by 1999. In the integration process, the EMU was considered as an instrument to achieve the final goals of the EU itself.[1] Such final goals implicitly include a "real" convergence, i.e. a convergence in economic performances of individual member States, allowing the achievement of similar performances of real variables as well as the catching-up of backward countries and regions.

Therefore the Maastricht Treaty has purported the view that nominal convergence[2] is a pre-requisite for candidate countries to enter the EMU, that in the long-run would lead to real economic convergence.[3] On the

---

[1] Including "economic and social progress, a high level of employment, balanced and sustainable development" (as stated in the article 2 of the Treaty).
[2] The justification for nominal convergence criteria has been critically assessed by many authors (e.g. Buiter, 2004; De Grauwe and Schnabl, 2005). In particular, the excessive insistence on fiscal conditions has been criticized (Buiter et al, 1993).
[3] The Maastricht convergence criteria (on inflation, interest rate, exchange rate, public deficit and debt) were, for the first time, verified in 1998, allowing to define a list of 11 members that in January 1999 gave birth to EMU, that now comprises 19 members. The following countries joined in the subsequent years: Greece (2001),

contrary, well-known economic theories – see the literature on "optimum currency areas" (OCA)[4] – maintain that the similarity in real economic conditions of candidate countries is a requirement to accomplish an effective monetary union; in fact, the homogeneity in economic structures makes more symmetric the economic shocks, so real variables tend to respond more similarly to possible economic shocks.

Moreover, the adjustment aftershocks would be easier, even in monetary unions (where the use of the exchange rate instrument is excluded), in presence of an adequate degree of flexibility in prices and wages, high labour mobility and a sufficiently centralized public budget.

When the EMU project was launched, in the '90s of last century, many economists doubted that such conditions of "real economic similarity" were satisfied in the EU. A complementary question, once the policy decision to start the EMU was taken, was whether real convergence would be likely to increase or decrease as a consequence of the integration process. Krugman (1993), for example, was pessimist and argued that economic integration is likely to cause increasing specialisation, diverging economic structures, asymmetric developments, and widening differences in growth rates.[5]

According to a more optimistic view (sustained by EU institutions) convergence is instead a probable outcome of monetary unification, thanks to macroeconomic stability (price stability and fiscal discipline), the removal of the exchange-rate risk, the reduction of uncertainty (concerning inflation and interest rates), the encouragement of investment and international trade, eventually leading to stronger economic growth.[6] In particular, the hope for formerly "deviating" countries was that they could be rewarded by the gains of EMU itself: disinflation and financial stability, lower interest rates and debt service.[7]

Slovenia (2007), Cyprus and Malta (2008), Slovakia (2009), Estonia (2011), Latvia (2014), and Lithuania (2015).
[4] The seminal works are by Mundell (1961), McKinnon (1963), Kenen (1969).
[5] For a more recent assessment, see Krugman (2012a). The emphasis on sector specialisation was originally placed also by Kenen (1969).
[6] See European Commission (1990) and also Buti and Sapir (1998).
[7] These gains should be added to the general benefits of monetary unions, in terms of lower transaction costs, lesser uncertainty, reinforced competition, etc.

The European crisis

Thus, a rejoinder to the pessimistic view was that the degree of similarity of economic systems could be enhanced by the integration process itself: increased competition, integration of markets, liberalisation of capital flows, etc. (see, for an initial account, Eichengreen, 1993). As a matter of fact, the "endogeneity of OCA's criteria" proposition maintains that even if such criteria are not satisfied ex-ante, they come to be endogenously confirmed ex-post: it is the monetary union itself that leads both to trade integration and to "structural convergence".[8]

The "similarity" of different economies has been empirically assessed with different methods. In some empirical studies, for example, the degree of synchronisation of business cycles between countries has been estimated by the computation of correlation coefficients of output or GDP: an increasing correlation of real variables would mean that shocks have become more symmetric across European countries. Real convergence has also been evaluated in terms of per capita income, productivity, labour market indicators, trade links, business cycle behaviour, etc.[9]

As to the most common results, we can say that the synchronicity of business cycles increased, before the recent crises, not only in the European "core" (the countries of Central Europe embracing Germany and the surrounding countries), but also in a wider area including some "peripheral" countries (for example countries in Southern Europe) and even many "new" members of Eastern Europe (NMS). Many empirical studies were carried out both in '90s (to assess the validity of the project before the birth of EMU) and in the new century. Therefore, the general empirical evidence prior to the crises (i.e. until 2007-08) made the concept of a "core" of European countries – more integrated than the "periphery" – less meaningful. Nevertheless, even in that period, some macroeconomic imbalances were mounting, as discussed below.

A more general consideration is that the process of monetary unification decreased economic growth, already in the '90s (De Grauwe, 2007), because of the deflationary effects of restrictive monetary and fiscal policies

---

[8] See the empirical contributions by Frankel and Rose (1998) and Rose (2000).
[9] See the review in Marelli and Signorelli (2010), where the links between real convergence, nominal convergence and institutional convergence are investigated.

undertaken by several countries at the same time. In particular, peripheral countries have been hurt because of the stringency of the Maastricht treaty nominal conditions.[10]

In any case, EU's response to the critiques about the scarce consideration of "economic growth" was the Lisbon Agenda of 2000 (followed by the more recent "Europe 2020" plan adopted in 2010); nevertheless, the quantitative targets that were introduced (e.g. concerning employment rates) were mere benchmarks, much softer than the Maastricht or Growth and Stability Pact (GSP) criteria. Consequently, economic growth has been lower in the EU as a whole in all years of the new century, even before the recent financial crisis, if compared to other leading economies in the world: China, India, most of emerging countries, but also to the United States.

On the other hand, nominal stability and convergence have been satisfactory in the pre-crisis period: e.g., the inflation rate has been in most countries very close to the 2% target set by the European Central Bank (ECB). A bit higher inflation was recorded in fast-growing countries, such as Ireland, Spain, Greece and some NMS. An implication of the different inflation rates is that the same short-term interest rate fixed by the ECB caused lower real interest rates in inflation-prone countries, thus fuelling investment in non-tradable activities as well as asset and housing bubbles. The final implication was a "structural divergence", since the periphery increasingly specialised – before the crises – in non-tradable goods and construction, while the centre was relying on exports and tradable activities (manufactures and services) (see Buti and Turrini, 2015).

Calmness dominated financial markets and interest rates were almost identical everywhere (the spread over the German bonds was 20 or 30 points at the most). The progressive financial integration promoted huge capital flows from the "centre" to the "periphery", favoured by the disappearance of the exchange rate risk and reduced default risk perceptions; in fact, intra-Eurozone private flows of capital, besides

---

[10] It should be noted that the bonus deriving from "nominal" convergence, especially lower interest rates, was not used by all countries to stimulate – also by means of accompanying structural reforms – higher economic growth and/or to improve public accounts sustainability (in countries with high debt levels).

supporting fast economic growth, were a substitute for the missing centralized public budget. However, this quiet environment hided growing (trade and debt) imbalances (in fact after the crises capital flows had a sudden reversal). The rise of debt in the periphery concerned primarily the private debt, rather than the public one; in the meantime, private banks of core countries were progressively exposed toward the periphery.

Concerning the OCA's criteria, we can add that price rigidity in the Eurozone, though still higher than in the US, has actually been decreasing; in fact, structural reforms in the product market have accelerated since euro's adoption (Alesina et al, 2008). The latter authors argue that wage moderation has also increased in the new monetary regime, despite the lack of significant reforms in the primary labour market; however we can add that wage rigidity for newly hired workers is lower and similar to the US's (Pasimeni, 2014). As regards labour, on one hand it is true that the geographical mobility of workers, as an adjustment mechanism to shocks, has increased over time in the EU;[11] but, on the other hand, it is still weaker than in the US (Dao et al., 2014) and too limited to offset the huge rise in unemployment and its persistence. Capital mobility, on the contrary, has been fully realized (Hale and Obstfeld, 2014), although the sovereign debt crisis (see section 4) caused a (temporary) segmentation of the financial markets of Eurozone countries.

The last, but not least, OCA's condition, in addition to the already discussed similarity of business cycles (that will be empirically assessed in the next section), is the fiscal capacity of the EMU. This has probably been the greatest failure of EMU's construction,[12] despite what was suggested by the theories (starting from Kenen, 1969, and many others) and advocated,

---

[11] Also the number of foreign-born residents in each EU country (published by Eurostat) is increasing over time; in particular, the "push" factors from origin countries played a crucial role in the crisis period. Labour out-migration ever more concerned high skilled workers, who frequently migrate to occupy medium or low skilled jobs in the core countries of the EU.

[12] The "major design failure" according to De Grauwe (2013). Notice that while in the US the Federal budget represents about 25% of GDP and the State ones about 10%, in the EU the corresponding figures are about 1% and 50% (not to mention that the Eurozone has not a specific budget). Thus, not only in the EMU is lacking a risk-sharing mechanism, but the additional no bail-out clause of the Maastricht Treaty implies that the impact of asymmetric shocks should have remained national.

already twenty years before the starting of euro, by the MacDougall Report (European Commission, 1977): on this crucial point we shall come back in the Conclusions.

Not only has economic growth been feeble in the EU, especially in the Eurozone, but it has been heterogeneous across the different countries. Overall, a certain degree of convergence has been insured by the catching-up of peripheral countries and many NMS of Central and Eastern Europe; on the contrary, some old members (e.g. Italy and Portugal) exhibited very low rates of growth. Moreover, many peripheral countries – the two mentioned countries with the addition of Spain and Greece – were suffering because of an increasing competitiveness gap; in the decade since 1999, the real exchange rate based on unit labour costs depreciated by about 10% in Germany and appreciated by 10-15% in Italy and Spain.[13] Thus, without the possibility to devalue the national currencies, trade and current account deficits were increasing in those countries, while Germany and the other "core" EU countries exhibited large surpluses.[14]

3. Real economic convergence in the long run: an empirical assessment

In the previous section, we have concluded that, since the euro's birth (1999), financial and macroeconomic stability was dominating the area, at least until the outbreak of the global financial crisis (2008). At the same time, real economic growth has been lower compared to other world partners and diverse across its members. In this section, we present some empirical analyses concerning long-run economic convergence, similarity of business cycles and trade integration within the euro area. This work partly integrates

---

[13] German competitiveness benefited both from productivity increases and from wage moderation, especially following the Hartz reforms (2003-05).
[14] See Berger and Nitsch (2010). Some authors also emphasized a possible link between persistent external imbalances and the sovereign debt risk (Giavazzi and Spaventa, 2010).

some recent research on ex-post assessment of developments in the EMU using OCA's and related theories.[15]

In the literature (Barro and Sala-I-Martin, 1995), both a "sigma convergence" approach, that investigates the evolution over time of some dispersion measures of the relevant variables (for instance GDP capita),[16] and a "beta convergence" approach have been used. Here we focus, first of all, on the *absolute beta-convergence*, by investigating whether GDP per capita of different countries is converging to a unique level. The regression can be specified as follows (*i* identifies an individual country):

$$(1/n) \ln (Y_{it}/Y_{i0}) = \alpha + \beta \ln (Y_{i0}) + \varepsilon$$

where Y is per capita GDP, 0 is the initial year, t the final year and n is the number of years from 0 to t (and ln stands for natural logarithm). If the estimated coefficient β is negative and significant, there is absolute convergence.

We have estimated this regression for the Eurozone countries, using annual per capita GDP data from Eurostat. Our intention was to distinguish between the pre-crisis period (1999-2007) and the crisis period (2008-14); however, for the first two years (1999 and 2000) Eurostat data set has many missing data, thus we prefer to present data for the period starting in 2001 (Table 1). The Eurozone refers to 11 countries for the pre-crisis period and to 19 countries for the crisis period.[17]

---

[15] For instance, Pasimeni (2014) focuses on factors mobility (capital and labour); price and wage flexibility; similarity of business cycles; common fiscal capacity (as a mechanism of shock absorption and risk-sharing).

[16] A recent analysis comparing the Eurozone members and other EU countries can be found in Marelli and Signorelli (2015); in addition to GDP per capita, other real variables (e.g. unemployment) and also nominal variables (interest expenditure, deficit/GDP, debt/GDP, etc.) have been considered.

[17] Although the new members of the Eurozone entered gradually from 2007 to 2015 (see footnote 4), they had to satisfy the requirement of fixed exchange rates (with the euro) for at least two years before entering, but many of them opted for fixed exchange rates even before. Thus, we can consider them all as Eurozone members for the crisis period. Notice that EZ11 refers to the 11 members in 1999 (Greece entered two years later).

The euro, long-run convergence and the impact of the crises

Table 1 shows that for the full period (2001-14) there has been a divergence in per-capita GDP, not statistically significant, for the Eurozone (EZ11); moreover, such divergence was statistically significant (at 5%) in the pre-crisis period. Finally, for the recent wider Eurozone (EZ19) it appears some convergence (significant at 10%): the reason is that some NMS, that recently joined the euro area, were growing fast thanks to their "catching-up".

An extension of the "absolute convergence" approach is based on the fact that for the GDP variable it is possible to get quarterly data; so, in order to exploit the full time-series information, we can adopt an *"extended" beta-convergence* approach (Canova and Marcet, 1995), that estimates some regressions of the following type:

$$(\ln Y_{i,t} - \ln Y_{i,t-1}) = \alpha + \beta \ln Y_{i,t-1} + \varepsilon$$

This specification implies that each country may converge toward its own steady-state; it can be estimated as a pooled regression, with fixed effects, and using as $Y_{i,t}$ the normalized per-capita income, i.e. national per-capita income divided by the average (EZ11 or EZ19) per-capita income: in this way, the lack of time-specific fixed effects can be justified, without jeopardizing the stationarity of the random disturbances.

Table 1 – Convergence in per capita GDP (Beta coefficients)

Absolute convergence (annual data)				Extended beta-convergence (quarterly data)			
Eurozone EZ11			EZ19	Eurozone EZ11			EZ19
Full period^ 2001-2014	Pre-crisis 2001-2007	Crisis 2007-2014	Crisis 2007-2014	Full period^ 2001.1-2015.1	Pre-crisis 2001.1-2007.1	Crisis 2007.1-2015.1	Crisis 2007.1-2015.1
0.0106	0.0114**	0.0051	-0.0119*	-0.0021	0.0007	-0.0032	-0.0058*
				-0.3854***	-0.6440***	-0.5721***	-0.3898***

Significance levels: 1%***, 5%**, 10%*
Source: elaborations on Eurostat data.
^ Note: the data in italics (second row of the Extended beta estimations) refer to estimations with fixed effects. Complete statistical results of the regressions are available upon request.

The results (right side of Table 1) of the estimations without fixed effects are quite similar to the previous ones: in the Eurozone there has not been convergence, apart from a partially significant convergence in the recent period (for the extended Eurozone). On the other hand, the estimations with Fixed Effects show a significant convergence for all groups of countries and for all periods.

Table 2 – Correlation coefficients of GDP growth (quarterly data seasonally adjusted) with European averages (EZ11 and EZ19)

	Correlation with respect to:			
	EZ11			EZ19
	1999.1-2015.1	1999.1-2007.1	2007.1-2015.1	2007.1-2015.1
Original EZ countries (11):	(0.790)	(0.620)	(0.827)	(0.791)
Austria	0.685	0.476	0.730	0.647
Belgium	0.853	0.622	0.915	0.860
Finland	0.846	0.583	0.879	0.883
France	0.880	0.767	0.895	0.856
Germany	0.820	0.612	0.931	0.916
Italy	0.919	0.751	0.939	0.873
Luxembourg	0.647	0.654	0.697	0.607
Netherlands	0.790	0.608	0.806	0.842
Portugal	0.702	0.547	0.721	0.644
Spain	0.760	0.578	0.758	0.784
New EZ countries (19):	(0.550)	(0.157)	(0.554)	(0.623)
Cyprus	0.531	0.511	0.343	0.346
Estonia	0.602	0.172	0.586	0.685^
Greece	0.478	0.133	0.338	0.347^
Latvia	0.367	-0.135	0.333	0.521^
Lithuania	0.756	0.318	0.739	0.840
Malta	0.354	-0.084	0.662	0.701^
Slovenia	0.765	0.185	0.879	0.919^

Note: ^ denotes a coefficient not statistically significant. Source: elaborations on Eurostat data.

The next step in our empirical investigations is to analyse the *similarity in business cycle evolutions*. The simplest way is to compute the *correlation coefficients* of quarterly GDP growth at constant prices (Table 2). We have considered the usual three periods (1999.1-2007.1, 2007.1-2015.1 and the full period). After the computation of the correlation coefficients for individual countries, we have computed the simple means of such coefficients for the two aggregates (shown in parentheses and italics in the table): EZ11 and EZ new members (i.e. the countries joining the Eurozone since 2007).

The coefficients are generally positive (the minus signs are really rare) and almost always statistically significant. As expected, the coefficients of the second sub-period (2007-15) are generally higher than those relative to the first sub-period (1999-2007): this reflects the fact that the fall in GDP in the Great Recession (2008-09) has been universal.

The highest coefficients are found in the EZ11 group, i.e. the original core of countries adopting euro since 1999. A possible interpretation is that EMU was realized within a group of relatively homogeneous countries (from the point of view of the business cycle); an alternative one is that the euro adoption has favoured their homogenisation (this is the "endogenous OCA proposition").

Concerning the individual countries, in the EZ11 group the correlation coefficients are in general very high (here it is better to consider correlation with the EZ11 average, i.e. to focus on the first three columns of Table 2): for the full period, they range from 0.919 of Italy[18] to 0.647 of Luxembourg.[19] In the late-comer group (in this case better look at the correlations with EZ19, i.e. the last column of Table 2), the correlations are lower, with notable exceptions (e.g. 0.840 for Lithuania and 0.919 for Slovenia); the lowest figures are found, as expected, in Greece and Cyprus.

A further step in our empirical analysis is to consider the *sensitivity of the business cycle* of individual countries with respect to the average European cycle, where by "average European" we refer once more to EZ11 and EZ19.

---

[18] This is a surprise, since this figure is even greater than the coefficient of 0.820 of Germany.
[19] In this case, the tiny size of its economy probably matters; furthermore, its growing specialisation in financial services makes its cycle different from the one of the industrial countries. In the first period the lowest coefficients are found in Austria and Portugal.

The European crisis

By using quarterly data (seasonally adjusted whenever possible) of real GDP, we can estimate some regressions of the following type:

$$\Delta \ln(Y_{i,t}) = \alpha_i + \gamma_i \Delta \ln(Y^{EU}_t) + \varepsilon_{i,t}$$

where Y is GDP at constant prices, t is the quarter, i is the individual country (and ln stands for natural logarithm). The coefficients γ represent the *elasticity* of each country quarterly growth with respect to the average European growth (EU11 or EU19 alternatively).

In this case, we are not so interested in the absolute values of the coefficients: they tend to be higher, *coeteris paribus*, in fast-growing countries, for instance in the NMS realizing catching-up processes. Instead, we are more interested in their statistical significance and in the overall goodness of fit: if the Adj. R2 is high, it means that the European cycle is by itself an important explanation of individual country performance (in terms of GDP), independently from idiosyncratic elements (notice that in the equation there are no control variables). According to Decressin and Fatàs (1995), a 20% of total variance explained by the regression is a good benchmark.[20]

In Table 3 we present our results, organized as usual considering three periods and two groups of countries. Regarding the original Eurozone member (EZ11), we see that the elasticities are generally significant and the Decressin-Fatas 20% condition (DF hereafter) is respected, with only one exception: Ireland. Rather low Adj. R2 values are also found, for the full period, in Luxembourg, Austria and Portugal. Finally, we observe that in the first period the goodness of fit was generally worse, i.e. in 1999-2007 idiosyncratic elements played a greater role in explaining the GDP dynamics.

In the second group of countries (new euro members), at least two countries did not respect the DF criterion: Cyprus and Greece; one more country was at the margin (Latvia). This evidence is detected in the case of elasticities

---

[20] This benchmark refers to an empirical investigation focused on the European regions; in the case of States, it is likely higher, but since in the Eurozone there are many tiny States (Luxembourg, Malta, the Baltic states, etc.) it is probably wise to keep the same 20% benchmark.

with respect to EZ19 (the last column of Table 3). However, if we consider the pre-crisis period, the DF criterion is hardly satisfied: Slovakia, Cyprus, Estonia are the partial exceptions.

Table 3 – Elasticities of countries' GDP growth (quarterly data seasonally adjusted) with respect to European averages (EZ11 and EZ19)

	Elasticities with respect to:			
	EZ11			EZ19
	1999.1-2015.1	1999.1-2007.1	2007.1-2015.1	2007.1-2015.1
Original Eurozone countries (11):				
Austria	0.890 (.5)	0.866^(.2)	0.930 (.5)	0.702 (.4)
Belgium	0.754 (.7)	0.761 (.4)	0.754 (.8)	0.603 (.7)
Finland	1.663 (.7)	1.227 (.3)	1.776 (.8)	1.519 (.8)
France	0.690 (.8)	0.783 (.6)	0.654 (.8)	0.532 (.7)
Germany	1.095 (.7)	1.014 (.3)	1.327 (.9)	1.111 (.8)
Ireland #	0.342^(.1)	0.641 (.5)	-0.112°(0)	-0.026°(0)
Italy	1.018 (.8)	0.892 (.6)	0.990 (.9)	0.783 (.7)
Luxembourg	1.493 (.4)	2.953 (.4)	1.336 (.5)	0.991 (.3)
The Netherlands	0.850 (.6)	0.796 (.3)	0.870 (.6)	0.773 (.7)
Portugal	0.853 (.5)	1.017^(.3)	0.775 (.5)	0.589 (.4)
Spain	0.774 (.6)	0.369^(.3)	0.593 (.6)	0.522 (.6)
New Eurozone countries (19):				
Cyprus	0.775 (.3)	0.849^(.2)	0.415^(.1)	0.355^(.1)
Estonia	2.068 (.3)	0.607 °(0)	1.941 (.3)	1.931 (.4)
Greece	1.123 (.2)	0.340°(0)	0.641^(.1)	0.562^(.1)
Latvia	1.184^(.1)	-0.585°(0)	0.933^(.1)	1.242^(.2)
Lithuania	2.588 (.6)	0.973°(0)	2.667 (.5)	2.580 (.7)
Malta	0.604^(.1)	-0.314°(0)	0.843 (.4)	0.759 (.5)
Slovakia #	1.055 (.2)	0.745^(.2)	1.457 (.3)	1.571 (.8)
Slovenia	1.443 (.6)	0.433°(0)	1.542 (.8)	1.372 (.8)

Significance levels: 1% everywhere, unless otherwise specified (^ means 5%; ° means 10% or less)
Adj. R2 in parentheses: for space limits only the first decimal is shown.
Source: elaborations on Eurostat data.

The European crisis

Let us analyse, finally, the economic integration from a different perspective. A possible question is whether the adoption of euro has increased the trade within the countries joining the monetary union (which should be true according to the "endogeneity" principle: see section 2).

If we consider data on *intra-EU trade* (exports by EU members to other EU members) and compute the ratios, by country, over GDP, from Eurostat data we can see that both in the 1999-2008 period and in the 2008-14 period there has been a prevailing increase in intra-EU trade in most countries:[21] the most evident exceptions are Malta, Ireland, Estonia in the first period, Belgium and Luxembourg in the second one.

Some relevant increases can be observed in the Netherlands (an old Eurozone country), in Slovenia and Slovakia (new euro members).[22] These trends are consistent with what found by other authors (Mongelli and Vega, 2006) concerning a moderate increase in intra-euro trade (by 5% to 10%, without any evidence of trade diversion) in the first years after the introduction of the euro. If we compute - for comparison purposes - the simple means of the ratios for EZ and non-EZ countries, we find that in the first period the intra-EU trade ratio has increased from 25% to 27% in the EZ and from 24% to 28% in the non-EZ; while in the second period it has decreased (from 27% back to 25%) in the EZ, but it has further increased (to 34%) in non-EZ. Thus, it seems that the crises have halted the trade integration process within the Eurozone, but they have reinforced trade integration in some EU countries not adopting the euro.

We can conclude that the analysis on long-run convergence does not allow to state that the adoption of euro did favour convergence trends (although it is true that correlation of business cycles seems higher in the original group

---

[21] As to the absolute values of the ratios, they depend, first of all, on the overall "degree of openness" of the countries: this is why small countries exhibit high ratios and big countries (including Germany, France, the U.K. and Italy) present rather small ratios. However, since we are considering "intra-EU" trade, some other elements – including sectoral specialisation, geographical location, historic links – become important: in fact, Cyprus and Greece exhibit the lowest ratios among all countries. On the contrary, it seems that the use of a common currency (the euro) has not been important for determining trade integration.

[22] And also in Hungary and the Czech Republic (among the non-euro members). Detailed results are available upon request.

of euro-area countries). As to intra-EU trade, its intensity seems higher and soaring in some non-euro members. These long-run features concerning to the impact of euro's adoption add to the fact that EMU construction does not appear ready to cope – as we shall explain in the next Section – with big shocks, such as the recent double crisis; in particular, the lack of common adjustment mechanisms dramatically increased the socio-economic divergences within the EMU (see also Pasimeni, 2014).

4. The double crisis in the Eurozone and the inadequate policy response

The global financial crisis originated in 2007-08 in the US and reached the peak with the Lehman Brothers crack; it determined a dramatic fall in confidence, with immediate effects on the credit and financial markets. The credit crunch, adverse expectations and systemic uncertainty subsequently caused detrimental real effects. The "Great Recession" (2008-09) has been the deepest contraction in economic activity since the Great Depression of the '30s. The recession propagated to Europe and many world countries. The unemployment rate rose everywhere.[23]

In late 2009, a recovery began in the US and in many other countries, also in Europe; it was facilitated by the manifold economic policy response: (i) wide rescue plans of banks; (ii) accommodating monetary policies, such that interest rates were reduced to almost zero and were accompanied by unconventional operations of liquidity management (e.g. "quantitative easing"); (iii) expansionary fiscal policies (in addition to the working of automatic stabilizers). Public budgets deteriorated, not only because of the recession and the rescue of banks, but also as a consequence of the fiscal stimulus packages. This triggered an increase in the deficit/GDP and debt/GDP ratios (see Table 4, where the largest EU countries and the "Piigs"

---

[23] It rapidly increased in the most flexible countries(e.g. in the US, the UK, Ireland, the Baltic states and Spain); in other countries, that for instance exploited "internal" flexibilities, the increase has been narrow, although in some cases postponed and more persistent.

are compared to the US), already rising because of the fall in GDP itself.[24] This worsening in the fiscal stance of many countries caused a new instability, especially in Europe; then the situation degenerated because of some news coming from Greece (2009-10).[25]

The further drop in confidence in the financial markets produced an increase in the spreads in interest rates on public debt, relative to the German bonds, not only in Greece but also - in the next two years - in the other peripheral countries of the Eurozone: the so-called "Piigs" (Portugal, Ireland, Italy, Greece and Spain). The "sovereign debt" crisis changed the perception of the risk compared to the previous decade; now, there was not only a deterioration in the perceived risk of default, but also the consideration of the possibility of some countries leaving the Eurozone or a break-up of the monetary union.

The uncertain, delayed and inadequate economic policy response also contributed – in addition to the "flight to quality" of capital movements – to the contagion in the Eurozone.[26] Some measures were taken in May 2010: bilateral loans to Greece, settlement of the European financial stability facility (EFSF), purchase of sovereign bonds on the secondary market by the ECB (through the SMP, Securities market program), but they were not sufficient to contrast the speculative attacks. The latter were to a certain extent bolstered by the EU Council decision to make private owners responsible for the losses in case of default or restructuring of the debt.[27]

---

[24] Notice that while in the Eurozone the deterioration of public budgets occurred at the member states level, in the US it took place mainly at the federal level (Pasimeni, 2014).

[25] In October 2009, the new Greek government (Papandreou) revealed that the true deficit/GDP ratio was equal to 12%, the double than previously announced.

[26] For example, in the Spring of 2010, when it was clear that Greece could not save itself, EU's intervention was postponed not only for legal problems (the no bail-out clause included in the Maastricht Treaty) or economic ones (moral hazard problem), but also for political reasons (the political situation in Germany advised to postpone any decision until the completion of elections in some Länders).

[27] A first restructuring of the Greek debt was realized in February 2012. A new restructuring or "re-profiling" is still likely, despite the new agreement reached after tough talks (with a concrete risk of "Grexit") in July 2015, agreement that led to the third financial help package (worth about 85 billion euro).

The euro, long-run convergence and the impact of the crises

Thus, the contagion reached Ireland and Portugal, that were helped through the EFSF in Autumn 2010 and Spring 2011, respectively; then, in the Summer 2011, Spain and Italy. The latter two countries are "too big to bail out" (because of the size of their public debts), but also "too big to default": their defaulting would certainly imply the collapse of EMU. The situation did not improve even after the institution of a new permanent fund (the European Stability Mechanism, ESM) and the adoption of the Fiscal Compact for the Eurozone countries, i.e. stricter fiscal rules on public deficits and debts, compared to the previous GSP. Instead, it was ECB President Draghi's declaration (July 2012) "we shall save euro whatever it takes" and the consequent adoption of the "Outright monetary transactions" (OMT) plan that crucially changed the financial situation; in fact, the systemic risk and the spreads reached low levels in the following years.

Despite the recent improvement in financial stability conditions (since the end of 2012), EU policies had globally a negative impact on the real economic trends. The strict austerity measures, added to the uncertainty created by the sovereign debt crisis itself, caused a new recession[28]: policymakers overlooked that public deficits and debts were not the cause of the financial crisis, but rather its consequence. As a matter of fact, austerity policies were imposed to Eurozone members, in order to improve the "confidence" of markets and to respect the new fiscal rules (not only for the assisted countries by the "troika" but also for all euro members by the Fiscal Compact).

From a theoretical point of view, while in the traditional Keynesian model a cut in public expenditure or an increase in taxation causes a more or less significant (multiplied) fall in production and income, in the Monetarist and New Classical Macroeconomic approaches there might be non-keynesian effects from fiscal consolidations. The latter include the crowding-in of private investment (thanks to the reduction in interest rates) and an increase in current consumption (thanks to the expectation of a long-run balanced budget, i.e. the "Ricardian equivalence"). The reduction in interest rates would be the consequence of the higher credibility of economic policies and

---

[28] The double-dip recession (De Grauwe, 2012), in the European countries with generalized falls of GDP in 2012-13, also contributed to the new global economic slowdown, assimilated by Krugman (2012b) to a true depression.

the better sustainability of public debt (this is the "confidence factor"). Thus fiscal consolidations, even severe fiscal contractions, can be expansionary.[29]

Table 4 – Key macro-variables for selected EU countries and the US

		US	EU	UK	D	F	I	E	PT	IRL	EL
Annual average change % (volumes)											
GDP	2004-08	2.3	2.3	2.4	2.0	1.8	1.1	3.1	1.2	3.7	3.1
	2009-13	1.2	-1.2	-0.2	0.7	0.2	-1.5	-1.4	-1.5	-1.0	-5.1
Private consumption	2004-08	2.4	1.8	1.9	0.5	1.8	0.7	3.0	2.0	4.8	4.1
	2009-13	1.4	-0.2	0	1.0	0.5	-1.4	-2.0	-2.2	-1.5	-6.3
Investment (total)	2004-08	1.3	3.5	3,1	2.9	3,7	0.9	3.7	0,1	4,1	2.6
	2009-13	0.2	-3.6	-3,2	-0.4	-5,4	-5,4	-8,5	-9.0	-11,3	-14,7
Investiment (equipment)	2004-08	4.5	5,0	0.7	6.9	3,5	1,7	5,6	5,4	7,1	7.9
	2009-13	-2.5	-3.2	-3.3	-1,6	-1,3	-5.0	-3,6	-7,1	-3.7	-12,8
Exports	2004-08	7.8	6.1	4.9	8.4	2.9	4.2	3.8	4.6	4.8	6.4
	2009-13	3.2	1.9	1.2	2.7	1.3	0.4	3.2	3.2	2.0	-2.8
Employment	2004-08	1.1	1.1	0.9	0.7	0.7	0.5	2.5	0.1	3.3	2.0
	2009-13	-0.6	-0.6	0.2	0.7	-0.2	-1.3	-3.8	-2,7	-2.6	-4.1
Productivity (per employm.)	2004-08	1.2	1.2	1.5	1.2	1.1	0.5	0.5	1.1	0.3	1.1
	2009-13	1.4	0.4	-0.4	-0.1	0.4	-0.3	2.5	1.5	1.1	-1.0
Unit labour costs	2004-08	2.5	1.7	2.4	-0.4	1.9	2.5	3.8	2.0	4.8	2.4
	2009-13	0.6	1.6	2.6	2.1	1.7	1.9	-1.1	-0.4	-2,5	-1.7
Inflation (GDP deflator)	2004-08	2.7	2.2	2.5	0.9	2.2	2.2	3.6	2.4	1.4	3.2
	2009-13	1.4	1.4	1.8	1.4	1.2	1.4	0.1	0.7	-0.6	0.4
% on GDP											
Trade balance (merchandise)	2004-08	-5.8	-0.5	-5.8	7.3	-1.6	0.0	-7.7	-11.2	15.1	-18.6
	2009-13	-4.4	-0.1	-6.5	6.2	-2.8	0.2	-3.2	-7.2	21.6	-13.1
Current account	2004-08	-5.2	-0.2	-2.0	6.0	-0.9	-1.4	-8.4	-10.4	-3.6	-14.2
	2009-13	-2.8	0.5	-2.7	6.6	-2.0	-1.6	-2.6	-5.9	1.7	-9.3
Government expenditure	2004-08	35.4	46.2	44.0	45.4	53.1	48.0	39.2	45.2	36.3	46.6
	2009-13	39.6	49.8	48.8	46.2	56.6	50.9	46.1	49.4	49.2	53.8
Public investment	2004-08	3.0	2.5*	1.7	1.5	3.2	2,3	3,7	3,2	4.2	3.4

---

[29] See the seminal paper by Giavazzi and Pagano (1990), the empirical investigation by Alesina and Perotti (1997) and the recent analysis by Perotti (2011).

The euro, long-run convergence and the impact of the crises

	2009-13	3.0	2,5	2.4	1.6	3,2	2,1	2,9	2.6	2.6	2.2
Government revenues	2004-08	30.8	44.2	40.5	43.7	50.1	44.9	39.5	40.9	36.1	39.6
	2009-13	29.5	44.8	40.4	44.5	50.8	46.9	36.6	42.1	34.6	42.1
Government balance	2004-08	-4.6	-1.9*	-3.5	-1.7	-3.0	-3.1	0.2	-4.4	-0.3	-7.0
	2009-13	-10.1	-5.0	-8.3	-1.7	-5.8	-4.0	-9.5	-7.3	-14.6	-11.7
Interest expenditure	2004-08	3.5	3.0*	2.1	2.8	2.7	4.8	1.7	2.8	1.1	4.7
	2009-13	3.8	2.8	2.9	2.5	2.5	5.0	2.5	3.6	3.3	5.4
Primary balance	2004-08	-1.1	0.7	-1.4	1.1	-0.3	1.7	1.9	-1.6	0.9	-2.3
	2009-13	-6.2	-2.2	-5.5	0.9	-3.3	1.0	-7.0	-3.7	-11.3	-6.2
Public debt	2004-08	..	69.0*	44.1	67.0	65.7	105.0	41.1	67.8	30.0	107.6
	2009-13	..	82.7	82.6	79.5	86.2	123.3	73.4	107.5	100.3	156.3
% on labour force											
Unemployment rate	2004-08	5.1	8.2	5.2	9.7	8.8	7.1	9.6	8.4	4.9	9.1
	2009-13	8.7	10.0	7.8	6.3	10.0	9.5	22.3	13.8	13.7	18.2

Note: (*) euro area.
Source: Marelli (2014); elaborations on European Commission, Autumn Forecast 2013.

However, the net result on production and income depends on the size of the "fiscal multiplier".[30] In fact, the supporters of tough austerity measures argue that fiscal multipliers are rather low and consequently restrictive fiscal policies do not cause large falls in income and production. The opponents argue that drastic austerity policies are likely to be "self-defeating", because the resulting loss of output is so large that the debt/GDP ratio increases (Gros, 2011).

Even the IMF (2012) eventually recognized that the value of the fiscal multipliers, since the Great Recession, has significantly increased, suggesting a more gradual fiscal adjustment.[31]

---

[30] See Marelli and Signorelli (2015), where the discussion on this point is more complete.
[31] Blanchard and Leigh (2013) admit that "in advanced economies, stronger planned fiscal consolidation has been associated with lower growth than expected", although they add: "the short-term effects of fiscal policy on economic activity are only one of

The European crisis

In the subsequent debate on fiscal multipliers, some other elements have been considered, supporting in general the assumption of high multipliers in the recent Eurozone situation: (i) the time horizon, because the short-run impact of fiscal consolidation is mostly negative; (ii) the cyclical phase, since multipliers are higher in recession periods rather than recoveries (Auerbach and Gorodnichenko, 2012);[32] (iii) the monetary conditions: when the nominal interest rate is zero the multipliers can be very large, because the fiscal tightening does not help in reducing interest rates, i.e. the "zero lower bound" (Christiano et al, 2011); (iv) the fact that many trade partners consolidate at the same time;[33] (v) the specific instrument of fiscal policy that is used.[34]

As a conclusion on this point, we can say that the size of the fiscal multipliers has been found large in the recent situation of the Eurozone.[35] For example, economists from leading institutions[36] found that the size of the multipliers is large, particularly for public expenditure and targeted transfers (Auerbach and Gorodnichenko, 2012). This "could be an issue if financial markets focus on the short-term behavior of the debt ratio, or if country authorities engage in repeated rounds of tightening" (Eyraud and Ankle, 2013).Thus, the miraculous virtues of the "expansionary austerity" did not

---

the many factors that need to be considered in determining the appropriate pace of fiscal consolidation".

[32] They are higher in crisis periods due to uncertainty about aggregate demand and credit conditions, the presence of slack in the economy, the larger share of consumers that are liquidity constrained.

[33] "Coordinated austerity in a depression is indeed self-defeating" (Portes, 2012). See also Blyth (2013) and the results of the "meta-analysis" by Gechert and Rannenberg (2014).

[34] Alesina et al (2015) maintain that adjustments realized through spending cuts are less recessionary than those achieved through tax increases. Moreover, according to them, spending-based consolidations should be accompanied by the "right" polices, including easy monetary policy, liberalisation of goods and labour markets, and other structural reforms.

[35] On the last point concerning the specific instrument of fiscal policy, some authors (including European Commission, 2012) found that the multipliers associated with public expenditure are higher than those observed for taxes (at least the first-year multipliers).

[36] IMF, OECD, European Commission (EC), European Central Bank (ECB), US Federal Reserve (FED), Bank of Canada. Such economists made use of eight different macro-econometric models (mainly DSGE models) for the US and four models for the Eurozone.

materialize; even the financial markets now seem to penalize countries for the feeble growth prospects rather than for temporary deviations from positions of a balanced budget (Shambaugh, 2012).

The consequence of the wrong or inadequate EU policies is that GDP is still below the pre-crisis levels in many Eurozone countries (see Table 4); the long and repeated recessions have led to a decrease of potential output too.[37] The unemployment rates have significantly risen and there are expectations of persistence at high levels for a long time. Social pain has spread in the continent and poverty indices have reached unprecedented levels (Darvas and Tschekassin, 2015).[38] As to the fiscal variables, the deficit/GDP ratios have been reduced because of the forced "austerity", but the debt/GDP ratios have been growing, due to the prevalence of the negative real effects on GDP with respect to the fiscal consolidation effects.

As regards the structural and macroeconomic imbalances, the peripheral countries have partly corrected the previous "structural divergence" (i.e. specialisation dominated by non-tradable goods and construction) and have tried to enhance their competitiveness by means of an "internal devaluation", obtained through the cut in wages or at least a restraint in the wage dynamics. In 2014-15 many Eurozone countries exhibited deflation conditions[39]. In many peripheral countries there was also an increase in productivity (Italy is one exception), however not thanks to an increase in output, but rather due to a reduction of employment (and corresponding rise

---

[37] The paradox is that this is causing further austerity (in fact the GSP requires the consideration of deficit/GDP ratios in terms of potential GDP) reducing again GDP and potential output. Notice, furthermore, that the EU Commission estimates of potential output have been criticized because very low, with a corresponding high value of "natural unemployment"; the effect is to determine an artificially high ratio between "structural" deficit and GDP.

[38] The workers' position in the labour market was already weaker as a consequence of long-run trends, for example those caused by the globalization processes. Nevertheless, after the crises, net job destruction, high turnover, workforce displacement (due to outsourcing) and loss of rights became part of the spectrum of management practices that emerged from the austerity guidelines, leading to precarious jobs and enhanced vulnerability of workers, mainly young people.

[39] Note that deflation itself, in addition to nil or small growth rates, has made very difficult the reduction of the debt/GDP ratios.

in unemployment).[40] In fact, wage moderation and labour market reforms did not produce, at least until 2014, significant increases in employment.

In any case, competitiveness gains triggered an improvement in current accounts[41], but in order to eliminate the competitiveness gap with Germany at least one decade of pain would be required; unless unit labour costs are mainly reduced through productivity increases, which requires strong innovations and investment (in R&D and equipment). It must also be added that the recent adjustment in current accounts is chiefly due to the fall in internal demand and in imports, rather than a significant improvement in export capacity.

In fact, many European countries – especially in the periphery – have suffered because of the collapse in internal demand. Consumption has been reduced because of the wage restraint, high unemployment as well as high fiscal pressure (consequent to fiscal consolidation measures), that have cut the disposable income.[42] Investment expenditure has plummeted: -15% is the cumulated loss in the 2007-13 period in the Eurozone (but the fall has been bigger in individual countries); also public investment has been slashed (see Table 4).

Thus, in order to have a strong recovery, we need also a demand-management strategy supporting both consumption and investment: in the former case, to guarantee viable conditions of social sustainability; in the latter case, to realize positive benefits also from the supply-side (on innovations, potential output and productivity dynamics).[43]

---

[40]As a consequence of extensive "internal flexibility" adjustments (i.e. working time reductions) the hourly productivity has increased in several countries.
[41]Wage deflation and labour market deregulation, i.e. "competitive austerity", were seen as a way to improve competitiveness; complementary to this, fiscal restraints – that in the first phase of the crisis were aimed at "expansionary austerity" (that failed to achieve the growth goals) – were functional, in a second phase, to improve current accounts (through increased competitiveness). However, this orthodox "neoclassical" view (Sinn, 2014) can be confuted on the basis of well-known "Keynesian" arguments (in which the link is from fiscal restraint to reduction of production and imports, to an improvement in current accounts): see Paternesi Meloni (2015).
[42] In addition, negative expectations and a growing uncertainty about the future increased the propensity to save.
[43] As for public investment, most of economic theories suggest its importance (e.g., on material and immaterial infrastructure) to sustain recoveries, but – paradoxically –

In conclusion, we can state that EU policies have been delayed in some cases and inadequate in other circumstances: this is the criticized "too little too late" approach. The monetary policy of the ECB has finally become sufficiently accommodative, but the fiscal stance has not substantially changed (as discussed in the next Section).

5. Conclusions and policy suggestions

The situation of feeble recovery, stagnation and deflation in the Eurozone, accompanied by high and persistent unemployment, requires some changes both in a long-run perspective, i.e. reforms in the governance of the EMU; and in the short-run, i.e. changes in the current macroeconomic policies.

As anticipated in Section 2, the EMU construction and governance present various weaknesses (see also De Grauwe, 2013). According to a former president of the EU Commission, the international financial crisis abruptly revealed the complete absence of an "economic axis" (see Delors, 2013). Probably the major flaw is the complete asymmetry between the two key macroeconomic policies: this is why EMU is sometimes defined as an "incomplete" monetary union (as warned many years ago by Goodhart, 1988).While monetary policy has been centralized, fiscal policy is still assigned to national governments (Obstfeld, 2013; Mody, 2015).

OCA's theories maintain that a working monetary union requires not only convergence of economic and institutional structures, together with an adequate degree of market flexibility and labour mobility, but also fiscal transfers stemming from a centralized budget. Thus, a tiny EU budget – 1% of GDP – is completely inadequate to carry out counter-cyclical policies, not to mention that Eurozone has not a proper budget.

It is true that there is an involvement by the EU also on fiscal policies, but it is just focused on rules and controls: fiscal policies are constrained by old and new rules. Although the GSP and the Fiscal Compact rules may be

---

often this kind of public expenditure is pro-cyclical; the key reason is that during recessions it is politically less costly to cut or postpone public investment than reducing current expenditures.

necessary (in general) for financial stability, in some cases they impose damaging constraints. Moreover, the emphasis on monetary and financial stability has triggered a neglect of effective mechanisms favouring long-run convergence among the economies. In the long run, a common currency cannot be maintained in a group of countries characterized by huge differences in competitiveness and current account balances.[44] The old "Lisbon Agenda" and the current "Europe 2020" plan could be (or have been) a proper solution only with adequate resources.[45] The resources of structural and cohesion funds (now about 0.4% of EU's GDP) should be significantly increased, in order to support investment, infrastructure, R&D, human capital, etc.

Looking at past trends (Section 3), our empirical analyses showed that real convergence (in terms of GDP per capita) was not evident in the Eurozone. Correlations of business cycles were significant in the original Eurozone countries (EZ11), but those concerning the current "ample" Eurozone (EZ19) are much lower. Sensitivity to a common business cycle (elasticities), initially rather low, have increased only as a result of the recent generalized crises. Finally, intra-EU trade is higher (and further increasing over time) for many non-euro countries also in comparison with euro area members.

Soon after the sovereign debt crisis, there were many doubts about the possibility of euro's survival. Now we can say that, in the short run, a break-up of EMU is unlikely, because a disintegration would be too costly. Also the exit from the Eurozone of individual countries will bear (for the exiting country) too many costs, much higher than the potential benefits: rising interest rates and capital outflows, worse public debt sustainability and much

---

[44] In principle, structural differences and macroeconomic imbalances can be acceptable even within monetary unions if they can be offset by proper fiscal transfers from a centralized budget, as occurs for example in the United States; also a region within a country can run a current account deficit indefinitely as long as there is a transfer of resources from the richer to the poorer regions. However, continuous and wide transfers of resources (from rich to poor areas) are not politically feasible, now and in the foreseeable future (permanent transfers are criticized even within national countries such as Germany or Italy). Thus, structural policies aimed at some "real convergence" are needed to reduce the largest differences across States.

[45] Also the new "macroeconomic imbalances" procedure, within the reformed GSP, is not the right solution: such imbalances cannot be eliminated only by means of new compelling rules and threat of fines.

higher risk of default, rising inflation (that will shortly reduce the possible benefits coming from an initial devaluation).[46]

Nevertheless, the long-run endurance of EMU will require – in addition to an effective support for real convergence (as already explained) – some shock absorption mechanisms and innovative crisis management instruments,[47] more effective than the "save-States" funds (EFSF and ESM).The principle should be that an authentic solidarity among the Eurozone countries goes hand in hand with stronger supra-national controls on all members (to face the "moral hazard" dilemma) and a more effective power allocated to the EU Commission. A separate budget and specific institutions (e.g. a Finance "minister") for the euro area appear appropriate.

All these radical changes will require a lengthy time, adequate financial resources and consistent institutional reforms (new Treaties should be approved). In June 2012, EU President van Rompuy presented (together with the Presidents of the EU Commission, Eurogroup and ECB) a document ("Toward a genuine economic and monetary union"), foreseeing a stronger integration, by means of: (i) a bank union, (ii) a budget union, (iii) an economic union, and (iv) (at the end) a political union. So far, a limited progress has been achieved only on the bank union, also in this case after many compromises.[48] It is even more disappointing that a fresh and similar document, presented in June 2015 by the "five" Presidents (the President of the Euro-Parliament has been added) is still vague and hesitant. At the end, a monetary union cannot be maintained without a continuous progress toward an economic and political union (O'Rourke and Taylor, 2013).

All these delays and mistakes in the integration process are worrying, particularly because in a globalized world, where the economic and political power is shifting to other world regions (in America, Asia and other continents), a fragmented Europe would be certainly fading. Thus, the hope for the long run is that open-minded policy makers will be able to introduce

---

[46] It should be also noted that – thanks to the new ECB measures undertaken by President Draghi – the contagion deriving from the possible exit of a single country (like Greece) is now much lower than in 2010-11.
[47] The debate on the usefulness of Eurobonds is continuing; see also Schäfer (2012).
[48] The bank union began in November 2014, but the ECB's direct supervision is limited to the biggest banks and financial institutions.

the required radical reforms, leading at the end to a "federal" Europe. Since this scenario is currently unrealistic, we could ask, to sum up, which changes in economic policies are shortly needed to improve the present economic and social situation.

First of all, austerity in fiscal policies should be lessened. Even the IMF, already in 2012 (IMF, 2012), advocated not only the maintenance of a very accommodating monetary stance, but also a smoothing of the fiscal adjustments. This is all the more true now, when most of the Eurozone countries are respecting the 3% ceiling of the GSP for the deficit/GDP ratio. Fiscal discipline – for the Eurozone countries in general and for countries demanding financial assistance in particular – should be assessed in a medium-term horizon, also because "structural reforms" can have a positive impact on growth and on debt sustainability only in the long run.[49] For the future, the requests to exclude public investment from the deficit definition, within the GSP rules, should be properly considered.

Secondarily, an improved coordination of national macroeconomic policies would be necessary as well: although a coordination was required by the Maastricht Treaty, it has not been realized at all. In fact, the repeated recessions and long stagnation in the euro area have also been caused by the wrong structure of macroeconomic adjustments: tight austerity has been imposed on the debtor (Southern) countries while the creditor (Northern) countries continued to follow balanced-budget policies (De Grauwe, 2012 and 2013). An alternative solution would be to convince countries with sound fiscal positions and that have room for fiscal manoeuvre – like Germany – to accept expansionary policies, through a coordinated domestic demand-led policy. Notice that internal devaluations in debtor countries, without rising inflation in the creditor ones, i.e. an asymmetric adjustment, is unsustainable on economic and political grounds (O'Rourke and Taylor, 2013).[50]

---

[49] "Not explicitly taking into account multipliers or underestimating their value could lead authorities to set unachievable debt (and deficit) targets" (Eyraud and Ankle, 2013); therefore, fiscal adjustment should be rebalanced and made more "growth-friendly" (Cottarelli and Jaramillo, 2012).
[50] Moreover, if all Eurozone countries adopt restrictive policies, who will provide the necessary source of demand? All world regions cannot have a surplus at the same time. The US recovery is satisfactory at present, but even China is exhibiting a

The euro, long-run convergence and the impact of the crises

In the third place, monetary policy is now sufficiently accommodative; not only the ECB has led the key interest rate to almost zero (since November 2014), but it has also adopted a battery of unconventional measures. The 2012 OMT plan (luckily never used up to now) has been crucial to reduce interest rates on sovereign debt and to guarantee, so far, euro's survival. Moreover, from the end of 2014 deflation (or conditions of zero inflation) were dominant in the Eurozone, hence the ECB had to intervene precisely on the basis of its mandate (2% target of inflation). This is the main reason justifying the "quantitative easing" operations commenced in March 2015 and partially extended in December 2015. At this point, one puzzle remains also for the monetary policy, since it is important to identify the most effective ways to ensure that the liquidity created by the ECB really flows to the firms and to the real economy.[51]

In the fourth place, monetary policy should be integrated by a real "growth policy" at the EU level. This necessity has a long-run dimension (as explained at the beginning of these Conclusions), but something could and should be done immediately. For instance, an increase of public investment expenditure would allow an immediate relief for the economy (demand side effect); in addition, investment in infrastructure, transport, communications (Digital Agenda), higher education and research would sustain long-run growth (supply side effect). From this point of view, the so-called "Juncker" programme (worth 310 billion euro of public and private investments) should be integrated by new resources (also through new credit lines from the ECB to the European Investment Bank) and rapidly implemented, because its start has been unsatisfactory.[52]

---

slowdown in economic growth and many emerging economies are hurt by serious crises. A "beggar-thy-neighbour" policy cannot be a proper solution.

[51] Moreover, as President Draghi has recognized in the Jackson Hole speech (ECB, August 2014), monetary policy is not sufficient to reinforce the feeble economic recovery in the Eurozone. He even accepted that structural reforms are fundamental for economic growth, but should be accompanied by policies to sustain aggregate demand.

[52] Another possibility could be, within a new "Eurozone budget", the emission of "project Eurozone bond" (for example up to 5% of Eurozone GDP) in view of financing public investment; with an interest rate near 2% (realistic but it might be even lower), the emission of ten-years Eurozone-bonds by an amount equivalent to 5% of GDP will imply an annual cost equivalent to 0.1% of Eurozone GDP.

The European crisis

On the other hand, private investments, that have collapsed in recent years, should benefit from the reversal of expectations (following the demanded growth-oriented policy) and from a more efficient working of the credit mechanism. Even on the supply side, growth-oriented policies should be grounded not only on "structural reforms" (liberalisations, reduction of the fiscal pressure, pro-market legislation, etc.) when necessary, but also on new industrial policies, putting R&D and innovation processes at the core.[53] In particular, the real manner by which peripheral countries can gain competitiveness is not only through wage and price moderation (the "internal devaluation" discussed above), but rather by means of an upgrade of the industrial structure and specialisation, product differentiation, technological content (as recently admitted also by the European Commission, 2013).

Finally, as long as the cost of the adjustment after the recent shocks fell mainly on labour (Pasimeni, 2014), an urgent action should be taken to fight the high unemployment rate, particularly huge in the peripheral countries of the Eurozone. The long period of stagnation and feeble recovery has caused the cyclical unemployment to become structural and persistent in some countries. In addition to more expansionary macroeconomic policies and more effective passive labour policies (on this point there are also some interesting proposals for a euro-wide system of unemployment insurance), active labour policies are also fundamental. This is even more important for young people, since they particularly suffer during economic crises and persistence is determining a "lost generation".[54] Some actions have been taken by the EU itself[55], but a radical correction of the "too little too late" approach is required, also to solve this troubling social problem.

---

[53] Instead of an indiscriminate support to all firms in all sectors, it would be appropriate to target the aid toward firms that actually expand "good" jobs or to those that act as leader in innovation processes, so that the benefits pour to the entire industrial and economic system. See Marelli (2014).

[54] See Scarpetta et al (2010), Brada et al (2014).

[55] The "Youth Guarantee" recommendation, launched in 2013, requires member States to put in place measures to ensure that young people (up to age 25) receive a good quality offer of employment, continued education, an apprenticeship or a traineeship, within four months of leaving school or becoming unemployed. However, also this programme is tempered by the limited available resources and by the heterogeneous implementation in the different countries.

References

Alesina, A. and Perotti, R. (1997) "Fiscal adjustments in OECD countries: composition and macroeconomic effects." *International Monetary Fund Staff Papers* 44(2) pp. 210–248.

Alesina, A., Ardagna, S. and Galasso, V. (2008) "The euro and structural reforms." *NBER Working Paper* 14479.

Alesina, A., Barbiero, O., Favero, C., Giavazzi, F. and Paradisi, M. (2015) "Austerity in 2009-2013." *NBER Working Paper* 20827.

Auerbach, A. J. and Gorodnichenko,Y. (2012) "Measuring the output responses to fiscal policy." *American Economic Journal: Economic Policy* 4(2) pp. 1–27.

Berger, H. and Nitsch, V. (2010) "The euro's effect on trade imbalances." *IMF Working Papers* 10/226 pp. 1-30.

Blanchard, O. and Leigh, D. (2013) "Growth forecast errors and fiscal multipliers." *IMF Working Paper* 13/1.

Barro, R. J. and Sala-i-Martin, X. (1995) *Economic growth*. New York: McGraw-Hill.

Blyth, M. (2013) *Austerity: the history of a dangerous idea*. Oxford: Oxford University Press.

Brada, J. C., Marelli, E. and Signorelli, M. (2014) "Young people and the labor market: key determinants and new evidences." *Comparative Economic Studies* 56(4) pp. 556-566.

Buiter, W. H. (2004) "To purgatory and beyond: when and how should the accession countries from Central and Eastern Europe become full members of EMU?" *CEPR Discussion Paper Series* 4342.

Buiter, W. H., Corsetti, G. and Roubini, N. (1993) "Excessive deficits: sense and nonsense in the Treaty of Maastricht." *Economic Policy* 16(8) pp. 58–100.

Buti, M. and Sapir, A. (eds.) (1998) *Economic Policy in EMU*. Oxford: Clarendon Press.

Buti, M. and Turrini, A. (2015) "Three waves of convergence. Can Eurozone countries start growing together?" *Voexeu.org*. 17 April.

Canova, F. and Marcet, A. (1995) "The poor stay poor: non-convergence across countries and regions." *CEPR Discussion Paper* 1265.

Christiano, L., Eichenbaum, M. and Rebelo, S. (2011) "When is the government spending multiplier large?" *Journal of Political Economy* 119(1) pp. 78-121.

Cottarelli, C. and Jaramillo, L. (2012) "Walking hand-in-hand: fiscal policy and growth in advanced economies." *IMF Working Paper* 137.

Dao, M., Furceri, D. and Loungani, P. (2014) "Regional labor market adjustments in the United States and Europe." *IMF Working Paper* 26.

Darvas, Z. and Tschekassin, O. (2015) "Poor and under pressure: the social impact of Europe's fiscal consolidation." *Bruegel Working Paper* 4.

De Grauwe, P. (2007) *Economics of the Monetary Union*. Oxford: Oxford University Press.

De Grauwe, P. (2012) "How to avoid a double-dip recession in the Eurozone." *CEPS Commentary* 15 November.

De Grauwe, P. (2013) "Design failures in the Eurozone: Can they be fixed?" *LSE 'Europe in Question' Discussion Paper Series*.

De Grauwe, P. and Schnabl, G. (2005) "Nominal versus real convergence – EMU entry scenarios for the New Member States." *Kyklos* 4 pp. 537-555.

Decressin, J. and Fatàs, A. (1995) "Regional labor market dynamics in Europe." *European Economic Review* 39 (9) pp. 1627-1655.

Delors, J. (2013) "Economic governance in the European Union: past, present and future." *Journal of Common Market Studies* 51(2) pp. 169-178.

ECB (2014) *Unemployment in the Euro area*, Speech by Mario Draghi, President of the ECB, Annual central bank symposium in Jackson Hole, 22 Aug 2014. Available via https://www.ecb.europa.eu/press/key/date/2014/html/ sp140822.en.html
Eichengreen, B. (1993) "European Monetary Unification." .*Journal of Economic Literature* 31(3) pp. 1321-1357.

European Commission (1977) *Report of the Study Group on the Role of Public Finance in European Integration (MacDougall Report)*.

European Commission (1990) "One market, one money: an evaluation of the potential benefits and costs of forming an economic and monetary union." *European Economy – Economic Papers* 4.

European Commission (2012) "Report on public finance in EMU." *European Economy– Economic Papers* 4.

European Commission (2013) *European Competitiveness Report*.

Eyraud, L. and Anke, W. (2013) "The challenge of debt reduction during fiscal consolidation." *IMF Working Paper* 67.

Frankel, J. and Rose, A. K. (1998) "The endogeneity of optimum currency area criteria." *Economic Journal* 108 pp. 1009-1025.

Gechert, S. Rannenberg, A. (2014) "Are fiscal multipliers regime dependent? A meta regression analysis." *IMK Working Paper* 139.

Giavazzi, F. and Pagano, M. (1990) "Can severe fiscal contractions be expansionary? Tales of two small European countries." In Blanchard, O. J. and Fischer, S. (eds.) *NBER Macroeconomics Annual 1990*. Cambridge (MA): MIT Press.

Giavazzi, F. and Spaventa, L. (2010) "Why the current account may matter in a monetary union: lessons from the financial crisis in the Euro area." *Centre for Economic Policy Research Discussion Paper* 8008.

Goodhart, C. (1988) "The two concepts of money: implications for the analysis of optimal currency areas." *European Journal of Political Economy* 14 (3) pp. 407-432.

Gros, D. (2011) "Can austerity be self-defeating?" *Economic Policy*. CEPS Commentaries.

Hale, G. and Obstfeld, M. (2014) "The euro and the geography of international debt flows." *NBER Working Paper* 20033.

IMF (2012). *World Economic Outlook -Coping with high debt and sluggish growth*. October.

Kenen, P. (1969) "The theory of optimum currency areas: an eclectic view." In Mundell, R. and Swoboda, A. (eds.). *Monetary Problems in the International Economy*. Chicago: University of Chicago Press.

Krugman, P. (1993) "Lessons of Massachusetts for EMU." In Torres, F. and Giavazzi, F. (eds.). *Adjustment and Growth in the European Monetary Union*. Cambridge: Cambridge University Press.

Krugman, P. (2012a) "Revenge of the optimum currency area." *NBER Macroeconomics Annual* 27. Chicago: University of Chicago Press.

Krugman, P. (2012b) *End this depression now!*. New York: W. Norton & Co.

Marelli, E. (2014) "Quali politiche dopo la crisi?" In Cappellin, R., Marelli, E., Rullani, E. and Sterlacchini, A. (eds.). *Crescita, investimenti e territorio: il ruolo delle politiche industriali e regionali*. Website "Scienze Regionali". eBook 2014.1.

Marelli, E. and Signorelli, M. (2010) "Institutional, nominal and real convergence in Europe." *Banks and Bank Systems* 5 (2) pp. 41-57.

Marelli, E. and Signorelli, M. (2015) "Convergence, crisis and unemployment in Europe:the need for innovative policies." *Croatian Economic Survey* 17(2) pp. 5-56.

McKinnon, R. (1963) "Optimum currency areas." *American Economic Review* 53 pp. 717-724.

Mody, A. (2015) "Living (dangerously) without a fiscal union." *Bruegel Working Paper* 3.

Mongelli, F. P. and Vega, J. L. (2006) "What effects is EMU having on the Euro area and its member countries? An overview." *European Central Bank Working Paper Series* 599.

Mundell, R. (1961) "A theory of optimum currency areas." *American Economic Review* 51(4) pp. 657-665.

Obstfeld, M. (2013) "Finance at center stage: Some lessons of the euro crisis." *European Economy Economic Papers* 493. April 2013.

O'Rourke, K. H. and Taylor, A. M. (2013) "Cross of Euros." *Journal of Economic Perspectives* 27(3) pp. 167-92.

Pasimeni, P. (2014) "An optimum currency crisis." *The European Journal of Comparative Economics* 11(2) pp. 173-204.

Paternesi Meloni, W. (2015) "Austerity and competitiveness: A misleading linkage." *1st World Congress of Comparative Economics*, Rome, 25-27 June 2015.

Perotti, R. (2011) "The 'austerity myth': Gain without pain?" *NBER Working Paper* 17571.

Portes, J. (2012) "Self-defeating austerity." *Social Europe Journal*, 31 October.

Rose, A. (2000) "One money, one market: The effect of common currencies on trade." *Economic Policy* 15(30) pp. 7-45.

Scarpetta, S., Sonnet, A. and Manfredi, T. (2010) "Rising youth unemployment during the crisis: How to prevent negative long-term consequences on a generation?" *OECD Social, Employment and Migration Working Papers* 6.

Schäfer, H. B. (2012) "The sovereign debt crisis in Europe, save banks not States." *The European Journal of Comparative Economics* 9(2) pp. 179-195.

Shambaugh, J. C. (2012) "The Euro's three crises." In Acemoglu, D., Parker, J. and Woodford, M. (eds.). *NBER Macroeconomics Annual* 27 pp. 157-231.

Sinn, H. W. (2014) "Austerity, growth and inflation: Remarks on the Eurozone's unresolved competitiveness problem." *The World Economy* 37(1) pp.1-13.

Chapter 2
A euro area government: a dream come true?
Tom Vleeschhouwer and Tara Koning

1. Introduction

Politicians have been debating the future of European integration for quite some time. Angela Merkel, Chancellor of Germany, has advocated a transition of the EU towards a political union (Press, 2012). Jean-Claude Juncker, president of the European Commission, has called for the same (Spiegel, 2015). This idea has also been theorized by several think tanks (Blockmans and Faleg, 2015), but economists also analyze the option that the euro area should separate (Begg et al, 2003; Dutta, 2011; Keuschnigg, 2012; Buiter and Rahbari, 2012). In many European countries political parties have emerged which also call for separation of the European Union, for example the UK Independence Party (Hunt, 2014). However, Eichengreen (2010) and Buiter and Rahbari (2012) signal that a breakup of the euro area has very severe consequences, and is therefore not desirable. Buiter and Rahbari (2012) acknowledge that politically, integration is a difficult subject. They therefore draw up the minimal institutions that can avoid a crisis in the future.

We propose to take a different point of view, namely that of assessing how a supranational government, i.e. integration of the euro area, transferring sovereignty to supranational institutions and drawing up such institutions, could solve problems that have emerged in the euro crisis. We feel that, although political reality is important, the economic consequences of a further transfer of sovereignty should be assessed first, and only after these have been identified, the political feasibility should be assessed. This paper will try to formulate an answer to the following question: Should the euro area create a supranational layer of government to tackle the problems that have led to the euro crisis, and if so, what should the tasks of this government be?

This paper focuses specifically on the euro area, not on the European Union. The currency integration has created some distinct problems which may have aggravated the euro crisis, or may have come to light because of the euro crisis. These problems may be solved by implementing an extra layer of government above the euro countries. The three clusters of problems that this paper will study are public debt accumulation and moral hazard, macroeconomic stabilization and competitiveness issues. Buiter and Rahbari (2012) discuss the inability of the euro area to deal with illiquid and insolvent banks and sovereigns and the emerging moral hazard. The other two problems involve externalities of fiscal policy and labor market policies and have been put forward by Pisani-Ferry (2012) and Fatas et al (2011). Each problem can essentially be boiled down to the allocation of costs; when looking at moral hazard, the costs of saving countries do not lie with that country. When it comes to externalities, countries conduct policies that imply costs for other countries.

In the first cluster, we will look at moral hazard in debt accumulation. In the second cluster, we will analyze how fiscal policy of a supranational government can improve coordination, internalize spillovers and provide macroeconomic stabilization. In the third cluster, we will analyze the source of macroeconomic imbalances of euro area countries.

This paper will specifically focus on fiscal policy, because those policies are conducted by national governments. Monetary policy, which is conducted centrally by the ECB, is therefore not in the scope of this paper. In the remainder of this paper, we will first examine the mentioned problems from a theoretical perspective, before assessing how important these problems are in the empirics section, and we will look at the existing institutions. Furthermore, we will see how likely it is that our proposed solutions will be politically feasible. We will then formulate an answer to the question we have posed above, and finally conclude with a summary of our findings.

A euro area government: a dream come true?

2. Theory

2.1 Moral Hazard and Public Debt

In the run-up to the euro crisis, interest rates of all euro countries converged. Eichengreen (2010) argues that this was the result of investors believing that all risk between countries had been eliminated, and that the no-bailout clause was incredible. Investors believed that when a country would become insolvent, the ECB or other countries would eventually rescue insolvent countries. Shambaugh et al (2012) too argue that the consequences of a sovereign default would be very large, as banks that hold large amounts of government debt would go bankrupt as well. The failing government, trying to support banks that go bankrupt, sees a lot of banks defaulting and can therefore not support them.

On the other hand, a defaulting sovereign induces austerity measures, which weakens the economy. The decrease in output lowers tax revenues, worsening government problems. Furthermore, because banks fail, the amount of credit provided to the economy is restricted, which slows down economic performance. In turn, a weak economy damages a bank's balance sheet through decreased asset prices and decreased credit demand, leading to bank defaults again. These effects are collectively referred to as the doom loop. Because usually not only domestic banks hold large amounts of sovereign debts, but also foreign banks hold sovereign debt, the sovereign debt crisis not only poses a threat to that country, but also to other countries. This is referred to as contagion. Austerity measures taken by the sovereign also affect other countries, and a failing of the banking system in other countries would, through a contraction of credit supply, also affect other (euro) countries. All these effects point to the disastrous consequence of not bailing out sovereigns, which led to the belief that this provision was incredible Eijffinger et al (2015). Interest rates on government bonds were especially lower for peripheral countries than they had been before the introduction of the euro.

Both the low interest rates and the belief that the no bailout clause was incredible led to countries accumulating unsustainable amounts of debt. Countries did not take into account the fact that their possible insolvency would create a large burden for other countries, which is moral hazard. Not only a solvency crisis can cause the problems as discussed in the previous paragraph. A liquidity crisis, in which the sovereign only faces illiquidity, but not yet insolvency, can eventually lead to a sovereignty crisis through two mechanisms (De Grauwe, 2011; Buiter and Rahbari, 2012) because perceived risk increases interest rates, repayment of current debt becomes harder. Furthermore, because the government has to repay more, it is forced into austerity. This leads to lower growth of the country's economy, making it even more difficult to repay debt, as less taxes are collected. As a fear of default often hits a country which is already in recession, the adjustment mechanism of stimulating fiscal policy is taken away, because countries are forced into austerity. This aggravates the budgetary problem of the country.

To break the loop that has been described above, Buiter and Rahbari (2012) argue that a bailout fund is needed, which acts as a sovereign debt restructuring mechanism (SDRM). This bailout fund is needed to guide the debt restructuring of defaulting sovereigns, as letting a country default completely would on the one hand create the doom loop described above, not only within the defaulting country, but also through contagion to other (euro) countries. On the other hand it would also cause a debt overhang problem; the country, having failed on its previous outstanding debt, can no longer acquire new funds to finance its expenditures. Furthermore, by having such a fund in place, investors will not push the country into a self-fulfilling prophecy of illiquidity and then insolvency, as there is an institution that backstops this (Lane and Pels, 2012).

Countries have created such a fund, in the ESM. Therefore, the severe economic consequences of a sovereign default that we have described above are less likely to occur. However, countries will be more inclined to accumulate public debt to finance their expenditures, as they will be bailed out. This is called moral hazard. Conditionality on bailout funds cannot solve this moral hazard problem; if the bailout fund would impose very strict conditions on accessibility of its funds, countries will not be able to use this bailout fund, and default. We have just established that letting countries default is undesirable, and advocating so is an incredible threat. Strong conditions are therefore an incredible threat as well (De Grauwe, 2011). Also, imposing strong conditions on countries upon receiving funds and assistance is not helpful to other countries either; a country receiving assistance is already in trouble, and punishing such a country would lead to higher unemployment and less economic performance, which also hurts other countries. Conditions can thus not be too harsh, but therefore they fail to solve moral hazard.

There are rules from the Maastricht Treaty concerning the amount of debt and deficit a country may accumulate. Wyplozs (2012) argues that such fiscal rules can, on a theoretical level, eliminate a bias of a government towards budget deficits. Governments experience this deficit bias because of two reasons: first, governments experience a common pool problem, where the benefits of public spending are experienced now, while the burden of deficits used to finance them is not experienced now, but by future generations. Second, Wyplozs (2012) also recognizes that a government anticipating to be bailed out by a supranational government (or institution) is also more biased towards deficits. Pisauro (2003) supports this conclusion.

We have argued earlier that harsh conditionality of a bailout fund is time inconsistent, as it is undesirable to punish a country that is already insolvent. The bailout fund, in the euro area embodied by the ESM, therefore induces moral hazard; countries accumulate too much debt, knowing that they can be bailed out. Fiscal rules, limiting the accumulation of debt and deficit, can backstop this moral hazard. Assuming that they are enforceable, countries may be inclined to borrow more, but are simply not able to do so. Wyplozs (2012) argues that rules alone are not enough to prevent a country from a bias towards deficits and debt accumulation, as these rules can just as easily be changed as they have been implemented. He stresses that there must be different institutions that can enforce these rules. A first best solution would be a neutral, non-elected agency which regulates budgets. Wyplozs (2012), along with Wren-Lewis (2011) argues, however, that delegation of budgetary authority to such an agent is not politically feasible.
The Maastricht treaty rules are currently enforced by the European Commission, by imposing a fine as a percentage of GDP. We will argue in the empirical section that the effectiveness and enforcement of the current rules is lacking, however. This is based on the fact that enforcement of budget rules is done partly through the European Council, which consists of the heads of state of EU countries. We argue that in such a setup, countries

are reluctant to agree to punishing other countries, as they fear that they will face the same punishment in the future. By being compassionate towards another country, these countries hope to escape punishment in the future themselves. A government institution which is not made up of heads of governments does not face this conflict of interests, as the officials making up this government would not be responsible for the fiscal policy of their home country. However, a time inconsistency problem may still arise; countries may delegate some authority regarding budgetary enforcement to the supranational institution, but this institution may still be hesitant to impose fines or give any other type of punishment, as a country that has accumulated too much debt is often already troubled.

Because of this time inconsistency problem, delegating more authority or providing harsher punishments to a supranational government would not alleviate this problem. Instead, Gros and Mayer (2010) propose a solution to alleviate moral hazard problems in a somewhat different, and more sophisticated way. They propose to draw up an institution that they call the European Monetary Fund (EMF), which should act as a lender of last resort/bailout fund to sovereigns. As the ESM is now in place, the authority which they delegate to their EMF would be given to the ESM. They propose to establish a fund, used for bailout purposes, to which countries contribute according to the risk that they pose. More specifically, they propose to calculate payments as follows:

- Countries contribute 1% annually of the stock of 'excess debt', which is defined as the difference between the actual level of public debt (at the end of the previous year) and the Maastricht limit of 60% of GDP. For Greece with a debt-to-GDP ratio of 115%, this would imply a contribution to the EMF/ESM equal to 0.55%.

- Countries contribute 1% of the excessive deficit, i.e. the amount of the deficit for a given year that exceeds the Maastricht limit of 3% of GDP. For Greece, the deficit of 13% of GDP would give rise to a contribution to the EMF/ESM equal to 0.10% of GDP.

This proposal would imply a contribution of 0.65% of GDP for Greece over 2009. Gros and Mayer (2010) argue that this is a large enough amount to prevent moral hazard, while not being so large that countries could not bear this contribution. We do have some concerns with this proposal. As countries only contribute when violating the Maastricht criteria, the same time inconsistency problem may arise; the enforcing institution may be inclined not to collect the contribution because the countries is already in distress. We propose to amend the proposal such that all countries contribute to the fund, regardless of their Maastricht compliance. We would imagine the scheme to be different:

• Countries contribute 0.5% annually of their actual level of public debt of the previous year. For Greece with a debt-to-GDP ratio of 115% (2009), this would imply a contribution to EMF/ESM of 0.575%.

• Countries contribute 0.5% of their actual deficit as a percentage of GDP. For Greece, the deficit of 13% of GDP would give rise to a contribution to the EMF/ESM equal to 0.065% of GDP.

This way, the contribution of Greece in 2009 would be around 0.64% of GDP, annually. This scheme would imply a contribution of all member countries, making the time inconsistency problem less likely. All countries now contribute to a fund that could help them overcome illiquidity or insolvency.

These contributions are made every year, in every economic situation, and even by countries who do not violate Maastricht rules. In fact, currently all countries that take part in ESM also contribute money, also those not violating Maastricht. This way however, the collection of funds also helps in preventing moral hazard.

2.2 Macroeconomic Stabilization

Macroeconomic stabilization in a country is typically achieved through both monetary and fiscal policy (Burda and Wyplosz, 2012; Marrewijk, 2012). Since the euro area countries have formed a currency union, monetary policy is now centrally carried out by the ECB. The problem here is that monetary policy, through interest rate setting, is an instrument that must adhere to the problems of each member countries; the ECB cannot differentiate its policy for each member country. Therefore, the importance of fiscal policy has increased, especially because booms and busts still occur at a national level instead of a euro level. This is because apart from monetary policy, all macroeconomic policy is still carried out at a national level.

The first important issue is fiscal policy coordination. Oates has described several externalities of decentralized policy. In his 1972 book on Fiscal Federalism (Oates, 1972) he describes tax competition; he suggests that decentralized governments try to keep taxes low, so as to attract businesses to settle in their district. This way, taxes collected are lower than optimal, resulting also in less spending than optimal. In the Eurozone, applying this theory would imply that Eurozone countries set tax rates lower than would be optimal, such that also public spending is less than optimal. However, also non-competitive decision making of decentralized governments has external effects. Oates points out that the argument in favor of transferring fiscal authority to a federal government is internalizing spillovers. He gives an example of poor relief programs; when one district (or country) would start a poor relief program, enhancing wealth of their individuals, this increases economic activity, which may easily spill over to other districts (or countries) through imports. Molle (2006) also emphasizes that spillover effects of fiscal policy work largely through imports, and that therefore in the integrated market of the European Union, where there is one currency, no import tariffs and no border control, imports are very large, and therefore spillover effects are large as well.

Austerity, on the other hand, has negative externalities for other countries, as some of the austerity results in decreases in import from other European countries Zezza (2012). The rationale for decentralized governments is that if public goods would be provided at a central level, the centralized government would fail to diversify the provision of public goods across regions; Oates (1999) argues that decentralized governments are better able to provide the level of public goods that is optimal in that specific area, at the cost of not internalizing inter-jurisdictional spillovers. This theory, named the first-generation theory of fiscal federalism by Oates in his 2005 paper, is elaborated upon in a second-generation theory. Oates (2005) adds the insight, put forward by Besley and Coate (2003) and Tommasi (2003), that

A euro area government: a dream come true?

politicians may not have the social interest at heart, and that therefore accountability of politicians plays an import role. He argues that a benefit of having decentralized governments is that they are better at controlling public officials, as their policies are more observable. The trade-off is then accountability versus externalities. The fact that the European Union and euro area have a very small 'central' government may point out that the emphasis is on accountability, even though externalities may be substantial. We will survey the empirical literate on the magnitude of fiscal spillovers in the next chapter.

The previous paragraph discussed policy making by a decentralized government, and the spillovers that may arise. Governments may become aware of these spillovers, and may try to coordinate policies with other governments for this reason. (Engwerda et al, 2002) develop a model where countries can execute cooperative or non-cooperative fiscal stabilization policies, which is essentially a prisoners' dilemma. Countries can agree to coordinate, but this is cheap talk if the 'game' is played only once (i.e. if governments only once try to cooperate). It is shown that countries coordinate on a Nash equilibrium where they do not coordinate their policies. However, it would be a Pareto improvement to have both countries coordinate policies. Policy coordination can be regarded as an infinitely repeated interaction game, where this repeated interaction could be used to coordinate on the Pareto efficient outcome (Aumann and Maschler, 1995). A country can either 'free-ride' on expansionary policy of its neighbor country once, and never be trusted again, or it can cooperate with the neighbor country, and have cooperation in all future periods (Brunila, 2002). Which of the two alternatives is reached depends on the valuation of the future. As coordination is done by politicians, who can be preoccupied with their next term instead of all other future periods, this may pose a problem. A more detailed example of this problem is elaborated upon in the appendix.

Internalizing spillover effects by transferring fiscal authority to a federal government solves a problem. Transferring money between decentralized governments through federal taxes goes beyond that, but is often used in federal frameworks as well (Oates, 1972). Transferring between countries implies that resources are distributed from rich to poor countries. This can provide risk sharing; if a country is hit by an exogenous shock, its GDP will drop. If taxes and subsidies are based on GDP, or on unemployment for example, such a shock will automatically be stabilized, as less taxes have to be paid and more subsidies are collected. When macroeconomic stabilization is carried out by decentralized governments, governments can only provide very limited fiscal stabilization when the economies are open, due to import leaks (Oates, 2005). Oates also argues that when there is large integration between regions or countries, macroeconomic stabilization through federal-local government transfers becomes increasingly important. Ter-Miniassian (1997) stresses this as well. A fiscal transfer mechanism can imply, however, than some countries which are performing better-than-average end up to be a net payer. Germany may be hesitant to join such a system, as they fear they might not benefit from it.

However, when viewed on a long-term basis, this system is basically an insurance against exogenous shocks for each member. Persson and Tabellini (1996) develop a model with two heterogeneous regions, in the sense that one has a larger variance in its economic performance than the other. These countries can engage in cross-country transfers. Two models of decision making are explored: federacy-wide voting under majority rule where each citizen within the two countries has a vote, and Nash bargaining between the two countries. Under majority voting, even though citizens within a country are heterogeneous in the sense that they can be employed or unemployed, Persson and Tabellini show that voters within a country are homogenous in their preference for the amount of transfer. If their country is likely to experience a shock, they agree on a higher transfer. Voters in the other country are also homogenous. This means that, under majority voting, the country with the most citizens wins. Persson and Tabellini conclude that this only exacerbates interregional differences.

However, when countries are involved in a Nash bargaining game, countries end up somewhere in the middle of their respective preferences, as one country may threaten to disagree, leaving no risk insurance for the other country (this is the participation constraint). Their main insight is that countries are willing to engage in risk sharing through transfers, but that direct voting does not lead to desirable outcomes. This provides an argument why we cannot simply subject all supranational economic policy issues to a euro area wide vote. Gong and Zou (2002) elaborate upon the model put forward by Persson and Tabellini. They develop a framework with two heterogeneous agents per local district. Two local governments sets a marginal consumption tax so as to maximize the social welfare function, constrained by public good provision. Then, the optimal federal income tax, used to finance subsidies to local governments and public good provision, can be either negative or positive, depending on parameters. As the optimal federal tax is nonzero, Gong and Zou conclude that fiscal transfers can be utility and welfare-enhancing through the reduction of income variance.

A supranational government would be able to do two things. On the one hand, by conducting part of the public goods provision and fiscal policy, it could internalize spillover effects of policies between countries, perhaps at the cost of accountability of politicians. Furthermore, by having taxes and subsidies flow between national governments and a supranational government, macroeconomic shocks can be absorbed, increasing utility of individuals, especially since the ability of national governments to do so is limited (Oates, 2005).

In this section we have discussed fiscal policy by local governments and supranational governments. This type of spending is affected by fiscal multipliers (Ramey, 2011; Aiyagari et al, 1992). We have argued that with small open economies, national governments are unable to provide macroeconomic stabilization, as there is an import leak. Furthermore, we have argued that transfers from one region to another, through federal taxes and transfers, can have stabilizing effects. When countries would not coordinate fiscal policy, and all conduct austerity, the spillover effects worsen the effect of this policy on the economy. Eggertson (2010), Christiano et al (2011) and Woodford (2011) all argue that when the zero lower bound is reached the interest rate is (almost) zero, and therefore monetary policy cannot stimulate the economy anymore, as the interest rate cannot be lowered multipliers are large.

This is due to the fact that under normal circumstances, expansionary policy is 'hindered' by a central bank increasing interest rates leaning against the wind. Admati et al (2013) argue that when the economy has been hit by a deleveraging shock, the interest rate can end up being stuck at the zero lower bound, and monetary policy cannot increase the interest rate.

Christiano et al (2011) shows for example that when interest rates are held constant for 3 years, multipliers may be as large as 2.3. However, if governments conduct austerity, while the interest rate cannot be lowered, the negative effect of this austerity is multiplied by the same number. Failure to coordinate fiscal policies is therefore even more severe in harsh economic conditions when a central bank cannot intervene. A supranational government, which has internalized fiscal spillovers of austerity policy, would not pursue austerity to the extent that national governments would.

Given the arguments in favor of a supranational government conducting fiscal policy, we propose to start moving towards such a government, as in conducting fiscal policy, the supranational government is concerned with the effects of this policy on the whole euro area, and can internalize spillovers and provide stabilization. In their 1996 paper by Persson and Tabellini, a distinction is made between direct, euro area wide voting on fiscal policies, and bargaining or execution of fiscal policy by a supranational government. They show that under area wide voting, one country can be completely exploited by the other country. This result does not occur under bargaining or fiscal federalism. Oates (2005) does show, however, that if countries end up sharing risks through fiscal transfers, a moral hazard problem occurs. Countries will be less inclined to save funds for 'rainy days', as they know that the shock will be absorbed partially by the other country.

2.3 Competitiveness Issues

In the run up to the euro crisis, the poorer, peripheral countries have run large current account deficits (Eichengreen, 2010). In principle, this is not surprising, but exactly what would be expected: Blanchard and Giavazzi (2002) explain that poorer countries have a higher expected rate of return to investment, and that therefore capital flows to these countries. If these poor countries use this capital to invest in their productivity, they are 'catching up' to the richer countries whose capital they are using, so that the difference between the rich and poor countries diminishes. This suggests that we should not worry about current account imbalances in the periphery, and for a long time, no-one has (Giavazzi and Spaventa, 2010). However if the current account deficit is a signal of a lack of competitiveness, i.e. if a country is importing goods without using them for long-term productivity gains, then the accumulated liability to other countries cannot be repaid, implying insolvency issues for the deficit country. Even if productivity is maintained, but financing is restricted, countries may face difficulties repaying their foreign liabilities. Thus, current account imbalances may be problematic if they arise due to a lack of competitiveness relative to other countries, instead of a catching up-effect (Belke, 2010).

A country may pursue a beggar-thy-neighbor policy by lowering wages (or moderating them), while other countries increase them. Eichengreen and Sachs (1986) study such policies on a theoretical basis in a gold standard setting (a fixed exchange rate system, and therefore relevant to the euro area). They argue that beggar-thy-neighbor policies can have two effects on foreign output, which are counteracting. If wages are moderated (a country thus devaluates internally), two effects occur; on the one hand, competitiveness of the moderating country increases, which raises its output, and lowers output in other countries.

However, if under the gold standard this change is followed by a gold stock change, money stock in the foreign country could increase, such that output is increased through this channel. The increase may be so large that it counteracts the competitiveness output decrease. Hein (2002) applies this insight to the euro area (EMU area at the time of his paper), and argues that a beggar-thy-neighbor policy will increase domestic output, while reducing foreign output. Also, it will allow for lower inflation, which may improve domestic output. He further argues that such effects only occur when large countries, such as Germany pursue a beggar-thy-neighbor policy. Fritsche et al (1999) use an Oxford Economic Forecasting Model to model the effects of wage moderation by Germany on output and employment on other euro countries. They show that for Germany, foreign output and employment would decrease, while for smaller countries such as the Netherlands such effects would not occur.

It is important to note that a floating exchange rate between countries would provide an easy solution to the posed problem; countries experiencing negative effects from beggar-thy-neighbor policies could devaluate their currency, regaining relative competitiveness (Mundell, 1961). This instrument can obviously no longer be used in the euro area, since the introduction of a common currency has shifted monetary policy to the ECB.

It should further be noted that if one country pursues a beggar-thy-neighbor policy, the foreign country suffering from it may lower (or moderate) its wages as well, restoring relative competitiveness. While this may lead to a race to the bottom (countries alternately lowering wages), it may also provide a signal to the other country that it does not lead to the desired effect (Hein, 2002). What could be worse, is if countries are unable to lower their wages in response to the beggar-thy-neighbor policy, as their relative competitiveness position deteriorates, and leads to the effects described above. Schmitt-Grohe et al (2003) develop a Keynesian model where they analyze the effect of downward wage rigidities (the extent to which a country can adjust wages downward) during a currency peg in a small, open economy. They show indeed that wage rigidities prohibit a country from adjusting after a shock to their economy.

This indicates that facing high nominal wages rigidities as a Eurozone country (which is an open economy due to EU membership) prevents countries from absorbing negative effects from a beggar-thy-neighbor policy. In a 2010 paper by the Dutch Central Bank (DNB, 2010), the Central Bank shares this view; stating that part of the current account divergence in the euro area was caused by wage moderation in Germany, while wages in the periphery increase more than the productivity. Gros and Mayer (2010) provide a different explanation for wage divergence; they argue that when domestic demand increases, financed by foreign debt due to low interest rates, this leads to an excess demand of labor, thereby driving up wages. This view does not explain why a country would have its wages grow with less than productivity growth, and therefore ignores the fact that countries may actively try to keep wages low.

Thillaye et al (2014) also recognize the role of wage divergence in current account deficits. They propose two ideas to counter this divergence. Their first proposal is in line with Watt (2010), and entails a 'golden wage rule'. This would imply that "nominal wage growth in each country equals medium-run national productivity growth, plus the target inflation rate of the central bank, plus/minus a competitiveness correction in surplus/deficit countries".

Their proposal is to give more autonomy to the European Trade Union Confederation and European Trade Union Federation, so as to come to a European level of trade unions. They argue that while trade unions may be reluctant to give up autonomy over their national bargaining power, the alternative would be deflationary policies imposed on deficit countries, which would not be in the interest of workers. Hein and Detzer (2014) also propose wage coordination through European trade unions. The second proposal is a 'minimum wage rule'. Here, minimum wage levels would be applied uniformly to all member countries, to halt deflationary pressures.

3. Empirics

3.1 The lender of last resort and moral hazard prevention

Both Buiter and Rahbari (2012) and De Grauwe (2013) stress the theoretical importance of the existence of lender of last resort for sovereigns. In their empirical paper De Grauwe and Ji (2011) find that government bond markets in the Eurozone are more fragile and more sensitive to self-fulfilling liquidity crises than stand-alone countries (countries with their own currency and an own central bank). They estimate regressions with linear and non-linear specifications where the bond spreads are regressed on a number of country and government specific indicators. Their analysis is not flawless, however. The countries that function as a control group, the stand-alone countries, are EU countries which have wished not to join the euro. This may be due to various reasons, but their exclusion from the euro is not random. Furthermore, bond rates are (or should be) a representation of the bond markets assessment of a country stability. It is therefore likely that these market indicators predict bond spreads, but this makes the regression less informative. Despite the flaws of their research the conclusions seem to point in the right direction.

With the existence of bailout and lending facilities, the problem of moral hazard arises. Dell'Ariccia et al (2002) assess how important moral hazard was around 1998, when Russia was not bailed out, and the perceived probability of future crisis lending decreased, which should have decreased moral hazard. They estimate a regression using Capital Data's Bondware dataset and the EMBI Global dataset to explain bond spreads both before and after the non-bailout of Russia, using OLS regression and a GARCH(1,1) estimation. Independent variables include macroeconomic performance variables, grouped into domestic economic indicators, foreign sector indicators and international interest rates. Both methods find that bond spreads differ significantly between the pre- and post-period, implying that perceived risk by investors has changed due to the non-bailout of Russia. They find furthermore that the sensitivity of spreads to macroeconomic indicators has increased after the non-bailout, and that there was more divergence between spreads of different countries. This indicates that moral hazard was indeed present.

Lane and Philips (2002) use a somewhat similar approach to identify the effect of other, less important events, such as the announcement of an increase of the IMF funds limits, to determine whether such events have an effect on bond spreads. They too use EMBI data to test for a significant change in bond spreads. They find that minor events, such as IMF funds announcement do not change bond spreads in the expected direction. They do find that major announcement, such as the non-bailout of Russia, does increase bond spreads. Their conclusion is that very severe cases of moral hazard, whereby investors fully rely on bailout of the IMF are unlikely, but that moral hazard may exist to some extent.

Haldane and Schebe (2004) look at the valuation of banks in Britain, and make a distinction between assets that they hold in countries with IMF support, and in countries without support. The change in market value of individual UK banks is then regressed on the change in UK equity market index, with each observation being a major IMF announcement, including two day before and after this event. Interventions such as those in Argentina, Turkey and Brazil yield significant exceeding of the market index of UK bank value, but only for banks with a large share of assets in emerging markets. This implies that IMF intervention raises the value of the assets in emerging markets, implying that IMF intervention increases moral hazard. These papers indicate that there is at least some level of creditor moral hazard; creditors are more inclined to provide funds to sovereigns when they expect that the country will be bailed out. All these authors stress that their research focuses on the creditor side, as this is easier to research empirically. They stress however that for each creditor, there is a debtor willing to borrow, and that borrowers, in this case sovereigns, suffer from debtor moral hazard.

We stressed that fiscal rules could help in preventing moral hazard, as they simply restrict public debt accumulation. Heinemann et al (2014) empirically assess how fiscal rules influence bond spreads of that country. Using a fixed effects and Fixed Effects Vector Decomposition (FEVD) estimation, they regress bond spreads on the European Commission's assessment of the strength of fiscal rules of 15 countries, while controlling for macroeconomic indicators. They find that strict fiscal rules can lower government bond spreads, even though a country already be geared towards stable policy, and that implementing stricter rules can also decrease bond spreads. Feld et al (2013) have similar findings. They analyze data on bond spreads of Swiss cantons from 1981 to 2007. It should be noted that the rates are compared to Swiss federal bonds. Feld et al (2013) use their own fiscal rules strength index, and regress canton bond spreads on this index, on a dummy which takes on value 1 after the ruling of the Swiss supreme court that municipalities could not be bailed out by cantons, and on control variables. They find bond spreads are significantly lower for cantons with stronger fiscal rules, and that a credible no-bailout regime also decreases bond spreads. This suggests that strict fiscal rules can help countries to prevent moral hazard.

Enforcement of the budgetary rules in the EU is essentially twofold. The Fiscal compact requires states to implement the budgetary rules within their national legislation, and to implement an automatic correction mechanism, which stabilizes these figures if they exceed a certain threshold (European Commission, 2012a,b). On the other hand, the European Commission and European Council can start an Excessive Deficit Procedure. This procedure can be advised by the European Commission to the European Council. This Council then decides whether it sets any recommendations, deadlines or targets to the failing country. It is important to note that is the Council which decides whether an excessive deficit procedure must be started; this Council is made up of the heads of states, and these heads of states may be reluctant to move for the imposing of fines and such, as they may fear that they may become subject to such fines themselves in the future (Bird and Mandilaras, 2013). To prevent this block-forming, the procedure has been changed somewhat. A recommendation by the European Commission is adopted, unless the European Council decides with a qualified majority (≥ 255 out of 345 weighed votes) not to do so (Barnes et al, 2012). Votes are weighed according to a scheme. In the current system, a blocking majority must thus gain 255 weighed votes, whereas under normal qualified majority voting, a minority of 91 votes could block passing of a recommendation. Even though voting has been changed to make it more difficult to block a recommendation of the Commission, the time inconsistency in enforcing the Maastricht rules still exists. The Commission may still feel that punishing a distressed country is not desirable.

To combat moral hazard and to urge countries to comply with fiscal rules, to refrain them from accumulating debt and deficit, and in the end to prevent them from becoming insolvent, we have followed to some extent the proposal of Gros and Mayer (2010) to implement a bailout/lender of last resort fund, and we mainly discussed the contribution to this fund, as this could prevent moral hazard, as it was tied to accumulation of debt and deficit. Currently, the ESM can provide liquidity and can help countries to restructure debt. The funds that the ESM uses are partially collected from the countries that have joined it, and are partly financed by bonds. We feel that changing the contribution scheme to the ESM from the current GDP based scheme to a debt and deficit scheme, would imply a small change of the current setup; countries are already providing funds to the ESM. The only change would be the way of calculating the contribution.

Fahrholz and Cezary (2010) assess that the contribution that countries would make under the proposed scheme by Gros and Mayer is substantial, but not so large that countries could not bear them. They also recognize that in the scheme proposed by Gros and Mayer (2010), a time inconsistency problem still occurs; countries that are exceeding the Maastricht rules may not be held to their contribution, as they are distressed. They too claim that a contribution should be made regardless of the level of debt and deficit, as in the scheme that we have proposed. Countries taking part in the ESM have contributed about 5.7% of their nominal 2010 GDP, while our proposal suggests a contribution of around 0.64% of GDP annually for very indebted countries such as Greece. Belke (2010) argues that such contributions are bearable by countries and therefore politically feasible. In the scheme that we have proposed, as well as in the Gros and Mayer (2010) scheme, the fund would have collected 120 billion by 2009, had it been in place since the start of the euro. They argue that this would have been enough to provide the ESM package to Greece of 110 billion, and the required package would have likely been lower, given that countries would have accumulated more debt. Changing the contribution scheme of the ESM would allow it to continue providing liquidity and solvency assistance, while at the same time combating moral hazard.

3.2 Macroeconomic stabilization

In the theory section it was argued that fiscal policy could be conducted partially at a supranational level, because it has several benefits; it can internalize external effects of fiscal policy and it creates fiscal insurance against macroeconomic shocks.

Empirical evidence indeed finds that spillovers of fiscal policy are significant. t'Veld (2013) calculates the magnitude of spillover effects of fiscal consolidation, by regressing domestic GDP on foreign GDP, domestic and foreign unemployment, government spending, imports, exports and real exchange rate indicators. Specifications for each country are made according to the European Commission QUEST model. t'Veld identifies the spillover effect of Spain's consolidation policy as 10% of domestic GDP drop. Foreign european countries thus experience a ten times smaller drop in GDP than the drop in Spanish GDP due to consolidation policy.

B´enassy-Qu´er´e and Cimadomo (2006) analyze the effect of German fiscal shocks on 7 euro area countries, using 17-year OECD quarterly data. GDP is regressed on both domestic and foreign net taxes per capita, real government spending per capita, real GDP per capita, GDP deflator inflation rate and 10-year nominal interest rate. The multiplier of a German fiscal shock ranges between 0.6 and 1.8, depending on the country. Hebous and Zimmerman (2013) develop a GVAR model in which they regress domestic output on foreign output, domestic fiscal shocks and foreign fiscal shocks. 12 euro area countries are included, and data is derived from the OECD economic outlook. They estimate that the aggregate multiplier of a foreign fiscal spending shock ranges between 0.5 and 2.0.

The European crisis

The second argument we made was that transfers between countries can help to smooth asymmetric shocks to one member country. It should first be noted that the size of the current European Union budget is about 1% of EU GNP. This budget is largely used for agricultural policies (Common Agricultural Policy, European Commission, 2013)) and transfers to regions that are economically troubled. Each of these policies make up about one-third of the EU budget. The regional policy can be regarded as a transfer from the richer to the poorer countries, as the receiving regions lie in the former Soviet Union, former Yugoslavia, southern Italy, Greece and the Iberian peninsula (European Commission, 2008). Most European countries have government spending in the range of 30 to 50 % of GDP. Macroeconomic stabilization is therefore at this point nonexistent. Buiter and Rahbari (2012) and Fuest and Peichl (2012) too stress that, for the supranational government to carry out macroeconomic stabilization, it would need a far larger budget than the EU has now.

Furceri and Zdzienicka (2013) analyze EU, U.S. and Germany panel data from 1979 to 2010. They identify several channels through which an output shock can be smoothed, including international factor income flows, capital depreciation, and net international taxes and transfers. The last variable is our variable of interest. Using OLS regressions, where shocks are regressed on the aforementioned factors, they find that in Germany 91% of shocks is smoothed through national (federal) taxation. They calculate that when euro countries would contribute between 3.3 and 4.5 % of their GNP, full fiscal insurance against asymmetric shocks could be provided. They even find that the contributions needed to smoothen serially correlated shocks remains at almost the same level. Feyrer and Sacerdote (2013) find that further fiscal integration of euro area can also lead to more unemployment smoothing. They regress the difference in spending between years on the difference in income per capita while controlling for year effects. They find that unemployment insurance spending increases when countries move towards more fiscal integration. They point out that a similar effect is observable for the U.S.

Sorensen and Yosha (1998) regresses U.S. state GDP shocks on smoothing federal factors such as unemployment benefits, using 1963-1990 data derived from the Bureau of Economic Analysis. He finds that 16.6% of shocks to state GDP is absorbed through direct transfers, grants and unemployment benefits. He points out that these 3 factors made up around 10% of the U.S. federal budget, and therefore concludes that with a relatively small budget, not only in the U.S. but also in the EMU area, sizable fiscal insurance can be provided.

We addressed the fact that financial flows between countries are affected by fiscal multipliers. Transferring from low marginal propensity to consume countries to high marginal propensity to consume countries could theoretically lead to transfer benefits. Burriel et al (2010) employ a VAR approach on quarterly data of euro area spending from 1987 to 2007, to calculate the aggregate spending and taxing multiplier. They find that the net effect (spending minus taxes) is positive for the first 8 quarters, and after these 8 months the effects dies out. Ramey (2011a) calculates the multiplier during the 1939-1947 period, when interest rates were held constant, using a similar VAR approach, but does not find a larger multiplier for this period.

Policy coordination in the current situation is governed by the Treaty on Stability, Coordination and Governance. All EU countries have pledged to work towards debt and deficit levels in line with the Maastricht treaty, and the treaty also provides very general rules stating that countries should coordinate their fiscal policies. In an ECB monthly bulletin paper (ECB, 2012), it is assessed that the treaty has very little impact on policy coordination in the sense of spillovers. They point out that the wording of the treaty is very broad, lack specificity and does set not concrete targets, measures or guidelines, and that therefore it is unable to provide enough coordination between countries.

So far we have argued that a supranational government could internalize fiscal policy spillovers, enhance risk sharing by fiscal transfers, and even redistribute resources. They electoral system heavily influences the policy decisions of a government. A majority system, where representatives are elected per district in a winner-takes-all system leads to completely different spending patterns of the government than a proportional representation system. Persson and Tabellini (2003) and Milesi-Feretti et al (2002) find that in majority systems, representatives are preoccupied with their own district, and tend to settle on policies that target smaller groups of citizens. A supranational government, whose parliament is elected by a proportional representation system and whose interest lie with all euro countries, is much better able to make policies that are targeting a larger group of people; coordination of policy between countries can be regarded as a system where heads of state are chosen as the representatives of their district.

Politically, transferring fiscal sovereignty to a supranational government can be difficult. Bargain et al (2013) use micro data of individual households concerning labor supply, income, etc., from 11 euro countries, and simulate the effect of a transfer scheme in Europe using the tax-benefit calculator EUROMOD. They find that in their model, more than half of the voters would benefit from transferring alone. In some countries, however, more than half of the voters would lose disposable income. This model does not take into account macroeconomic stabilization nor internalizing externalities of fiscal policies. No empirical evidence is available where these aspects are included. However, as argued in the theory section and as mentioned above, their separate effects have a positive effect on the economies of countries.

Furthermore, in a paper by Kuhn and Stoeckel (2014), Euro-barometer data is used to assess the attitude of the European people towards European economic governance and european integration. They find that while support for European integration has declined during the course of the euro crisis, the support for European economic governance has not. They use the Euro-barometer responses and group questions into either European integration or European economic governance. The questions regarding economic governance report a Cronbach's alpha of 0.85, indicating that these questions are able to testify well as to the feeling of the public towards this topic.

On a scale of 0 to 10 (where 0 is no support and 10 is full support), a score of 7.2 with a standard deviation of 2 is reported, indicating that the european people are fairly positive towards European economic governance. Stracca (2013) also employ Euro-barometer data to assess how important European people find macroeconomic stabilization. He finds that people report that their life satisfaction negatively depends on unemployment, while positively on lifetime income. This effect is fairly homogenous for all countries. He concludes that providing macroeconomic stabilization can be utility enhancing for European citizens.

Based on the empirical literature, we think that a supranational government can provide substantial benefits to countries and citizens. While European integration may be less politically feasible, the European people do not seem to have a negative attitude towards European economic governance. Krugman (2012) also advocates to set the first steps towards a supranational government for the euro area.

3.3 Competitiveness Issues

In the previous section we discussed the absence of a devaluation mechanism for euro countries, and their problems to implement real devaluation through wage cuts. We argued that having one country conduct a 'beggar-thy-neighbor' policy, in the sense that this country keeps wages at a same level, while other countries increase them. This can lead to a current account deficit, building liabilities to other countries.

We will first try to assess whether the current account deficits of peripheral countries were caused by a competitiveness deterioration. Gaulier and Vicard (2012) argue that unit labor costs have played no role in the current account divergences. They argue that the increase in ULC has largely taken place in the non-tradable sector, therefore not influencing trade and current accounts. Giavazzi and Spaventa (2010) temper this argument, stating that "the distinction between traded and non-traded goods has a high degree of arbitrariness: any non-exportable good or service from a haircut to housing services becomes tradable to the extent to which it is consumed by visiting foreigners".

Jaumotte and Sodsriwiboon (2010) show that peripheral countries were already running somewhat large current account deficits, before the euro crisis. They acknowledge that these deficits were mainly caused by low interest rates due to entering the Eurozone, which facilitated foreign borrowing and discouraged domestic saving. They show that during the euro crisis, the capital inflow stopped, therefore increasing savings, which should have reversed the current account deficit into a surplus.

However, current account deficits have remained. They show that wages in countries like Greece and Spain were in fact already higher than Eurozone averages, and thus argue that the divergence in wages was not part of catching up to Germany, but was a result of different wage policies. Kang and Shambaugh (2013) come to the same conclusion. Belke (2010) use euro area data from 1982-2011 on 11 euro countries to separate the interest rate and competitiveness effect. They find that both effects had a significant impact on current account balances, but do note that wage increases may be endogenous, in that they are increased due to capital inflows.

We will now investigate whether Germany has indeed pursued a beggar-thy-neighbor policy. Germany featured constant wages from 1999 to 2008, while countries like France, Italy, Belgium and the Netherlands faced annual increases of 2 to 3% (Wren-Lewis, 2014). Keuschnigg (2012) also signals that while German wages remained constant, Greek wages increase with 133% over the 1999-2008 period.

Kollmann et al (2015) point to the same conclusion, and calculate the impulse response function of several German policy interventions, by linearizing a DSGE model. The impulse response function for the nominal wage moderation shows that for the rest of the euro area, domestic demand decreased, real GDP declined and trade balance decreased. Hein and Detzer (2014) come to a similar conclusion, arguing that Germany has tried to shift problems to other European countries, in a mercantilist view.

Table 1. Annual wage increases from 1998 to 2008

Countries	Annual wage increase %
Germany	0
France	2.0
Italy	3.0
Belgium	2.1
The Netherlands	2.3

Source: Wren-Lewis (2014).

We have argued that nominal wage rigidities limit the capability of a country devaluating, and therefore counteracting the negative effects of a beggar-thy-neighbor policy of another country. Behr and Potter (2005) estimate downward wage rigidities in 11 euro countries. They employ yearly data from the User Data Base of the European Community household panel to compare a hypothetical wage rigidity (an absence of wage rigidity) to the actual observed wage change distribution. They find that in Italy, Portugal and Greece nominal wage rigidity is much higher than in for example Germany, the UK and Belgium.

We have established that peripheral countries have been unable to correct their current account deficits due to high wage rigidity. The European Union has implemented a Macroeconomic Imbalances Procedure, which can be compared to the Excessive Deficit Procedure. It is also initiated by the European Commission, but the entrance of the corrective arm, which puts a country under surveillance, is decided upon by the European Council, made up of national representatives. This procedure is flawed and cannot force countries to adapt variables concerning competitiveness (DNB, 2010). Penalties that can be imposed suffer from the same time inconsistency as the Excessive Deficit Procedure, which we discussed in the previous section (Essl and Stiglbauer, 2011). These authors also argue that the order to take corrective measures is much more difficult than under a government spending deficit; wage growth and trade is at least partially conducted in the private sector, and cannot be regulated as easily.

Federal countries like the U.S. and Germany have nation-wide minimum wage regulations[1] and trade unions, such that unit labor costs cannot diverge too much within the federacy. As explained in the theory section, countries may be reluctant to adapt wages for political reasons. It is therefore very important to have a supranational government that can organize a minimum wage and improve cooperation between trade unions. Also the Macroeconomic Imbalances Procedure has difficulties to correct a divergence of wages, as it suffers from the same time inconsistency problem as the Excessive Deficit Procedure. Furthermore, the European Commission has decided not to place countries with excessive deficits under the corrective arm of the Excessive Deficit Procedure, because these countries are already receiving liquidity from the ESM/EFSF, and are therefore already under surveillance of these institutions (Rehn, 2014).

---

[1] Germany has only adopted a minimum wage on January 1st, 2015.

The ESM conditions imposed on current account deficit countries are focused on government debt restructuring, instead of labor market policies. An extension of the powers of the European Trade Union Confederation and European Trade Union Federation, along with more room for European trade unions, may help in preventing countries pursuing a beggar-thy-neighbor policy. Glassner and Pochet (2011) establish too that more coordination is needed, and that unions have, especially when the euro was just introduced, made efforts to coordinate wage demands transnationally. They argue that because wage coordination was not ranked high on Europe's political agenda, these efforts have failed. They argue that when coordination would be facilitated more by European law, beggar-thy-neighbor policies cannot be pursued.

4. Policy recommendation

We will now try to answer the question that we have posed in introduction: What should the tasks of a supranational government be? And how should it be designed? With regard to preventing moral hazard, we have seen that punishing countries, in any way possible, always suffers from a time inconsistency problem. This implies that a supranational government, no matter how it is designed nor how much powers it has, it cannot deal optimally with moral hazard.

The best solution, in our opinion, is to alter the funding scheme of the ESM, as we have argue in section 2.1: Countries contribute 0.5% annually of their actual level of public debt of the previous year, and countries contribute 0.5% of their actual deficit as a percentage of GDP. This way, the time inconsistency problem is improved; countries pay contributions over their accumulation of debt and deficit. Once a country faces liquidity problems or must be bailed out, this fund can be used. Because these contributions are made every year, regardless of the level of debt, no discretionary decision has to be taken by any governmental body. The contributions are large enough to induce countries to decrease their debt levels, but at the same time are not so large that they will be problematic.

A euro area government: a dream come true?

When it comes to macroeconomic stabilization, we have argued the importance of coordination and internalizing spillovers. A lot of governments have pursued austerity during the euro crisis, which has worsened economic conditions both in their own and other countries. Having more economic governance by a European or euro area wide government, can internalize spillovers and improve coordination. This type of governance is supported by the European public. Therefore, we propose to slowly transfer more budgetary powers towards the European Union, or to create a supranational government for the euro area alone, as the euro area itself suffers most from lacking fiscal policy. This government should then receive budgetary powers and should collect taxes, such that it can provide stabilization and coordination, while being controlled by an elected parliament. This mechanism would induce individual countries to save less for rainy days, however, and induce them to finance expenditures using debt. The ESM contribution scheme is meant to tackle this problem of deficit bias, however.

When it comes to the actual legal framework of such a government, there are several models one could think of. There could be a "euro parliament", elected proportionally by all euro area citizens, which would control a euro government, and would have a role in passing bills. On the other hand, the euro area is based on the frameworks of the European Union. Therefore, one could think of an extension of the powers of the European Parliament and the European Commission, in the sense that apart from the sovereignty regarding the European Union, it would also have the above-mentioned sovereignty regarding the euro area. A similar model over government exists in Belgium. This is a question for legal scholars, however.

When it comes to macroeconomic imbalances, we have argued that part of these imbalances was caused by countries pursuing beggar-thy-neighbor policies. Therefore, we propose to give more authority to the European Trade Union Confederation and European Trade Union Federation. Also, the supranational government, primarily occupied with fiscal policy, should encourage unions to cooperate at a European level, and should make a legal framework in which a minimum wage is possible. Furthermore, it should create a legal framework in which wage negotiations between European trade unions, employees and the supranational government has binding power within the union.

We feel that the change of the ESM contribution scheme is a marginal change which can provide a lot of benefits. The creation of a supranational government with budgetary powers, and a development of European wide unions is a larger change. However, these could provide mechanisms to decrease the magnitude of asymmetric shocks, and enhance cooperation between euro countries. Politically, the European public seems to be in favor of some economic governance, and theoretical models show that a majority of voters can benefit. The move towards a supranational government with tax and spending powers should be a long-term goal of European policy makers, as De Grauwe (2011) and Krugman (2012) have argued as well.

5. Conclusion

We started our analysis by identifying that countries in the Eurozone faced several coordination problems in the policy they conduct. We found that, because countries have joined a currency union, monetary policy is no longer at their disposal, and a lender of last resort was lacking. Moral hazard was and is not combated well. The proposed change in the contribution scheme to the ESM can help to counter this problem better, while not implying a large amount of sovereignty transfer.

A second problem we discussed concerned fiscal policy. Countries do not coordinate their fiscal policies, and therefore create externalities. Furthermore, risk of asymmetric shocks can be shared better through fiscal transfers.

The supranational government conducts fiscal policy and therefore provides insurance to asymmetric shocks and unemployment. Even though some countries may end up being net payers in the near future, their citizens benefit from the fact that they face less variance in income. Furthermore, a majority of European voters would benefit, and a majority of European voters also seems to be in favour of more economic governance.

A third problem concerned the fact that Germany had conducted a beggar-thy-neighbor policy by intentionally keeping labor wages low. Peripheral countries faced high downward wage rigidity, and therefore were pushed into a current account deficit. This meant that they were building up liabilities to other countries, which they could eventually not pay back. When unions would coordinate wage demands euro area wide, and when the supranational government would make a legal framework in which wage negotiations have legal power, beggar-thy-neighbor policies can be prevented.

Appendix: an infinitely repeated government interaction

Two governments can either pursue expansionary fiscal policy or austerity. Austerity is negative for the other country, while expansionary policy is beneficial for the other country. Let the payoffs be as follows:

	Austerity	Expansionary
Austerity	(100, 100)	(150, 50)
Expansionary	(50, 150)	(125, 125)

Now, if countries value the next period with δ, countries will only coordinate on expansionary policy if

$150(1 - \delta) - 100\delta \leq 25$
$150 - 250\delta \leq 25$
$-250 \delta \leq -125$
$\delta \geq 1/2$

So, if governments value future periods enough, they will coordinate on the Pareto efficient, non-Nash equilibrium.

References

Admati, A. R., De Marzo, P. M., Hellwig, M. F., Pfleiderer, P. C. (2013) "Fallacies, Irrelevant Facts, and Myths in the Discussion of Capital Regulation: Why Bank Equity is Not Socially Expensive." SSRN, October 22, 2013.

Aiyagari, R., Christiano, L., and Eichenbaum, M. (1992) "The output, employment and interest rate effects of government consumption." *Journal of Monetary Economics* 30 pp. 73–86.

Aumann, R. and Maschler, M. (1995) *Repeated games with Incomplete information.* Cambridge: MIT Press.

Bargain, O., Dolls, M., Fuest, C., Neumann, D., Peichl, A., Pestl, N. and Siegloch, S. (2013) "Fiscal union in Europe? Redistributive and stabilizing effects of a European ta-benefit system and fiscal equalization mechanism." *Economic Policy*, pp. 375–422.

Barnes, S., Davidson, D. and Rawdanowicz, L. (2012) "Europe's new fiscal rules." *OECD Economics Department Working Papers* 972, 21 June 2012.

Begg, I., Hodson, D., and Maher, I. (2003) "Economic policy coordination in the European union." *National Institute Economic Review* 183 pp. 66–77.

Behr, A. and Potter, U. (2005) "Downward wage rigidity in Europe: A new flexible parametric approach and empirical results." *German Economic Review* 11(2) pp. 169–87.

Belke, A. (2010) "Reinforcing EU governance in times of crisis: The Commission proposals and beyond." *Discussion Papers of DIW* 1082.

B'enassy-Qu'er'e, A. and Cimadomo, J. (2006) "Changing patterns of domestic and cross-border fiscal policy multipliers in Europe and the US." *CEPII Working Paper* 24.

Besley, T. and Coate, S. (2003) "Centralized versus decentralized provision of local public goods: A political economy approach." *Journal of Public Economics* 87 pp.2611–2637.

Bird, G. and Mandilaras, A. (2013) "Fiscal imbalances and the output crises in Europe: Will the fiscal compact help or hinder?" *Journal of Economic Policy Reform*, 16(1) pp. 1–16.

Blanchard, O. and Giavazzi, F. (2002) "Current account deficits in the euro area: The end of the Feldstein-Harioka puzzle?" *Brookings Paper on Economic Activity*, 2 pp. 147–209.

Blockmans, S. and Faleg, G. (2015) "More union in European deference." *EU Foreign policy CEPS Task Force Reports*. February 2015.

Brunila, A. (2002) "Fiscal policy: Coordination, discipline and stabilization." *Bank of Finland Working Paper* 7.

Buiter, W. and Rahbari, E. (2012) "The European central bank as lender of last resort for sovereings in the eurozone." *Journal of Common Market Studies* 50 pp. 6–35.

Burriel, P. B., De Castro, F., Garrote, D., Gordo, E., Paredes, J. and Javier J. Pérez (2010) "Fiscal multipliers in the euro area." Mimeo.

Burda, M. and Wyplosz, C. (2012) *Macroeconomics* Oxford: University Press.

Christiano, L., Eichenbaum, M. and Rebelo, S. (2011) "When is the government spending multiplier large?" *Journal of Political Economy* 119 pp. 78–121.

De Grauwe, P. (2011) "Managing a fragile eurozone." *CESifo Forum* 12(2) pp. 40-45.

De Grauwe, P. (2013) "The European central bank as lender of last resort in the government bond markets." *CESifo Economic Studies* 59(3) pp. 520–535.

De Grauwe, P. and Ji, Y. (2011) "The governance of a fragile Eurozone." *CEPS Working Document* 346, May.

Dell'Ariccia, G., Schnabel, I., and Zettenmeyer, J. (2002) "Moral hazard and international crises lending: A test." *SSRN Scholarly Paper* 80258.

DNB (2010) *Enhanced coordination on macroeconomic imbalances in the euro area* 3 August 2010.

Dutta, M. (2011) "The United States of Europe: European union and the euro revolution." *Emerald Insight*. Revised edition.

ECB (2012) "A fiscal compact for a stronger economic and monetary union." *Monthly Bulletin*. May 2012 pp. 79-94.

Eggertson, G. (2010) "What fiscal policy is effective at zero interest rates?" *NBER Macroeconomics Annual*.

Eichengreen, B. (2010) *Europe and the Euro*. Chicago: The University of Chicago Press.

Eichengreen, B. and Sachs, J. (1986) "Competitive devaluation and the great depression: A theoretical reassesment." *Economics Letters* 22(1) pp. 67-71.

Eijffinger, S., Kobielarz, M., and Uras, B. (2015) "Sovereign debt, bailouts and contagion in the eurozone." *VOXEU*.

Engwerda, J., van Aarle, B. and Plasmans, J. (2002) "Cooperative and non-cooperative fiscal stabilization policies." *Journal Economic Dynamics and Control*, 26 pp. 451–481.

Essl, S. and Stiglbauer, A. (2011) "Prevention and correction of macroeconomic imbalances: The excessive imbalances procedure." *Journal of Monetary Policy*, (4)pp. 99–113.

European Commission (2008) *Working for the regions*. Office for Official Pulications of European Communities.

European Commission (2012a) "Fiscal sustainability report 2012." *European Economy* 8.

European Commission (2012b) "Report on public finances in emu." *European Economy* 4.

European Commission (2013) "The common agricultural policy after 2013." *Agricultural Policy Perspectives Brief* 5.

Fahrholz, C. and Cezary, C. (2010) "The European council summit and the political economics of the Emu crisis." *CEPS Policy Brief* 217.

Fatas, A., Abbas, S., Bouhga-Hagbe, J., Mauro, P. and Velloso, R. (2011) "Fiscal policy and the current account." *IMF Economic Review*, 59(4) pp. 603–29.

Feld, L. P., Kalb, A., Moessinger, M.-D., Osterioh, S. (2013) "Sovereign Bond Market Reactions to Fiscal Rules and No-Bailout Clauses – The Swiss Experience." *IEB Working Paper N. 2013/028*, SSRN, June 13.

Feyrer, J. and Sacerdote, B. (2013) "How much would US style fiscal integration buffer European unemployment and income shocks? (a comparative empirical analysis)." *American Economic Review*, 103(3) pp. 125–8.

Fritsche, U., Horn, G., Scheremet, W., and Zwiener, R. (1999) "Is there a need for a coordinated European wage and labor market policy?" Aldershot: Ashgate Publishing Group.

Fuest, C. and Peichl, A. (2012) "European fiscal union: What is it? does it work? and are there really 'no alternatives' ?" *IZA Policy Paper*.

Furceri, D. and Zdzienicka, A. (2013) "The euro area crisis: A need for a supranational fiscal risk sharing mechanism?" *IMF Working Paper* 198.

Gaulier, G. and Vicard, V. (2012) "Current account imbalances in the euro area: Competitiveness or demand shock?" In Banque de France, *Quarterly Selection of Articles* 27.

Giavazzi, F. and Spaventa, L. (2010) "Why the current account may matter in a monetary union: Lessons from the financial crisis in the euro area." *CEPR Discussion Paper* 8008.

Glassner, V. and Pochet, P. (2011) "Why trade unions seek to coordinate wages and collective bargaining in the Eurozone: Past developments and future prospects." *Etui Working Paper* 3.

Gong, L. and Zou, H. (2002) "Optimal taxation and intergovernmental transfer in a dynamic model with multiple levels of government." *Journal of Economic Dynamics and Control* 26(12) pp. 1975–2003.

Gros, D. and Mayer, T. (2010) "How to deal with sovereign default in Europe: Towards a euro(pean) monetary fund." *VoxEU Policy Brief*.

Haldane, A. and Schebe, J. (2004) "IMF lending and creditor moral hazard." *Bank of England Working Paper* 216.

Hebous, S. and Zimmerman, T. (2013) "Estimating the effects of coordinated fiscal actions in the euro area." *CESifo Working Papers* 3912.

Hein, E. (2002) "Monetary policy and wage bargaining in the emu: Restrictive Ecb policies, high unemployment, nominal wage restraint and rising inflation." *WSI-Discussion Paper* 103.

Hein, E. and Detzer, D. (2014) "Coping with imbalances in the euro area: Policy alternatives addressing divergences and disparities between member countries." *Economics Working Papers* 816.

Heinemann, F., Osterloh, S. and Kalb, A. (2014) "Sovereign risk premia: The link between fiscal rules and stability culture." *Journal of International Money and Finance* 41 pp. 110–27.

Hunt, A. (2014) "Ukip: The story of the Uk independence party rise." *BBC News*.

Jaumotte, F. and Sodsriwiboon, R. (2010) "Current account imbalances in the southern euro area." *IMF Working Paper* 139.

Kang, J. and Shambaugh, J. (2013) "The evolution of current account deficits in the euro area periphery and the Baltics: Many paths to the same endpoint." *IMF Working Paper* 169.

Keuschnigg, C. (2012) "Should Europe become a fiscal union?" *CESifo Forum* 1.

Kollmann, R., Ratto, M., Roeger, W., in't Veld, J. and Vogel, L. (2015) "What drives the German current account? And how doest it affect other Eu Member States? *Economic Policy* 30(81) pp. 47–93.

Krugman, P. (2012) "Revenge of the optimal currency area." *NBER Macroeconomics Annual* 27(1) pp. 439–48.

Kuhn, T. and Stoeckel, F. (2014) "When European integration becomes costly: The euro crisis and public support for European economic governance." *Journal of European Public Policy* 21(4) pp. 624–41.

Lane, P. and Pels, B. (2012) "Current account imbalances in Europe." *IIIS Discussion Paper* 397.

Lane, T. and Philips, S. (2002) "Does Imf financing encourage imprudence by borrowers and lenders?" *IMF Working Paper Economic Issues* 28.

Marrewijk, C. V. (2012) *International Economics*. Oxford: Oxford University Press.

Milesi-Feretti, G., Perotti, R. and Rostagno, M. (2002) "Electoral systems and the composition of government spending." *Quarterly Journal of Economics*, 117 pp. 609-57.

Molle, W. (2006) *The Economics of European integration: Theory, practice, policy.* Farnham, Surrey: Ashgate Publishing Group.

Mundell, R. (1961) "A theory of optimum currency areas." *American Economic Review* 51(4) pp. 657-665.

Oates, W. (1972) *Fiscal Federalism.* New York: Harcourt Brace Jovanovich.

Oates, W. (1999) "An essay on fiscal federalism." *Journal of Economic Literature* XXXVII pp. 1120-1149, September.

Oates, W. (2005) "Toward a second-generation theory of fiscal federalism." *International Tax and Public Finance* 12 pp. 349–73.

Persson, T. and Tabellini, G. (1996) "Federal fiscal constitutions: Risk sharing and redistribution." *Journal of Political Economy* 104(5) pp. 979–1009.

Persson, T. and Tabellini, G. (2003) *The Economic Effects of Constitutions.* Cambridge: MIT Press.

Pisani-Ferry, J. (2012) "The euro crisis and the new impossible trinity." *Policy Contributions* 674.

Pisauro, G. (2003) "Fiscal decentralization and the budget process: A simple model of common pool and bailouts." *Società Italiana di Economia Pubblica Working Paper* 294.

Press, A. (2012) "Merkel urges gradual political union in europe." *Bloomberg Business* 7 June 2012.

Ramey, V. (2011) "Can government purchases stimulate the economy?" *Journal of Economic Literature* 49(3) pp. 673–85.

Rehn, O. (2014) *Speaking points by Vice-President Olli Rehn on the 2014 Convergence Report.* Brussels 4 June 2014.

Schmitt-Grohe, S., Ravn, M. and Uribe, M. (2003) "Downward nominal wage rigidity, currency pegs, and involuntary unemployment." *Journal of International Economics* 61 pp. 163-185.

Shambaugh, J., Reis, R. and Rey, H. (2012) "The euro's three crises." *Brookings Papers on Economic Activity* pp. 157–231.

Sorensen, B. and Yosha, O. (1998) "International risk sharing and European monetary unification." *Journal of International Economics* 45 pp. 211–38.

Spiegel, P. (2015) "Juncker revives Eurozone integration proposals." *Financial Times* 12 February.

Stracca, L. (2013) "Financial imbalances and household welfare." *ECB Working Paper Series* 1543.

Ter-Miniassian, T. (1997) *Fiscal federalism in theory and practice*. New York: IMF.

Thillaye, R., Kouba, L. and Sachs, A. (2014) "Why institutions matter in the Eurozone: Reforming EU economic governance." *Policy network paper* July pp. 1-17.

Tommasi, M. (2003) *Centralization vs. decentralization: A principal-agent analysis*. Mimeo.

t'Veld, J. (2013) "Fiscal consolidations and spillovers in the euro area periphery and the core." *European Economy: Economic papers* 506. October.

Watt, A. (2010) "From end-of-pipe solutions towards a golden wage rule to prevent and cure imbalances in the euro area." *Social Europe Journal* 23 December 2010.

Woodford, M. (2011) "Simple analytics of the government spending multiplier." *American Economic Journal: Macroeconomics* 3 pp. 1–35.

Wren-Lewis, S. (2011) "Comparing the delegation of monetary and fiscal policy." *Department of Economics, Oxford University Discussion Paper* 540.

Wren-Lewis, S. (2014) "The untold story of the Eurozone crisis." *Mainly Macro* 29 October 2014.

Wyplozs, C. (2012) "Fiscal rules: Theoretical issues and historical experiences." *NBER Working Papers* 17884.

Zezza, G. (2012) "The impact of fiscal austerity in the Eurozone." *Review of Keynesian Economics* Autumn pp. 37–54.

The European crisis

Chapter 3
Varoufakis' plan B, parallel currencies, and the euro
Jacques Sapir

1. Introduction

The last round of the Greek crisis has epitomized the European institutions nasty behavior. It has also put on the forefront the issue of the Euro. The European Monetary Union has turned into an instrument of enforcement of austerity and deflation all over the Eurozone. Its nasty consequences are going far over the Eurozone by the way. The crisis ended temporarily with an agreement that was forced upon the Greek government. It will have enduring consequences. But, in the process of this crisis have emerged the possibility of another way. What has been called Yanis Varoufakis "plan B" was an attempt to create a parallel payment system, and possibly a parallel currency. It was not intended to be a short road for Greece to return to the Drachma but it could have been so. But this "plan B" has also another meaning. It exemplified an alternative possible out of the straightjacket the Eurozone is. This is why it has such an impact on the "left".

This paper is then to study the process of this so-called "plan B", and why the idea of a "plan B" emerged, in the light of previous experiment with parallel currencies. In this process we will turn on to a very old debate: is money only a payment system or it is something else? This is quite important to understand the issue of so-called "parallel currencies" and their possible effects. What is at stake here is the precise status of money either as a "central" institution of capitalism or, more accurately, as part of an institution nexus. Then we will go back to the "plan B" idea and will look at reactions it provoked.

2. Why the idea of a "plan B" emerged in Greece?

The very idea of a "plan B" for Greece was not born in a vacuum. It was generated by the more or less clear understanding by some Syriza leaders, among them Alexis Tsipras and Yanis Varoufakis, of the coming struggle against European institutions (Sapir, 2015). Varoufakis own previous specialization with game theory[1] led him to understand that an alternative had to be built in a credible way if he wanted to achieve success with the initial Greek government proposals. But, in the same time, to build a credible alternative with the then present situation, what is called "plan B", could make possible the switch toward this new situation. Here was lying the critical issue of the Greek government negotiation strategy. There is no doubt about the commitment of both Tsipras and Varoufakis to the European project. Nevertheless to build an alternative, which could bolster the Greek position in the negotiating process, it was necessary to seriously envisage a break with the European project. As weeks went on after the fateful January 2015 elections a divergence emerged between the two men. Tsipras clung to his commitment to Europe (and the Euro) and Varoufakis understood more and more clearly that there would be no possible future for Greece if it stayed in the European Monetary Union. Both men really wanted to "change" the European process. But Tsipras still hold the view that the existing structure was better than nothing.

2.1 The economic situation of Greece

Greece has committed itself to a three-year agreement with the Board of Governors of the European Stability Mechanism (ESM) for stability support in the form of a loan. In accordance with Article 13(3) of the ESM Treaty, it details the conditionality attached to the financial assistance facility covering the period 2015-18. This mean that in return for a loan of the ESM, which will go mostly to pay principles and interest of past debt, Greece had to agree with a new "memorandum", actually the third one, which would imply more austerity and would let no place for growth (Barro, 2015). This bail-out agreement has been forced upon the Greek government under the threat of an expulsion from the Euro and very clearly we are back to the notorious

---

[1] As it can be seen from Varoufakis (1991) or Hargreaves-Heap (2004).

notion of "limited sovereignty", the so-called "Brezhnev's doctrine" implemented to crush the Prague uprising in August 1968 (Weeks, 2015). But it is doubtful if even this will ultimately prevent Greece exit from the Eurozone (Komileva, 2015).

The agreement that has been reached at by Greece and its creditors after a lengthy negotiation is actually a bad agreement, and this is former Greece minister of finance Yanis Varoufakis opinion[2]. The 85 billion foreseen in this agreement are, at present, woefully insufficient to cure situation of Greece. It could not have been otherwise. For this text is the logical conclusion of the *diktat* imposed on Greece on July 13th, 2015, by its creditors. And this *diktat* was never conceived with the aim of bringing true support to Greece, even at the price of enormous sacrifices, but solely in order to humiliate and discredit its government. This *diktat* is the fruit of a political vengeance and is plainly devoid of economic rationality.

Doubts have been voiced on this agreement. It has been denounced at length in various columns (Evans-Pritchard, 2015). It will increase austerity in a country where the economy is in a free fall since the maneuverings of the European Central Bank beginning on June 26th. The shock on the Greece economy has been tremendous. Provisional data on July and August are pointing to a massive negative effect on industrial production[3]. The IMF is already forecasting another round of depression for year 2015, with a fall of GDP of -2,5%, and another one in 2016. And it is clear that such estimates are conservative. The actual truth could be considerably bleaker. In such a context it is clear that increasing the tax levy in an economy in recession is nonsensical. The VAT hike is to destroy what was left of output potential. One should, in the contrary, massively inject liquidities into the economy in order to jump start production. Everybody knows this[4], the Greek government as well as its creditors. Yet the latter persevere in their error.

---

[2] http://www.lepoint.fr/economie/grece-le-plan-d-aide-ne-marchera-pas-affirme-yanis-varoufakis-12-08-2015-1956351_28.php
[3] http://www.latribune.fr/economie/union-europeenne/grece-l-economie-s-est-effondree-au-troisieme-trimestre-530994.html
[4] http://russeurope.hypotheses.org/4148

The European crisis

This is raising the issue of how such a disaster could have been avoided, as the final result is not just undermining Greece sustainability but EU viability too, as forecasted by Jörg Bibow (2015). To a large extent the discussion then focuses on the so-called "Varoufakis' secret plan" and the possible introduction of a parallel currency in Greece. But in other terms it raises too the issue of relations between "technical decision" and politics. And this issue is clearly a fundamental one.

2.2 Re-throning politics?

Varoufakis actions have to be seen in the context of a move initiated by the January 25th election, which bring Syriza, the Greek "Radical Left" party to power. It was a move to put back politics in command. A lot of people are getting confused by "plan B" technicalities. But the very idea of a "plan B" has never been technical. It was political since its very beginning. However to understand the real nature of the so-called "plan B" it is to be understood where it stands in the ongoing struggle between politics and economics. To do this implied to some extent a move toward re-throning politics.

This expression is coined from a seminal paper written by R. Bellamy about the liberal Hayekian thought and a process of "Dethroning politics" (Bellamy, 1994). The lead idea in Bellamy's paper was that a true liberal would want to replace political decisions by a behavior grounded on norms. Bellamy shows also the limits of such a thought, an in particular explains contradictions of the late Hayek's thought. As a matter of fact dethroning politics imply to kiss goodbye to democracy. What is important is the fact that this process of dethroning politics in the context of what was called "liberal democracy" has been quite well described by a far-right author in the early 1930: Carl Schmitt. Carl Schmitt (1936) is not someone to be followed on all counts but he has also been one of the most powerful thinkers of its time in Constitutional right (Balakrishnan, 2002; Scheuerman, 2001).

In his book "Legality and Legitimacy", he carefully analyses inherent contradiction of what he call "liberal democracy" (Schmitt, 1932 and 2004). One of his avenues of attack is the complete lack of realism inside the "liberal democracy" thinking (Schmitt, 2004, pp. 73-54). Then he focuses to the fact that a power established only through "legality" or the rule of law would benefit of what he called a "majority presumption" and then would turn into a tyranny because it didn't specify who could discuss the principles of this rule of law (Schmitt, 2004, pp. 78-79). He also discusses at length the pretense to replace political decision by rules, be they legal or technical, which is embedded in the modern – i.e. post industrial revolution – liberal democracy system. Actually the "liberal democracy" with its reduction of decisions to the very application of norms and its emphasis on the rule of law is the end of the Right and will lead to a special kind of tyranny (Schmitt, 1985). One special point is that Schmitt highlights the role of homogeneity in what he call "democracy" but is actually parliamentary democracy: "Democracy therefore, requires, first homogeneity and second – if the need arises – elimination or eradication of heterogeneity" (Schmitt, 1985, p. 9). This point has been thoroughly discussed by Chantal Mouffe (1999).

But, it was in the name of pre-established rules and norms that Jean-Claude Juncker, the President of the European commission and one of the main opponents to Syriza government attacked the newly elected Greek government. Even more important, the focus put on homogeneity is a characteristic of neo-classical economics (Sapir, 2000 and 2001-a). We can see here how economics and politics are mixing. Some ideas at the very heart of neo-classical economics, like agents homogeneity, a completely probabilistic environment, are playing in the hands of a specific tradition in politics, the one of "liberal democracy".

2.3 *Rules or discretion? the path toward a naturalization of economics*

The debate about the possible substitution of rules to the political decision raised by Carl Schmitt is of course extremely relevant now. As a matter of fact the *Eurogroup*, a non-elected and legally non-existent institution has enforced its rules against the political decision of sovereign Greece. Arguments in the process have been mostly confined to the "technical" sphere and have largely drawn to mainstream economics. This is showing a kind of congruence between what Schmitt call a "parliamentary democracy" and the very spirit of mainstream economics. Actually we can see a huge literature focusing on norms and rules against discretion, beginning with the famed Kydland and Prescott (1977) paper. The relevance of norms and rules has become one of the most central points in macroeconomics and particularly in monetary economics (Stiglitz, 1994 and Taylor, 1993). However, it is well known that for rules and norms to become the only way to take a decision would imply a perfect probabilistic world. This is, of course, one of assumptions of mainstream economics and econometrics (Haavelmo, 1944, p.48.).

This led to a "naturalization" of economics (Le Gall, 2002). This is a process describing as "natural" things that are not and which frequently is just a front to advance interests based position in what is thought a "non-contestable" way. This probabilistic turn has been enshrined in mainstream economics by the famous Robert Lucas' (1976) paper. To a large extent, this has been largely integrated in the current governance of "modern" liberal democracies (Rose, 1996; Barry, 1996; O'Malley, 1996). This has however been fiercely opposed (Van Lear, 2000), either in economics where authors have highlighted the various deficiencies of the probabilistic world (Davidson, 1996), the problem raised by endogenous money (Davidson, 1994 and Wray, 1998), or in politics. A rules only way of governing has been faulted on the basis of applied psychology (Kahneman and Tversky, 1974).

As a result, the role of discretion is now more and more emphasized. But discretion is not just to be "legal" or it will run into Schmitt argumentation. Discretion has to be legitimate. Raising the issue of legitimacy bring us back to the sovereignty issue, as described in the XVI Century by Jean Bodin (1993). Sovereignty can't be *technically* limited even if there are some technical constraints on any government action (Goyard-Fabre, 1989). One understands that even the most powerful nation would be left without possibility to stop an earthquake or any other natural event. This does not means that consequences of such an event would not be managed by political decision or that the possibility of such a natural catastrophe could not give birth to a *policy* trying to limit possible damages if and when this catastrophe would occur. Then sovereignty is not *technically* limited as the government could decide before and after the natural catastrophe. But the fact that there could be no *technical* limitation of sovereignty goes further. The very impact of a lot of so-called "natural" events is the product of political decision taken long before and of the ability of a given nation to make these decisions. Difference between hurricane impacts in Cuba and

Varoufakis' plan B, parallel currencies, and the euro

neighbor countries was the result of discretion, not rules, in the application of Cuban decision-making (UN/ISDR, 2004 and OXFAM, 2004).

This is why we could find much more into Varoufakis so-called "secret plan" than just a *technical* attempt to circumvent forecasted European Central Bank actions. Varoufakis' plan was actually, even if, himself, he has not understood completely the issue, an attempt to regain Greece sovereignty against the Eurogroup tyranny. It was then a political fight and not just a technical or an economic issue. The very meaning of the "plan B" was the struggle to regain sovereignty. This was the actual context in which this "plan B" was drafted.

2.4 Varoufakis' secret plan

One possible way to avoid this result could have reposed on the famous Varoufakis' Plan B, a plan subject to a lot of debate since last July. This plan would have involved the creation of a dual monetary circulation system, with the creation of a parallel currency. The intent was in no way to explicitly exit from the Euro (or more precisely form the European Monetary Union). It is to be reminded that Yanis Varoufakis – and this is making a big difference with other radical economists like Costas Lapavitsas[5] – is a staunch defender of the Euro. However such an exit could have been contemplated at any time. But the "plan B" was quite sophisticated and would have induced some important changes in the situation. At that point, it is interesting to have a look on what Varoufakis explains and what said when discussing with OMFIF people about this plan:[6]

> "What we planned to do was the following. There is the website of the tax office, like there is in Britain and everywhere else, where citizens – taxpayers who go to the website – they use their tax file number and they transfer to web banking moneys from the bank account to their tax file

---

[5] Lapavitsas (2012); see also Lapavitsas and Flassbeck (2015).
[6] Telephone conversation of July 16th, 2015, between Yanis Varoufakis and OMFIF senior adviser
http://www.omfif.org/media/1122791/omfif-telephone-conversation-between-yanis-varoufakis-norman-lamont-and-david-marsh-16-july-2015.pdf

number so as to make payments on VAT, on income tax and so on and so forth. We were planning to create, surreptitiously, reserve accounts attached to every tax file number without telling anyone, just to have this system functioning under wraps. At the touch of button that would allow us to give pin numbers to tax file number-holders (tax payers). So take for instance a case where the state owed a million [euros] to some pharmaceutical company for drugs purchased on behalf of the National Health Service, we could immediately create a transfer into that reserve account of the tax file number of the pharmaceutical company, and provide them with a pin number. They could use this as a kind of parallel payment mechanism which to transfer whichever part of those digital moneys they wanted to any tax file number to whom they owed money. Or indeed to use it in order to make tax payments for the state."[7]

It is obvious that, in Yanis Varoufakis' mind, the system (called "Plan B") was intended to alleviate the European Central Bank pressure upon Greece and specifically to solve the liquidity crisis engineered by the ECB through its imposed "capitals control". This plan he drafted with Alexis Tsipras as early December 2014, that is *before* Syriza success in January 25th elections, was thought mostly as a *technical* response to a possible ECB action. Political implications seem to have been largely tacit. But actually it was more than that. The main failure of both Tsipras and Varoufakis was to have not understood that. Austerity was much more than a misguided policy. Austerity was the result of a system of governance largely based on the Euro (Fusaro, 2014). When these both men began to plan a fight against austerity, they would have understood that such a fight would put them on a collision course with the Euro.

About the possibility that the plan could lead to a Greece exit from the Euro Varoufakis then add: "That would have created a parallel banking system while the bank were shut as a result of ECB aggressive action to give us some breathing space"[8]. Note then that it was not technically a parallel

---

[7] Transcript of the phone conversation, page 3.
[8] OMFIF Transcript of Varoufakis' phone conversation, page 3.

currency but only a parallel banking system. However, in the next paragraph, Varoufakis admits: "And of course this could be euro-denominated, but at the drop of a hat it could be converted to a new drachma".

It is very clearly stated then that the development of a parallel payment system was not intended as a step to move out from the EMU but could actually have become one at short notice. But to be ready to do so the Greek government, and particularly Alexis Tsipras, would have figured out what was at stake from the beginning, but for Greece and for the Eurozone. That they have not is now history. However, this raises of course the whole issue of parallel currencies and the possible option of a "Grexit".

3. What is at stake with parallel currencies?

The Varoufakis' idea is first to be seen in the frame of the old and long debate on money. Is money just a "payment system" or it is more than that? Mainstream economists have largely explained money as an improvement on barter, mostly for transaction costs reasons (Samuelson, 1973). This had been expanded into the development of "credit money" and the banking system expansion (Schweikart, 1991). This quite obviously misses the fact that with the development of "credit money", and the emergence of capitalism, money changed of nature (Wray, 1990). The distinction between what was traditionally called "money" and financial assets became blurred (Gurley and Shaw, 1960). This does not mean that money is not a transaction system, but this points that the link between production and money has subtly changed in centuries with the slow substitution of species by bank notes and the development of credit. As a matter of fact debts have taken a central place in present economies. Then if a parallel currency is to succeed it has to face the challenge of taking place into the process of debt emission. If a "currency" is limited to current transactions it is not a full-fledged currency. But, to pass the debt issuing test a "currency" is to be backed by specific institutions without which it could not function normally. This is showing that money is not THE central institution of a capitalist economy[9] but part of a nexus of institutions (Sapir, 2005, chapters 3 and 4).

---

[9] Thesis advocated by Aglietta and Orléan (1982) and Orléan (1999).

The European crisis

An important part is trust-generating institutions, without which no currency could actually exists.

3.1 Parallel currencies

The very notion of possible parallel currencies has been raised as a tool to solve the issue of Greece remaining in the Eurozone *and* of managing a possible break with the Eurozone (Cohen-Setton, 2015). But parallel currencies have a long history in economics. In historical times bullions emitted by different countries have freely circulated in a given one. The issue came up as a specific one when paper money was introduced (Ögren, 2006). Experiments with parallel currencies were not a plenty in the XX century but are still noteworthy to examine. An important point here is the fact that from a theoretical point of view it would be important to strictly separate attempt of creating parallel payment systems and genuine attempt to create parallel currencies. But, actually, both are becoming quickly blurred.

One well known and quite publicized experiment in the creation of parallel currency was the so-called "Dated Stamp Script", which circulated concurrently with Canadian dollars, in the Canadian province of Alberta in 1936-1937 (Coe, 1938). This attempt ended up in a failure and most of the paper refused to stay in circulation. But, it is interesting to look at because economic problems in Alberta were mirroring in some ways what is happening in Greece. Alberta has been beset by seven years of distress associated with low farm prices and bad crop yields in the wake of 1929 crisis. Unemployment was pretty high by 1935. The new government elected at Provincial elections was not ready to implement a truly radical reform. It decided then to implement a system of "stamp" to pay for public works done by unemployed people, with e redemption delay of two-years. But, by the end of 1936, it offered the possibility for Albertans to redeem their certificates for Canadian dollars, and most of people chosen to do so.[10] This proofs that confidence in this parallel payment system was quite low. The main reason was that most banks refused to take any part in this system. Irving Fisher (1933) has forecasted this development in a book he wrote in

---

[10] http://jpkoning.blogspot.fr/2015/05/alberta-prosperity-certificates-and.html

1933 about the stamp scrip system. Actually, we were facing a *special kind* of the Gresham law (Bernholz and Gersbach, 1992). It was no more a case of the "bad money" ousting the good one. Coe himself went so far to write: "Bad money obviously does not drive out good money when the government is willing to redeem the bad money in good money" (Coe, 1938, p. 88).

This point is important. As "stamps" were actually guaranteed by the provincial government, economic agents had no doubts they could switch back to Canadian dollar quickly and without cost. There was then no difference in using Canadian dollars or "stamps" as provisional savings.

Another experiment with parallel currency has taken place in Soviet Russia when the government introduced the Tchervonetz. The monetary reform that took place at the beginning of the NEP (Fitzpatick and al., eds., 1991) is a very interesting one.[11] In 1922 the Soviet government introduced a parallel currency, named "Tchervonetz", which was not (at first) legal tender but could be freely traded against the Ruble then the SovZnak. The introduction of the Tchervonetz parallel to the "SovZnak"[12] was an attempt to cure the huge hyperinflation crisis at the end of the Civil War. It worked, but progressively the "SovZnak" disappeared and the Tchervonetz was called just the Ruble (Voznesensky, 1935).

The idea of parallel currency refloated at different times since World War II but essentially as a possible solution either to hyperinflation or to dollarization in emerging economies (Agenor, 1992). The reasons behind the development of parallel currency markets ranges from the sudden influx of worker remittances (Banuri, 1989) to the development of drug trafficking (Thomas, 1989). Such a development is frequently blurring the difference between le legal and illegal, and leading to a huge fragmentation of capital circulation (Lindauer, 1989). By the way, all known examples are stressing that the development of parallel currency markets is a highly unstable situation.

---

[11] Goland (2006); see also Goland (1994), p. 1272.
[12] As was called the Rouble after the coming to power of Bolsheviki.

3.2 The Russian demonetization episode of 1993-1998 and its lessons for Greece

Before the 1998 crash, the Russian economic situation was marked by a number of important features indicating a trend toward a kind of return to a barter economy (Woodruff, 1999). This gave birth to a lot of heated debates. The important point was first the reasons for the development the demonetarization process from 1993 to 1998 (Dufy, 2008). This process resulted from the development not just of barter but also of "parallel currencies".

An important point was also their impact on the Russian economy. Actually they made it especially vulnerable to collapse. This demonetization was both a process of creating an alternate payment system (Comander and Mumssen, 1998) and, in some case, a genuine attempt to create parallel currencies leading to a genuine fragmentation of the Russian monetary space (Sapir, 1996). It is to be noted that this process was also the result of a non-functional budget and fiscal federalism in Russia (Sapir, 2001-c).

First, a large proportion of economic transactions were conducted through barter - by most estimates, at least 50% by May 1998 (Rozanova, 1998). But a significant part too was conducted in Veksels, which were theoretically a credit instrument between two agents without the possibility of transforming the instrument in money.

This can be seen from the following table data of which were compiled by a Russian scholar. What is particularly impressive in the following table is the growth of barter trade at a time when inflation (end of course inflationist expectations) decreased a lot. To some extent it was not hyperinflation that led to demonetization of the Russian economy but precisely the reverse process.

Table 1. Share of barter trade and Veksel use in inter-enterprise trade in Russia from 1993 to 1997 in %

Sectors	Barter share in 1993	Barter share in 1997	Share of trade using Veksels 1997
Chemicals	21	52	14
Metal working	14	46	8 / 5
Mechanical constructions	12	41	10
Wood and paper	12	46	8
Construction materials	11	59	13
Fuel	10	33	26
Textile and clothes	8	42	9
Food processing	6	25	5
Power generation	4	46	n.d.

Source : Rozanova (1998), p. 98.

As a matter of fact, if we add up barter and Veksels, between 60% and 70% of the inter-enterprise trade were done out of the ruble (Comander and Mumssen, 1998). It has to be added that enterprises were not alone to issue Veksels. Some regional administrations did so to pay regional civil servant. By doing so they crossed the border between a specific payment system and money.

In the Veksel column for 1997, the first figures in the metalworking line is for iron and ferrous metal and the second figure is for non-ferrous metals. And, these "regional" Veksels could be transformed into rubles. In the end, perhaps as much as 25% of transactions was conducted in Veksels, some of which have been emitted by regional authorities and were no more than proxy currencies or even regional currencies-in-the-making. Then, the border between what could be an alternative payment system and a genuine parallel currency became blurred. Actually, using official income and saving data we could see that the use of the ruble was steadfastly decreasing in some regions. The dual use of barter and Veksels led to a creeping demonetization of a part of Russia.

It is also important to note that demonetization increased simultaneously with the decrease in the inflation rate. Thus, barter was not a reaction to fears of a loss of value of the national currency. Rather, it was generated by fears of defection in transactional relations (Marin, 2000), induced by a shortage of liquidities that favored the actor who held money in any transaction. This has important and significant implications if we look at Greece today. Quite obviously the Greek economy is facing, and has faced since the end of June, an important shortage of liquidity. It is to be seen to what extent this would lead to the spontaneous creation of parallel payment systems like in Russia in 1993-1998. But it is also to be seen to what extent these systems, if created, are to lead to a massive tax-evasion and to induce a process of economic and then political fragmentation like the one which took place in Russia before the 1998 crash. Thus, the macroeconomic policy geared toward fighting inflation has largely destroyed money as an institution in Russia.

The rapid decrease of barter after the 1998 crash is also noteworthy. Barter trade went down to 26% in September 2000 and the use of Veksels also retreated. This was to a very large extent the product of two major changes. First, following the process of State rebuilding initiated by the then Prime minister Mr. Evguenny Primakov transactions were more and more effectively enforced and confidence between economic agents progressively returned (Durkheim, 1991). Second, liquidity was increasing in Russia, partly because the Central Bank policy had been less stupidly rigid it was before the crash and partly because the economic rebound Russia witnessed after the crash implied more profits and enterprises financial situation improvement (Sapir, 2001-b).

There are important lessons from these events in Russia for Greece. The first one is then the value of the link between liquidity flows and institutional stability and the stability of monetary relations. A second important lesson is that "austerity" policies when implemented without a view on the actual situation, when leading to a critical shortage of liquidity, could well generate the opposite of what they are aimed at (Sapir, 2002). The main raison here is that illiquidity could provoke as much damage than insolvency and that solvency is not a guarantee that you will be liquid. Increase in barter transaction in Greece is just a proof that illiquidity could provoke demonetarization and that without institutional stability monetary transactions could become more and more difficult[13]. Actually these austerity policies are weakening the institutional nexus that is required to maintain the hegemony of a specific currency on a given territory.

3.3 *The case of Greece*

The idea of parallel currencies was refloated in the context of the sovereign debt crisis in the Eurozone (Andresen, 2012). Two issues were actually mixed. The first one was how to avoid engaging into painful and not very effective internal devaluation. This is why parallel currencies were mostly proposed to "Southern" Eurozone countries (Butler, 2011). But a second issue came to front then: could the Euro be transformed into a kind of supplementary currency, to be used only with non-Eurozone countries? Then every country would recover its own currency for internal trade and inter-Zone trade, and would use the Euro only for trading (in goods and financial operation) with non-Eurozone countries.

Actually the first issue has concentrated most of attention. A great number of the authors who are considering parallel currency proposal are actually focusing on a mechanism that will facilitate economic recovery in the crisis-struck countries. Introduction of parallel currencies are seen as able to boost domestic economic activity and to reduce the dependence on imports. It is then expected that, in return, parallel currencies will increase the export performance and competitiveness of these countries (Vaubel, 2011). Some authors are also seeing the introduction of parallel currencies as a mean to allow the affected states to reduce the interest rate levels for loans and investments and to systematically increase the amount of money in circulation, both for state debts and in the private sector (Goodhart and Tsomocos, 2010). Around one third see the parallel currency as a way of setting free non-used capacities (Schuster, 2012). One important opinion is that in view of the extremely differing economic situations in the European member states, parallel currencies might be a tool for economic self-help

---

[13] http://www.independent.co.uk/news/business/news/greece-debt-crisis-news-barter-is-booming-in-rural-areas-as-cash-dries-up-10427713.html
and http://www.nytimes.com/2015/09/22/business/international/trading-meat-for-tires-as-bartering-economy-grows-in-greece.html

and a means of boosting economic recovery (Butler, 2011). But, this implicitly means that for a large number of economists there is no hope for economic recovery under the current Euro system.

Still, the parallel currency idea raises the issue of how and by whom it is to be introduced. One possibility is of course that the parallel currency is being brought into circulation via the usual channels of the two-tier banking system. But this implies that the banking system would either agree with such an idea or could be coerced to implement it. The other possibility being that the State itself would play banker role and act as the issuer. In the great majority of plans we are seeing a process to bring the parallel currency into circulation on the basis of loans. This was the case for Varoufakis' Plan B and these loans would have been, at least at first, Euro denominated.

It is to be understood that would the State be the issuer, as in proposed IOU in Greece. However the issue of what role is to play the banking system would still be pending. Actually in Varoufakis' Plan B, the State would have played the main role because the Greek banking system was disabled by ECB actions. The logical solution would have been to make a "requisition" order (under the frame of a state of urgency) to assure control of the Greece Central Bank and most commercial banks. However, it was clear from the outset that such a move was the equivalent of a declaration of war against the ECB.

The whole IOU system was then envisioned without any constraints either on commercial banks or on the Central Bank. But, such a system is clearly just a stopgap. Its main role is to allow economic agents to work for some weeks, but it would be not quite a sustainable system. As noted above Varoufakis himself was admitting that the result could have been a fast Greek exit from the Eurozone. The main reason is that would a parallel currency system be implemented it would have implied some form of state control upon the Greek banking system. But, this control could not have been implemented without shortcutting the ECB (and this was part of the plan) and depriving it of its power on the Greek banking system. Then the ECB would have, quite probably, reacted by calling Euro circulating in Greece "false money" and cut all transactions (Target-2 accounts) with

Greece. The only possible then solution would have to be renaming the currency "drachma" to circumvent ECB action.

For all its alleged interests a parallel currency system is both highly dependent of the banking system and highly unstable, but if it is backed by a strong government will to make the "second currency" the first in a given time. This is one lesson we could draw from Alberta. May be the parallel currency could have been implemented in Greece with ECB approval but certainly not *against its will*. Then, the only advantage of the parallel currency for a country like Greece would have been to allow for an exit from the EMU in quite an orderly way. But this was a point where opinions clashed inside the Syriza government and even Varoufakis was not, at least till end June 2015, ready to face this reality. One of closest Varoufakis collaborators admits to have changed his mind about the so-called "Grexit" and now to favor it (Munevar, 2015). There is then some truth in the fact that designing an alternative payment system in a country facing huge financial difficulties like Greece could give birth to a change of currency. But in the end the political decision to cross the symbolic border is needed and Mr. Tsipras and his government for all their rhetoric were not ready to make this specific political decision?

4. Plan B consequences and after

The "plan B" designed by Yanis Varoufakis is now history for Greece. But like the famous cat in fairy tales it has still many lives to live. It is clear that the so-called "agreement" turns out to be inadequate and unable to treat the problem at the root, but one is beginning to realize that it will not bring any respite (Galbraith, 2015). The financial situation is just as tragic, because when production plummets, so do tax receipts, as well as the solvency of borrowers. The percentage of non-performing loans has sharply increased since last June 26th, 2015. The financing needs of Greek banks have gone from 7 to 10 billion euro at the end of June 2015 to 25-28 billions on July 15, and could reach 35 billion by the middle of the following week. In fact, pressures exerted by the European Central Bank had deliberately destroyed the Greek banking system. And these pressures were serving essentially political aims. The sums which will need to be granted to Greece simply to prevent the country from sinking into total chaos, should it stay in the Eurozone, amount no longer to 82-96 billion euro as estimated on July 13th, 2015, but more probably in the order of 120 billion euro. The Greek debt is at present no longer sustainable and the so-called agreement of July 13th did nothing to make it so (Barro, 2015).

Its disclosure raised a huge debate not just in Greece but in Europe as well. In Greece, but also from Brussels, the former Minister of finance has been attacked from the right side of the political spectrum. One suspects that his attitude during the negotiations from end of January to the end of June 2015 was largely the main reason for these attacks. There is however another dimensions here. The so-called "plan B" has become the rallying point for many opponents to the status-quo in the Eurozone. Because the Greek crisis showed the true nature of so-called "united Europe" (Milne, 2015) and clearly demonstrated that German policy was striving at no less than complete preeminence, Varoufakis' plan "B" has turned into something quite different to what its father envisioned at first. The idea of "parallel currencies" has gained a new strength in the Eurozone and this is to be understood to as a legacy of the June and July crisis.

4.1 The ongoing debate on Varoufakis' "plan B"

As the story goes, a parallel currency system was never implemented in Greece. But this was mainly for political reasons and not for economic or technical ones. In a more profound way Alexis Tsipras' capitulation on July 13th has provoked a deep change in mood and mind about both the Euro and the EU. The idea of a "left exit" or "Lexit" is now open on the table (Jones, 2015).

Yanis Varoufakis, as Minister of Finances, took the decision with the approval of the Prime Minister, Mr. Alexis Tsipras, to have the computer system of the Greek tax administration covertly penetrated. He took this decision about the computer system of the Greek tax administration *because the latter was in reality under the control of persons of the "Troika"*, that is, of the International Monetary Fund, of the European Central Bank and of the

Varoufakis' plan B, parallel currencies, and the euro

European Commission. This was reported to be the famous "plan B"[14]. And this is what he is being reproached for. It is therefore the conservative Prime Minister, M. Samaras, who was beaten in the elections of January 25th, who in reality has committed this act of *High Treason* in entrusting the tax administration to one (or several) foreign powers. It is he, and he alone, who carry the total responsibility for what happened then.

Varoufakis' decision aimed at implementing a parallel payment system, which would have allowed the Greek government to circumvent the blocking of the banks, which was organized by the European Central Bank starting at the end of June 2015. This would have been necessary in order to avoid the destruction of the Greek banking system provoked by the action of the European Central Bank. This actually illegal action of the ECB imperiled the whole banking system, when one of its very missions, *duly inscribed in the charter of the ECB*, was precisely to ensure the good and regular functioning of this banking system.

If Yanis Varoufakis were to be indicted in the future, it would then be logical and just for the President of the ECB, M. Draghi, as well as the President of the Eurogroup, M. Dijsselbloem, to be indicted too. It is true, as we demonstrated, that this parallel payment system could *also* have allowed a very rapid shifting from the Euro to the Drachma, and would probably have triggered such a shift, but Varoufakis, according to his statements reported by *The Telegraph*, considered this only as a very last extremity[15]. Actually what Greek crisis demonstrated was the unwillingness but also the impossibility to act under the framework of previously established rules. That was true for the ECB and that was true for the Eurogroup but that was true also for the Greek government. But it is to be noted that in this crisis it was the Greek government that bowed to these rules when they were cynically discarded or forgotten by most of its opponents.

---

[14] http://russeurope.hypotheses.org/4148
[15] http://www.telegraph.co.uk/finance/economics/11764018/Varoufakis-reveals-cloak-and-dagger-Plan-B-for-Greece-awaits-treason-charges.html

4.2 An absurd decision

Indicting M. Varoufakis is therefore absurd. The fact that he is now being defended by personalities such as Mohamed El-Erian, the chief economist of Allianz and President of a comity of economic experts around the President of the United States[16] indeed goes to show that what he did, he did *for the greater good of the State which he was serving as Minister of Finances.* This indictment, should it be confirmed, could only happen with the complicity of Alexis Tsipras who would then have dropped his Minister of Finances and would not be taking on his own responsibilities. This indictment, were it to happen, would be an odious act, an act of pure political justice and of vengeance on the part of the European authorities, against a man who dared, with the support of his people, to defy them.

Whatever the difference we could have with Mr. Varoufakis, and definitely I don't share his affection for the Euro as it has very deleterious effect on many Eurozone economies (Bibow, 2007), whatever the judgment we could form about his own reluctance to implement this alternative course of action, there is nothing in what he has done that could be considered as *High Treason*. All economists have to stand up and be counted in support of Yanis Varoufakis. Such an indictment would also be very revealing of the *neo-colonialist* attitude of the European authorities today towards Greece, as well as towards other countries.

But what happened in Greece has also other implications. Stefano Fassina, former Vice-Minister of Finances of the Italian government, an MP and one of the prominent members of the Italian *Democratic Party* presently in power, wrote in a text published on the blog of Yanis Varoufakis[17]:

> "Alexis Tsipras, Syriza and the Greek people have the undeniable historical merit of having ripped away the veil of

---

[16] http://www.project-syndicate.org/commentary/varoufakis-agenda-defended-by-mohamed-a–el-erian-2015-07

[17] See Fassina Stefano: «For an alliance of national liberation fronts», article published on the blog of Yanis Varoufakis by Stefano Fassina, Member of Parliament (PD), on 27 July 2015, available via
http://yanisvaroufakis.eu/2015/07/27/for-an-alliance-of-national-liberation-fronts-by-stefano-fassina-mp/

Europeanist rhetoric and technical objectivity aimed at covering up the dynamics in the Eurozone."

He adds:

"We need to admit that in the neo-liberal cage of the euro, the left loses its historical function and is dead as a force committed to the dignity and political relevance of labor and to social citizenship as a vehicle of effective democracy."

He concludes:

"For a managed dis-integration of the single currency, we must build a broad alliance of national liberation fronts."

These are strong words.

But, this perspective is at present entirely justified. The Eurozone has indeed revealed itself to be a war machine at the service of an ideology, neo-liberalism, and vested interests, those of finance and of an oligarchy without borders. The perspective offered by Stefano Fassina is the only one at present open to us, meaning, constituting an "alliance of national liberation fronts" of the countries of the Eurozone to bring the tyrant to bend and to dismantle the Eurozone. It is to be understood then that regaining sovereignty could be defined as a top priority. Without sovereignty there is no possible democratic change. And this is why the struggle for sovereignty could include broad alliances with forces not just on the left but also on the democratic right.

4.3 The German responsibility

One often points at the responsibility of Germany. In fact, Germany insists on tying this agreement down to a strict conditionality, when the conditions put to the previous help plans since 2010 have resulted in a 25% drop in GDP and an explosion in unemployment. Similarly, Germany wants to impose on Athens an important pensions-reform, when these same pensions are playing the role of shock absorbers in the crisis, in a country where intergenerational transfers are replacing unemployment benefits, which have become very scant. This will result in impoverishing a little bit more the population and deepening the recession. Finally, Germany wants to impose wide-ranging privatizations. It is clear that the latter would allow German companies, which are far from being choir-children when it comes to Greece (the Greek branch of Siemens being at the heart of an enormous tax scandal) to proceed with its shopping-list at ramshackle prices. One can see that incompetence seems to reach hands with cynicism.

The responsibility of Germany is evident. In fact, the only hope – if Greece were to remain in the Eurozone – would be to annul a large part, between 33% and 50%, of the Greek debt. But the German government wants to hear nothing about this at the very moment when it is becoming known that it has drawn large profits from the Greek crisis, as acknowledged by a German expertise institute[18]. Yet, there is something in the murderous obstination of the German government towards the Greek people that is going far beyond the « rules » of a very conservative management, or of special interests. In fact, the German government wants to punish the Greek people for having brought to power a party of the radical left. In this, there is a clearly political will at work, not an economic one. But the German government also wants to make an example out of Greece, while putting its sight on Italy and France, as noted by the former Minister of finances Yanis Varoufakis[19], in order to show who is the boss in the European Union. Actually, Jörg Bibow has been forecasting it in a 2013 paper where he describes contradictions between France and Germany about the Euro future the real issue (Bibow, 2013).

But to be forecasted such a move is certainly most alarming indeed. It is to be noted that even Romano Prodi, a former Italian PM and European commissioner is actually deeply worried by the turn taken by German policy (Prodi, 2015). But, Germany is acting in such a way because it has no other choices. For to act differently would be tantamount to accepting what

---

[18] "Greek Debt Disaster: Even If Greece Defaults, German Taxpayers Will Come Out Forward, Says German Assume Tank" in the *Observer*,
http://www.observerchronicle.com/politics/greek-debt-crisis-even-if-Greece-defaults-German-taxpayers-will-come-out-ahead-says-german-think-tank/58504/
[19] http://www.omfif.org/media/1122791/omfif-telephone-conversation-between-yanis-varoufakis-norman-lamont-and-david-marsh-16-july-2015.pdf

Varoufakis' plan B, parallel currencies, and the euro

Romano Prodi is implicitly proposing namely a *federal* organization of the Eurozone. However, this is not possible for Germany. If one doesn't want the Eurozone to be the straitjacket which it is presently, allying economic depression to austeritarian rules, it would be necessary indeed for the countries of the North of the Eurozone to transfer between 280 and 320 billion Euros per year, over a period of at least ten years, to the countries of Southern Europe. Germany would have to contribute to this sum probably to the tune of at least 80%. This means that it would have to transfer every year 8% to 12% of its GDP, depending on hypotheses and estimations (Sapir, 2012-a).

One must state flatly that this is not possible. All those who burst into the great *lamento* about federalism (Aglietta, 2012) in the Eurozone with sobs in their voices or with martial posturing have either not done the sums, or they cannot count very well. One can, and one must criticize the German attitude towards Greece because it amounts to a political *vendetta* against a legally and legitimately elected government[20]. But to demand from a country that it transfer *voluntarily* such a proportion (the highest figure of 12% has been computed by Natixis chief economist Artus, 2012) of the wealth it produces every year is not realistic. It is then to be said that for a third time in a century, Germany is actually destroying Europe but this time not by design but by incapacity to exert a sensible view of its hegemony.

It may be that the whole EMU project has been a political one from the outset. The very possibility it was a cover for a hidden federalist agenda has been noted (Sapir, 2012-b). But, this project has turned into something to be feared by population of Eurozone countries. As a matter of fact we are still decades away from the federalist future, and maybe we would never reach it, and in a terrible economic situation (O'Rourke, 2014). The turn toward a non-democratic, to say the least, governance is also notorious. To have not understood that has doomed Syriza experiment, even if it seems that by end June Varoufakis has came to this conclusion or at least accepted it could become the result of his actions. It is time now to dismantle the EMU, and if possible to do it in a cooperative way. But we are not to be afraid would this

---

[20] As done by Nicole Gohlke and Janine Wissler, two Bundestag MP belonging to *Die Linke* in *Jacobin*, https://www.jacobinmag.com/2015/07/germany-greece-austerity-grexit/

occur in a non-cooperative way. On this point, the idea of parallel currencies or parallel banking system could be useful transitional tools toward a general dismantling of the Eurozone, but certainly not stable ones. Parallel currencies could also play a role in the context of a post-Euro situation, where the Euro itself could resurrect as a parallel currency for trade with non-zone countries. But this is a different story.

References

Agenor, P. R. (1992) "Parallel currency markets in developing countries ." *Essay in International Finance* . Princeton: University Press, 188, December.

Aglietta M. (2012) *"Zone Euro: éclatement ou fédération"*. Paris: Michalon.

Aglietta, M. and Orléan A. (1982) *La violence de la monnaie*, Paris: PUF.

Artus, P. (2012). " La solidarité avec les autres pays de la zone euro est-elle incompatible avec la stratégie fondamentale de l'Allemagne: rester compétitive au niveau mondial? La réponse est oui». *Natixis Flash-Economie,* 508, July 17.

Andresen, T. (2012) "What if the Greeks, Portuguese, Irish, Baltics, Spaniards, and Italians did this: high-tech parallel monetary systems for the underdogs?" *Real-world economics review*, 59, pp. 105-112.
http://www.paecon.net/PAEReview/issue59/Andresen59.pdf .

Balakrishnan, G. (2002) *The Enemy: An intellectual portrait of Carl Schmitt*. London: Verso.

Banuri, T. (1989) "Black Markets, Openness and Central Bank Autonomy" *World Institute for Development Economies Research (WIDER) Working Paper n°62*, Helsinki.

Barro, J. (2015) "The I.M.F. is telling Europe the euro doesn't work » *The New York Times*, July 14. http://www.nytimes.com/2015/07/15/upshot/the-imf-is-telling-europe-the-euro-doesnt-work.html?_r=1&abt=0002&abg=0

Barry, A. (1996) "Lines of communication and space of rule." In A. Barry, N. Rose and al., *Foucault and Political reason. Liberalism, neo-liberalism and rationalities of government*. London: UCL Press, pp. 123-42.

Bellamy R. (1994) "Dethroning Politics: Liberalism, Constitutionalism and Democracy in the Thought of F. A. Hayek". *British Journal of Political Science* 24 pp 419-441.

Bernholz, P. and Gersbach, H. (1992) "Gresham's Law: Theory." *The New Palgrave Dictionary of Money and Finance*, vol. 2. London: Macmillan pp. 286-288.

Bibow, J. (2015) *Euro Union – Quo Vadis?* , July 2nd, http://www.socialeurope.eu/2015/07/euro-union-quo-vadis/

Bibow, J. (2013) "On the Franco-German Contradiction and the Ultimate Euro Battleground." *The Levy Economics Institute of Bard College Working Paper 762*. Annandale-on-Hudson, April.

Bibow, J. (2007) "Global Imbalances, Bretton Woods II, and Euroland's Role in All This." In J. Bibow and A. Terzi (eds.) *Euroland and the World Economy: Global Player or Global Drag?* London: Palgrave.

Bodin, J. (1993) *Les Six Livres de la République* (1575), Librairie générale française, Paris, Le livre de poche, LP17, n° 4619. Classiques de la philosophie.

Butler, M. (2011) "Parallel currencies could boost euro." Comment in *Financial Times*, 10 Jan 2011. Available via http://www.ft.com/intl/cms/s/0/fdafbb0e-1cee-11e0-8c86-00144feab49a.html

Coe, V.-F. (1938) "Dated Stamp Scrip in Alberta." *Canadian Journal of Economics and Political Science/Revue canadienne de economiques et science politique* 4 pp. 60-91.

Cohen-Setton J. (2015) *The economics of parallel currencies*. June 8. Available via http://bruegel.org/2015/06/the-economics-of-parallel-currencies/

Comander, S. and Mumssen C. (1998) "Understanding Barter in Russia", EBRD/BERD, *Working Paper*, London.

Davidson P. (1996). *Economics for a Civilized Economy*. Armonk: Sharpe.

Davidson P. (1994) *Post Keynesian Macroeconomics Theory*. Cheltenham: Edward Elgar.

Dufy C. (2008) *Le troc dans le marché. Pour une sociologie des échanges dans la Russie post-soviétique*. Paris: l'Harmattan.

Durkheim E. (1991/1893) *De la division du travail social*. PUF. Paris: coll "Quadrige".

Evans-Pritchard A. (2015) "European 'alliance of national liberation fronts' emerges to avenge Greek defeat." *The Telegraph*, 29 July. Available via http://www.telegraph.co.uk/finance/economics/11768134/European-allince-of-national-liberation-fronts-emerges-to-avenge-Greek-defeat.html

Fisher, I. (1933). *Stamp Scrip*. New York: Adelphi.

Fitzpatick, S., Rabinowitch, A. and Stites R. (eds.) *Russia in the Era of NEP*. Bloomington: Indiana University Press.

Fusaro, D. (2014) *Il Futuro é Nostro*. Milano: Bompiani.

Galbraith, J. (2015) "Greece, Europe, and the United States." *Harper's Magazine*, 16 July. Available via http://harpers.org/blog/2015/07/greece-europe-and-the-united-states/

Goland, Y. (2006) *Diskussii ob economicheskoi politike v gody denezhnoi reformy 1921–1924*. Moscow: Magistr.

Goland, Y. (1994) "Currency Regulations in the NEP Period." *Europe-Asia studies*, 46 (8).

Goodhart, C. and Tsomocos, D. (2010) "The Californian Solution for the Club Med." *Financial Times* January 24.

Goyard-Fabre, S. (1989) *Jean Bodin et le Droit de la République*. Paris: PUF.

Gurley, J. and Shaw E. S. (1960) *Money in a theory of Finance*. Washington DC: Brookings Institution.

Haavelmo, T. (1944) "The Probability Approach in Economics." *Econometrica* 12 pp.1-118.

Hargreaves-Heap, S. (2004) *Game Theory: A critical text*. London and New York: Routledge.

Jones, O. (2015) "The left must put Britain's EU withdrawal on the agenda." *The Guardian*, July 14th. Available via http://www.theguardian.com/commentisfree/2015/jul/14/left-reject-eu-greece-eurosceptic

Kahneman, D. and Tversky A. (1974) "Judgment under Uncertainty: Heuristics and Biases." *Science*. pp. 1124-31.

Kydland, F. E. and Prescott E. C. (1977) "Rules rather than discretion: The inconsistency of optimal plans." *Journal of Political Economy* 85(3) pp. 473-490.

Komileva, L. (2015) "Another Bailout Won't Keep Greece in the Eurozone." *Foreign Policy*, August 12.

Lapavitsas, C. (eds.) (2012) *Crisis in the Eurozone*, London: Verso.

Lapavitsas, C. and Flassbeck H. (2015) *Against the Troika – Crisis and Austerity in the Eurozone*. London: Verso.

Le Gall, P. (2002) "Les représentations du monde et les pensées analogiques des économètres: un siècle de modélisation en perspective." *Revue d'histoire des sciences humaines*, 1(6), pp. 39-64.

Lindauer, D. L. (1989) "Parallel, Fragmented or Black? Defining Market Structure in Developing Economies." *World Development* 17 pp. 1871-1880.

Lucas, R. E. (1976) "Econometric Policy Evaluation: a Critique." In Bruner, K. and Meltzer, A. (eds.) *The Phillips Curve and Labor Markets, Carnegie-Rochester Conferences Series in Public Policy.* Vol. 1, Amsterdam: North-Holland pp. 19-46.

Marin, D. (2000) "Trust Vs. illusion: what is driving demonetization in Russia?" *CEPR Discussion Paper Series 2570.* London, September.

Milne, S. (2015) "The crucifixion of Greece is killing the European project." *The Guardian*, 16 July. Available via http://www.theguardian.com/commentisfree/2015/jul/16/crucifixion-of-greece-european-project-debt-colony-breakup-eurozone

Mouffe, C. (1999) "Carl Schmitt and the Paradox of Liberal Democracy." In Mouffe, C. (ed.), *The Callenge of Carl Schmit.* London: Verso, pp. 38-53.

Munevar, D. (2015) "Ecco perché ho cambiato idea sul Grexit." Available via http://www.socialeurope.eu/2015/07/why-ive-changed-my-mind-about-grexit/

O'Malley P. (1996) "Risk and responsibility." In Barry A., Rose N. and al., *Foucault and Political reason. Liberalism, neo-liberalism and rationalities of government.* London: UCL Press, pp. 189-207.

O'Rourke, K. H. (2014) "Wither the Euro?" *Finance & Development* March 2014, pp. 14-17.

Orléan, A. (1999) *Le Pouvoir de la finance.* Paris: Odile Jacob.

Ögren, A. (2006) "Free or central banking? Liquidity and financial deepening in Sweden, 1834–1913." *Explorations in Economic History* 43 pp. 64-93.

OXFAM (2004) *Weathering the storm, lessons in risk reduction from Cuba.* Available via http://www.oxfamamerica.org/publications/art7111.html .

Prodi, R. (2015) "L'Europa fermi l'inaccettabile blitz tedesco." *Il Mesaggero* 8 agosto, http://www.ilmessaggero.it/PRIMOPIANO/ESTERI/europa_fermi_inaccettabile_blitz_tedesco/notizie/1507018.shtml

Rose, N. (1996) "Governing 'advanced' liberal democracies." In Barry, A., Rose N. and al., *Foucault and Political reason. Liberalism, neo-liberalism and rationalities of government.* London: UCL Press, pp. 37-65.

Rozanova, M. (1998) "Alternativnye formy finansovyh rascetov mezhdu predprijatijami", *Problemy Prognozirovanija* 6 pp. 96-103.

Samuelson, P. (1973) *Economics*, 9th Edition, New York: McGraw Hill.

Sapir, J. (2015) "Un jeu complexe." Note posted on *RussEurope* blog, February 3. Available via http://russeurope.hypotheses.org/3389

Sapir, J. (2012-a) "Le coût du fédéralisme dans la zone Euro." Note posted on *Russeurope* blog November 10. Available via http://russeurope.hypotheses.org/453

Sapir, J. (2012-b) "Faut-il sortir de l'euro?." *Le Seuil*, Paris.

Sapir, J. (2005) *Quelle économie pour le XXI siècle?* Paris: Odile Jacob.

Sapir, J. (2002) "Troc, inflation et monnaie en Russie: tentative d'élucidation d'un paradoxe." In Brama S., Mesnard M. and Zlotowski Y. (eds.) *La Transition Monétaire en Russie - Avatars de la monnaie, crise de la finance (1990-2000)*. Paris: L'Harmattan, pp. 49-83.

Sapir, J. (2001-a) *K Ekonomitcheskoj teorii neodnorodnyh sistem - opyt issledovanija decentralizovannoj ekonomiki* (Economic Theory of Heterogenous Systems – An Essay on decentralized economies). Moscow: Higher School of Economics Press.

Sapir, J. (2001-b) "The Russian Economy: From Rebound to Rebuilding." *Post-Soviet Affairs* 17(1) pp. 1-22.

Sapir, J. (2001-c) "Différenciation régionale et fédéralisme budgétaire en Russie." *Critique Internationale* 11, avril, pp. 161-178.

Sapir J. (2000) *Les trous noirs de la science économique*. Paris: Albin Michel.

Sapir, J. (1996) "Désintégration économique, transition et politiques publiques." In Delorme, R. *A l'Est du nouveau. Changement institutionnel et transformations économiques*, Paris: L'Harmattan, octobre, pp. 303-335.

Scheuerman, W. E. (2001) "Down on Law: The complicated legacy of the authoritarian jurist Carl Schmitt." *Boston Review* XXVI(2), April-May.

Schmitt, C. (1936) *Légalité, Légitimité* (translated from German by W. Gueydan de Roussel), Librairie générale de Droit et Jurisprudence, Paris.

Schmitt, C. (1985) *The Crisis of Parliamentary Democracy*, Cambridge, MA: MIT Press.

Schmitt, C. (2004) *Legality and Legitimacy*. Durham NC: Duke University Press.

Schuster, L. (2012) *Parallel Currencies for the Eurozone*. The Veblen Institute. Available via
http://www.veblen-institute.org/IMG/pdf/schuster_parallel_currencies_for_the_eurozone_final.pdf .

Schweikart, L. (1991) "US Banking System: a Historiographical Survey." *Business History Review* 65, Autumn.

Stiglitz, J. E. (1994) "The Role of State in Financial Markets." *Proceedings of the World Bank Annual Conference on Development Economics*, World bank, Washington D.C. pp. 19-52.

Taylor, J. B. (1993) "Discretion versus Policy Rules in Practice." *Carnegie-Rochester Conference Series on Public Policies* 39 pp. 195-214.

Thomas, C. Y. (1989) *Foreign Currency Black Markets: Lessons from Guyana*. Kingston, Jamaica: University of West Indies.

UN/ISDR (2004) *Cuba: A Model in Hurricane Risk management*, UN/ISDR Press release 2005/05, September, New York. Available via www.unisdr.org

Van Lear, W. (2000) "A Review of The Rules versus Discretion Debate in Monetary Theory." *Eastern Economic Journal* 26(1) pp. 29-39.

Varoufakis, Y. (1991) *Rational Conflict*. Oxford: Blackwell.

Vaubel, R. (2011) "Plan B für Griechenland." *Working paper*, 19 Oct 2011. Available via

http://vaubel.unimannheim.de/publications/plan_b_fuer_griechenland_19_10_11.pdf

Voznesensky, N. A. (1935) "O sovetskih den'gah", in *Bol'chevik*, 2.

Weeks, J. (2015) *A specter is Haunting Europe*, July 31st
https://www.opendemocracy.net/can-europe-make-it/john-weeks/spectre-is-haunting-europe-—-spectre-of-democracy

Woodruff, D. (1999) *Money Unmade: Barter and the fate of Russian Capitalism*, Cornell: University Press.

Wray, L. R. (1998) *Understanding Modern Money*. Cheltenham: Edward Elgar.

Wray, R. L. (1990) *Money and Credit in Capitalist Economies: The Endogeneous Money Approach*. Aldershot: Edward Elgar.

The European crisis

Chapter 4
The euro area's experience with unconventional monetary policy

Cristiano Boaventura Duarte and André de Melo Modenesi[*]

1 Background: banking and sovereign crisis

The use of unconventional monetary policies in the euro area began in 2008, in the aftermath of the international financial crisis, with its epicenter in the United States and global implications. After the collapse of Lehman Brothers in September 2008, the world's leading central banks, including the ECB, acted quickly to avoid a more severe spread of the crisis to the financial sector and to the real economy. In this regard, they took not only conventional measures (e.g.: rapid and significant reduction of interest rates), but also a series of unconventional measures, such as extensive liquidity provision operations and foreign exchange swap agreements to ensure the liquidity needs of banks in foreign currency, according to Lane (2012). European banks also had significant exposures in the US subprime market. In this sense, the action of central banks in 2008 has helped to contain panic and avoid a massive failure of banks.

However, the worsening of the crisis in the euro area in 2009 showed that the situation was not just an "external shock" originated in the USA, but a crisis with roots deeply inserted into the monetary union. In the view of authors like Bibow (2012), this intrinsic crisis had two natures: balance of payments and banking. Indeed, since the adoption of the euro as the single currency in 1999, it was hoped that the monetary union would promote an improvement of the economic and financial integration and, coupled by the output expansion that occurred in the 2000s, would help euro area's least developed countries (*periphery*, namely: Greece, Ireland, Portugal, Spain,

---

[*] The views expressed in this Chapter are those of the authors, and do not reflect those of the Central Bank of Brazil.

Italy, Cyprus) in a movement towards convergence with the development level achieved by euro area's *core* countries (namely: Germany, Netherlands, Austria, Finland, Luxembourg, France, Belgium).

Nevertheless, what actually happened was a deepening of the zone's economic asymmetries. According to Miranda (2014), the divergence increased significantly in the period 2000-2008, with core countries specializing in manufacturing and capital goods' exports, while the periphery was left with the supply of basic goods, services and construction sectors. This implied that Germany, Netherlands, Finland and Luxembourg widened their current account surplus, while the other countries increased their current account deficits, especially in the periphery. Additionally, the periphery also lost competitiveness to their main trade partner in the period (Germany) due to lower wage growth rates in this country. According to authors like Brenke (2009), net real wages barely grew in Germany in the 2000's, and actually fell between 2004–2008. The reasons behind this would be the relative loss of bargaining power from labor unions (mainly in industry), and labor market reforms implemented in 2002 and 2008, which increased labor market flexibility and reduced employees' benefits. Those factors are possible explanations why unit labor costs grew much less in Germany than in the periphery. Also, taxes were shifted away enterprises towards individuals. That allowed Germany to increase manufacturing production and exports, keeping lower levels of domestic consumption and imports. Within the monetary union, in the absence of a mechanism to adjust the exchange rate, while Germany could improve its surplus, the periphery remained dependent of basic goods exports and capital goods imports, increasing their current account deficit.

During most of the 2000s, current account deficits were financed by capital flows from the core to the periphery, fostered by the abundance of liquidity and low interest rates (sovereign debt yields from the periphery were close to the ones of core countries). Banks in the core lent money to enterprises and banks in the periphery, which in turn could pay for its imports and lend money domestically cheaply. Credit expansion was accelerated in the periphery in the 2000s, especially in the real estate sector of countries like Spain and Ireland. After the 2008 financial shock in the USA, due to the scarcity of liquidity, banks in the core interrupted their flows to the periphery and claimed their loans' payment there. Then, banks in the periphery claimed their loans' payment to enterprises and households. This provoked a sharp rise in non-performing loans and default rates, and fire sales of assets. At this point, the banking crisis affected severely private agents and impacted directly the real economy.

Those imbalances in the banking system and the private sector were transferred to the periphery's public sector through the fiscal channel. Since the 2000's, peripheral countries already had fiscal deficits, once an important share of their economic growth counted on public expenditure. After 2009, the abrupt drop in income and the growth in expenditure needs to rescue banks/firms in difficulty and pay unemployment benefits forced public deficits to rise quickly. At the same time, public debt, which until then was relatively manageable in most peripheral countries (except for Greece, which at that time was 120% of GDP), increased rapidly. This took sovereign yield curves to steepen in these countries. At that time, mechanisms for the mutualization of risks within the monetary union were temporary or insufficient (e.g., the ECB did not state the lender-of-last-resort status, as suggested by Arestis (2015). Then, each national government had to assume the liabilities of its own banks and private agents. This is what actually turned a banking crisis in each country into a sovereign debt crisis. To make matters worse, since 2010 the sovereign crisis assumed a nature of "contagion": high yields on a single peripheral country's public debt began to transmit to other peripheral countries, perceived by the market as facing similar macroeconomic problems.

This phenomenon began with Greece, which disclosed a record fiscal deficit in late 2009, starting a process that led to the announcement of three rescue programs: € 110 billion in May 2010, € 130 billion in February 2012, and € 86 billion in August 2015, totaling € 326 billion. Rescue packages by the Troika were also announced for Ireland (€ 85 billion in November 2010) and Portugal (€ 78 billion in May 2011), and later for Spain (availability of up to € 100 billion for banks in June 2012, of which € 41 billion were used in recapitalization) and Cyprus (€ 10 billion in March 2013).

Having presented the basic features of the euro area's banking and sovereign debt crisis, the chapter's following sections will discuss the monetary policy actions taken by the ECB after 2008, evaluating to what extent they were able to contain the crisis and influence the macroeconomic performance of euro area countries as a whole in the period. Section 2 will discuss conventional and unconventional measures taken between 2008 and 2014, before the implementation of Asset Purchase Programs (APPs). Section 3 will focus on the programs implemented from September 2014 onwards, mainly on APPs and their effects on the monetary union. Section 4 will present the main conclusions and challenges ahead for the monetary, financial stability and economic policies in the euro area.

2. Pre-asset purchase programs

Before discussing ECB's unconventional measures in the post-2008 period, we will present a brief overview of conventional monetary policy, particularly the evolution of ECB's benchmark interest rate during in the period.

2.1 Benchmark interest rate

With the adverse events of the financial crisis in the USA in September 2008, the ECB promoted a rapid reduction of the benchmark interest rate, from 4.25% in September 2008 to 1.0% in May 2009, 325 basis points (bps) on total.

The rate has remained at that level until April 2011, when it rose 25 bps, and increased again by 25 bps to 1.5% in July 2011. ECB's Governing Council President at that time was Jean Claude Trichet. He justified the rate hikes based on two reasons: (i) To control inflation expectations' acceleration (headline inflation was at that time 2.6% YoY, above the ECB's objective (ii) To avoid the formation of new "asset bubbles", due to the accommodative liquidity conditions since the end of 2008. Those rate hikes were criticized by many people, as the increase in headline inflation was caused by temporary factors (such as high international commodity price levels), but core inflation remained under control (around 1.6%, as can be seen in the chart 1).

Chart 1- Euro area - Benchmark Interest Rate and HICP (Headline and Core % YoY)

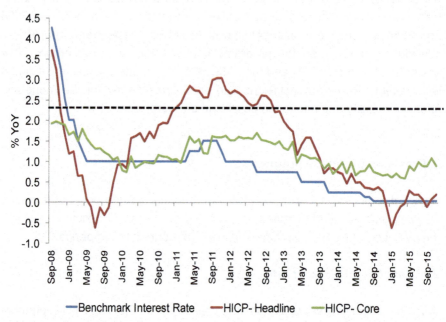

P.S.: Euro area's core inflation excludes energy, food, alcohol and tobacco.
Source: Eurostat

Critics argued that those rate hikes brought further restrictions to the then difficult financial conditions on the monetary union, and had negative spillovers from smaller peripheral countries (Greece, Ireland, Portugal) to larger nations (such as Spain and Italy). Hence, there would be no funds available to rescue all those countries together. In fact, with higher interest rates and the worsening of the sovereign crisis, the euro area experienced a sharp financial volatility during the second half of 2011.

However, it was just in November 2011 (when Mario Draghi assumed as the new President of ECB's Governing Council) that rates began to change their course. Benchmark interest rate was reduced in November (-25 bps) and December (-25 bps), to 1.0%. Since then it was established a downward trend. Between 2012 and 2016 the rate was reduced 100 bps: first to 0.05%

in September 2014, and then to the historic low of 0% in March 2016. Interest rates should be kept at this level or lower levels for an extended period, according to the forward guidance mechanism in place.

2.2 Enhanced credit support and covered bond purchase program

When it comes to unconventional monetary policies in the euro area, some initial measures had already been implemented in 2008, but a formal ECB unconventional program only began in July 2009, with a set of initiatives that was called "Enhanced Credit Support": (i) The conduct of full allotment auctions for liquidity supply at fixed rates; (ii) A broader range of asset types (public and private) accepted as collateral for loans from the ECB; (iii) The extension of ECB's liquidity operations maturities (from 3 months up to 1 year); (iv) The provision of liquidity in foreign currency (mainly dollars) through swap agreements with central banks; (v) The purchase of covered bonds issued by banks.

Regarding the Covered Bonds Purchase Program (CBPP), the universe of assets purchased by the ECB included securities issued by banks in the primary and secondary markets in emissions of at least € 100 million, with a minimum of investment grade rating (BBB- or similar) and backed by public or private guarantees. The first phase of this program (CBPP1) occurred between July 2009 and June 2010. The objectives of the program were: i) To promote lower interbank's market rates; ii) To reduce funding restrictions for credit institutions, and indirectly to non-financial companies; iii) To encourage credit institutions to expand their loans; iv) To improve liquidity conditions, particularly in the private debt market. In the first phase, the ECB bought a nominal amount of € 60 billion, 27% in the primary market and 73% in secondary. The maturity of the purchased securities was between 3 and 7 years, with an average duration of 4.1 years, according to Beirne et al (2011). Despite the CBPP1 managed to buy the previously announced amount of € 60 billion, and in general terms fulfilled its four objectives, it was not enough to prevent covered bonds yields' to steepen in peripheral countries affected by the sovereign banking crisis.

A second phase of the program (CBPP2) was launched in November 2011, the same month the ECB started cutting the benchmark interest rate again.

In the second phase, the ECB announced an intention to buy a nominal amount of € 40 billion in covered bonds until October 2012. It required that securities to be purchased by the ECB had to come from bank emissions with at least € 300 million. The CBPP2 lasted until the intended date, but the more stringent conditions in bank bond markets and from the program itself led to ECB's purchases of only € 16.4 billion (36.7% in the primary market and 63.3% in the secondary).

2.3 Long term refinancing operations

Before 2008, the ECB usually offered Long Term Refinancing Operations (LTROs) monthly, to be repaid in 3 months. In 2008, it began to offer also operations to be repaid in 6 months. In June 2009 it added also to its tender procedures operations with repayment in 12 months. In November 2011, when the ECB noticed the sovereign crisis had worsened of and the liquidity available to the banks and the economy as a whole had shrunk, the institution announced two major three-year LTROs, which were held in December 2011 and February 2012. On those occasions, the ECB lent to banks amounts to be paid over three years, charging only the benchmark interest rate (then in a level of 1.0%). The first operation amounted € 489.2 billion, and the second operation € 529.5 billion, thus totaling a liquidity injection of € 1018.7 billion by the ECB within three months. However, due to the high uncertainty level in the euro area, a large amount of this liquidity had two undesired destinations: i) The ECB's balance sheet itself, parked at the current account or deposit facility (the latter yielded 0.25% until July 2012, being reduced to zero thereafter); ii) Carry trade, speculative operations that used cheap money to buy assets with higher returns, including short term sovereign debt of the periphery. Thus, although three-year LTRO operations have avoided a massive bank deleveraging and promoted a short term positive effect in sovereign yields (as stated by Pattipeilohy et al, 2013), those large liquidity injections did not achieve their goal of restoring credit market's dynamics and channel funds to the real economy.

2.4 Securities markets program

This program was implemented in May 2010, same month when the first Greece aid package was agreed, but markets priced high spreads between German's and peripheral countries' bonds. In order to reduce the financial fragmentation in the euro area and improve monetary policy transmission, the ECB engaged in purchasing peripheral countries' securities, in an attempt to prevent their yields to rise.

Although the program also legally allowed corporate bond purchases in primary and secondary markets, its implementation was through government bond purchases in secondary markets. The program focus was not to make monetary policy more expansionary or to finance member countries. As a consequence, the ECB conducted weekly open market operations to provide fixed-term deposits (with a weekly duration), in order to sterilize the liquidity injected through its purchases.[1]

In the beginning (May 2010 to February 2011), purchases were limited to bonds of Greece, Ireland and Portugal. After a pause between February and July 2011, the ECB resumed its purchases in August 2011, including also bonds of Spain and Italy. The program was officially terminated in September 2012, although purchases have actually occurred until February 2012. According to ECB data, the program has acquired bonds with an average maturity of 4.3 years and a nominal amount of € 218 billion, of which almost half belonged to Italy, as shown in Table 1.

When it comes to the evaluation of SMP impacts, there are several studies working with different methodologies to verify its effectiveness. In general, most authors agree that interventions have managed to reduce the yields of peripheral countries, but only in the short term (a few weeks, as Pattipeilohy et al, 2013, or even a day, as Doran et al, 2013). According to Doran et al, even after ECB's intervention and yields falling in the same day, with adverse macroeconomic events and a possible lag for a new intervention, yields resumed rising up to pre-intervention levels the next day. From the point of view of private investors, what concerned them the most was that

---

[1] The ECB interrupted SMP portfolio weekly sterilization operations since July 10, 2014.

the ECB had seniority over them from a legal point of view. This implied that private investors would be the first to bear the losses of any default in these countries, and the ECB could be charged only after all private investors had been wiped out. This was one of the reasons why SMP's interventions had only very short-term effects, with yields soon returning to rise again.

Table 1 ECB - SMP - Amount purchased by country and average bond maturity

Issuer Country	Nominal Amount (€ billion)	% per country	Average Maturity (years)
Italy	102.8	47.2%	4.5
Spain	44.3	20.3%	4.1
Greece	33.9	15.6%	3.6
Portugal	22.8	10.5%	3.9
Ireland	14.2	6.5%	4.6
Total	**218**	**100.0**	**4.3**

Source: ECB

Indeed, the great controversy both in public opinion and among ECB members themselves were factors that contributed to the interventions be discontinued in time, and actually interrupted seven months before the official end of the program. The disagreement within the ECB was such that it was appointed as a reason to the resignation of Bundesbank President Axel Weber and ECB's Chief Economist Jurgen Stark.

Helm (2012) states that ECB core countries' members (notably Germany) considered that the program did not respect ECB's mandate to keep price stability. According to them, SMP just tried to disguise monetary financing of peripheral governments (although the program didn't purchase government securities in the primary market, it allowed peripheral countries to delay the much "requested" fiscal adjustment measures).

2.5 Verbal intervention strategy and the OMT

With debt yields of peripheral countries rising to unsustainable levels and sovereign contagion threatening to reach even core countries (e.g. France), the ECB introduced a different communication approach. From July 2012 onwards, it started a "verbal intervention" strategy, trying to contain negative expectations on markets and aiming to increase monetary policy credibility. At its meeting of July 4, 2012, the ECB introduced the "forward guidance" mechanism, which affirmed that interest rates would remain at low levels for a prolonged period of time, signaling an accommodative monetary stance. On a speech in July 26, 2012, Draghi affirmed he would do "whatever it takes to save the euro".

This change in the communication strategy culminated in September 2012 with the end of SMP and the creation of a new program, named Outright Monetary Transactions (OMT). This new program intended to restore the transmission mechanism of monetary policy, which was notoriously disrupted. It opened the door for the ECB to buy sovereign debt of specific countries in the secondary markets, in order to stabilize their yields, once they signed a Memorandum of Understanding (MOU) with fiscal and reform conditionalities attached.

ECB purchases would be of bonds with maturities between 1 to 3 years, in unlimited amounts. The OMT focus wasn't on countries which were already receiving assistance from the Troika (Greece, Portugal or Ireland). Instead, it aimed to avoid spreading contagion to countries which had their debt trading on markets, but at high yields (e.g. Spain, Italy). Most importantly, the ECB would be treated *pari passu* with other creditors, eliminating the problem of ECB seniority that existed in the SMP. As the SMP, the OMT received a number of legal challenges in the German Constitutional Court (GCC) and the European Court of Justice (ECJ), related to accusations such as monetary financing of government debt. The OMT had a ruling of "approval with conditions" by the GCC on January 14, 2015. The ECJ dismissed OMT's charges in 16, June 2015. Nonetheless, the OMT was never activated, only remaining in the field of verbal intervention.

The euro area's experience with unconventional monetary policy

The ECB's OMT program is part of a broader set of other institutional actions taken by the EU in that period: (i) The creation in October 2012 of a permanent bailout fund, the European Stabilization Mechanism (ESM), to replace other previous temporary funds (European Financial Stability Facility- EFSF and European Financial Stabilization Mechanism- EFSM). The ESM would have a significant lending capacity (€ 500 billion) and stable guarantees; (ii) The beginning of the project to create a banking union. Under this project, from November 2014 onwards there would exist a Single Supervisory Mechanism, where the ECB would centralize most of euro area banking supervision authority under its responsibility.

Later, it would be established a Single Resolution Mechanism and a Banking Recovery and Resolution Directive, so that bank resolution costs would rely mostly on private (bail-in), rather that public (bailout) funds. Finally, the harmonization of Deposit Guarantee Schemes would protect euro area's depositors of up to € 100,000 from potential losses.

All of them intended to convey positive messages to the markets. In the case of the OMT, it showed ECB's unconditional willingness to take bold actions if necessary. The ESM ensured an increase in the amount and duration of rescue funds (now permanent). With the banking union, there would be a substantial advance in the monetary union banking supervision and resolution framework. The combination of these elements had an important role in reducing investors' risk perception about euro area's countries, so that from the end of 2012 onwards, the former trend of rising sovereign yields was stopped.

3. Asset purchase programs

3.1 Background

Despite the less volatile scenario in 2013 and 2014, with some countries of the periphery ending their assistance programs with "clean exits" (Ireland, Portugal, Spain for banks) and the gradual downward trend of sovereign yields, euro area economy still showed slow signs of recovery in credit and output in those years.

The European crisis

In the second half of 2014, the most serious concern became the threat of deflation, with signs that the low inflation level was not just a temporary phenomenon (related to an oil price drop), but a more lasting element, with second round effects that weakened the economic activity. The risk of falling prices was a heavier burden for an economy with difficulty to recover, which could generate a situation that entrepreneurs would no longer invest, families would postpone spending decisions and the real value of debts would rise. In this context, the ECB began to monitor more closely the medium/long-term inflation expectations. In August 2014, the 5Y5Y inflation swap rate (which reflects how inflation expectations for the next five years will be in the following five years) fell below 2% YoY for the first time on record.

3.2 CBPP3, ABSPP and TLTROs

In an attempt to avoid a deflationary spiral, in September 2014 the ECB launched new initiatives in order to improve the transmission of monetary stimulus to the credit market and the real economy. In terms of interest rates, the benchmark rate was reduced to its lowest level ever (0.05%). The deposit rate was also reduced to an even more negative level (-0.20%, from -0.10 in June 2014), in an attempt to avoid that banks kept parking liquidity on ECB's current account. In addition, it announced a set of three unconventional measures:

i) Covered Bond Purchase Program - CBPP3: a third round of ECB's purchases of covered bonds issued by banks;
ii) Asset Backed Security Purchase Program - ABSPP: purchases of securitized corporate bonds by the ECB, based on guarantees from private assets;
iii) Targeted Long Term Refinancing Operations - TLTRO: the provision of long-term liquidity lines to banks, with should target this liquidity preferably for loans to non-financial companies/households, except for mortgages.

Regarding the CBPP3, purchases of covered bonds by the ECB began in October 2014 and are expected to last until at least March 2017, without a predetermined amount. This third stage of the program has acquired an amount of bonds nearly the triple of the first stage. According to ECB data available until March 2016, an amount of € 165.8 billion have been acquired, with a vast majority of purchases in the secondary market (70%).

In terms of the ABSPP, the program started a month later, in November 2014, and is also expected to last at least until March 2017. Nevertheless, there are some technical difficulties in its implementation. This happens because the corporate bond securitization market in the euro area (based on guarantees offered by small private agents, such as auto loans, credit card bills, etc.) shrank considerably after the 2008 crisis, and the availability of collateral that meets ECB's requirements is small. The ECB has made some changes in the ABSPP framework in September 2015, with national central banks assuming a greater role in ABS purchases. However, it still remains to be seen if those changes can foster the program's implementation. Until March 2016, only € 19 billion of ABS were purchased by the ECB.

As for the TLTROs, it was decided that the ECB would hold eight operations between September 2014 and June 2016, all maturing in September 2018 (i.e., the operations will last between two and four years). The fees charged to banks would be 0.25% in the first two operations, dropping to the benchmark rate in the following six operations (0.05% until December 2015, and 0% in March and June 2016). The idea is that banks can borrow funds respecting their initial limit (7% of their loan portfolio in the first two operations), which can be gradually expanded in the following operations if their loan portfolio directed to non-financial businesses and households (except for mortgages) increase. However, there is no serious punitive mechanism for banks if the borrowed liquidity is not directed towards lending to the real economy. The only "punishment" is that the resources must be repaid two years earlier (September 2016, instead of September 2018). The ECB has offered a total of € 425.1 billion in the first seven operations (€ 82.6 billion in September 2014, € 129.8 billion in December 2014, € 97.8 billion in March 2015, € 73.8 billion in June 2015, € 15.5 billion in September 2015, € 18.3 billion in December 2015, € 7.3 billion in March 2016).

This amount fell far short of the ECB's own initial estimate, which was € 400 billion just in the first two operations. Several analysts sought to explain the initial low demand for loans from banks. At the first operation, one of the causes could be that banks avoided taking new loans until the results of the 2014 ECB Comprehensive Assessment were not disclosed (this release only occurred in October 2014, and capital adjustment needs in the banks were modest, a net amount of € 6.35 billion for eight banks). But according to Merler (2014), the main reason was that banks feared to extend new loans to businesses and households in a still uncertain scenario. The institutions were just swapping the "old LTRO" funds, which matured in February 2015 with a rate of 1%, for new TLTRO funds with lower rates. Thus, the net impact of expansion in ECB's balance sheet with the initial TLTRO was small.

In January 2015, it became clear that ECB's implicit objective to expand its balance sheet by € 1 trillion until September 2016 just with the programs announced in September 2014 would not be met. At the same time, with a sharp fall experienced by energy prices, the inflation rate in the euro area was -0.6% YoY, deepening in the negative territory (reached in December 2014 with -0.2% YoY) and fueling fears of a deflationary spiral.

In this context, most economic analysts converged to a view that a more incisive action was necessary. This view also became the most suitable alternative for the majority of ECB's Governing Council members, and tolerated by Germany, since the ultimate goal of ECB's purchases would not be monetary financing of governments, but to ensure euro area's price stability in the medium/long run. The institution was then ready to follow the path of Quantitative Easing (QE) also adopted by other major global central banks: Fed (USA), BOE (UK), BOJ (Japan), although well after them.

3.3 Public sector purchase program

It was at this scene that in January 2015 the ECB announced it would start in March its QE program, called Public Sector Purchase Program - PSPP. Its focus would be to make unsterilized purchases of bonds issued by governments, national agencies and EU's supranational bodies, initially at least September 2016. Additionally, the ECB would continue the programs announced in September 2014 (CBPP3, ABSPP and TLTROs). Together, they would promote an initial monthly expansion in ECB's balance sheet of € 60 billion, which implied a net expansion in the institution's balance sheet of over € 1 trillion, to levels observed in early 2012. The focus was on achieving a sustained path in inflation towards the level of below but close 2% over the medium term.

Here we perform a brief description of the main features of the PSPP, valid from March 2015 until December 2015.[2] First, bond purchases were made by the Eurosystem (ECB or National Central Banks - NCBs) in the secondary market, not to incur in monetary financing of governments (violation of Article 123 - Treaty of Functioning of the European Union). Purchases were being divided in a way that the ECB buys 8% of the securities and NCBs the remaining 92%. Of these 92%, NCBs acquired 12% from EU supranational bodies and 80% from their own government or national agencies.

Thus, although the program comprises the entire euro area, the mutualization of risks within the Eurosystem is low (only 20%), with 80% under each country's responsibility through its NCB. In terms of amounts acquired, they follow the share of each country in ECB's capital key, so that the largest countries are responsible for most part of the purchases. Germany (26.6%), France (21.1%), Italy (18.2%) and Spain (13.1%) supply 78.9% of the securities bought by the PSPP.

In terms of ECB's purchases, there was a limit of 33% per country, in order to prevent the ECB to concentrate its purchases in a single country. There was also a 33% limit per bond issued, to avoid that ECB purchases eventually distort the negotiation of a specific bond in the market. Assets purchased must have a minimum investment grade rating (BBB- or equivalent), except for Greece and Cyprus. These countries can only join the PSPP while fulfilling Troika assistance program conditionalities. In the beginning of the program, when Greece and Cyprus were undergoing revisions of their agreements, their bonds were not eligible.

By July 2015, Cyprus completed its review and also joined the program, while that still was not possible for Greece. If it turns out necessary to restructure a sovereign bond in the program, the ECB would receive *pari*

---

[2] All the features listed here are currently in place, except for the modifications mentioned in section 3.4.

passu (not senior) treatment with private creditors. Regarding the maturity of the securities, short and long-term bonds (between 2 and 30 years) were being purchased, with an average maturity of 8 years. The ECB/NCBs can buy bonds including ones with negative yields, provided that they are not below the deposit rate.

3.4 APPs concerns and modifications

Since the beginning of the APPs, several concerns related to the program's implementation emerged, related to the following issues: (i) The program's duration - too short to have the expected effects on inflation; (ii) The availability of assets to be purchased - scarcity of bonds in markets due to ECB' purchases and (iii) The level of yields - too low, undermining agents' profitability and bringing financial stability problems. Therefore, some important modifications were introduced in APPs in order to face some of those concerns, and try to increase its effectiveness.

In the December 2015 meeting, the ECB implemented the first round of changes. It was announced that APPs would remain at least until March 2017, what meant an extension of 6 months from the original date of September 2016. Furthermore, main refinancing operations and 3 month-LTROs would remain as fixed rate tender procedures with full allotment until at least the end of 2017. And securities bought under APPs would have their principal payments reinvested as they mature, which means the ECB would maintain an expanded balance sheet for as long as it considers adequate for its monetary policy objectives. In addition, it also lowered the deposit rate from -0.2% to -0.3%, so more bonds with negative yields could be bought. In addition, it included regional and local government bonds in the list of eligible assets for the program.[3]

In the March 2016 meeting, more incisive modifications were taken. First, not only the deposit rate was lowered 10 bps (from -0.3% to -0.4%), but also the main refinancing and marginal rates were lowered 5 bps (to 0% and 0.25%, respectively). The duration of APPs was kept at least until March 2017, but the volume of monthly purchases was increased from € 60 to € 80

---

[3] In July 2015, the ECB had already added 13 new national agencies in the list of agencies whose securities are eligible for the PSPP.

billion per month. The availability of assets to be purchased would also be increased in the following ways: (i) Lowering the yield floor for purchases, with the deposit rate cut; (ii) Increasing the issuer and issue limit of bonds purchased from international organizations and multilateral development banks from 33% to 50% (although the share of those securities in total purchases would fall from 12% to 10%, and ECB's purchase would be increased from 8% to 10%); (iii) Including investment grade non-bank corporate bonds in the list of eligible assets to be purchased, starting from June 2016 onwards. The intention to increase the availability of credit to the real economy was strengthened not only through this decision to buy corporate bonds, but also through the announcement of a new round of TLTROs.

TLTRO 2 will be a series of four quarterly operations, from June 2016 up to March 2017. Banks can borrow money for four years, and there will be no requirement for early repayment within two years, as it was the case for TLTRO 1 (banks can roll from TLTRO 1 to TLTRO 2). The limit for each counterparty to borrow will be up to 30% of the stock of eligible loans as at the end of January 2016 (higher than the 7% limit established in the TLTRO 1). But the main change is the incentive introduced for banks to provide credit to the real economy, enabling the ones which lend more to non-financial corporations and households (except for housing) to have lower rates.

For each operation, the interest rate will be the main refinancing operation prevailing at that time (ex: 0%). But for banks who exceed their loan benchmark to the real economy, the interest rate can be as low as the deposit rate (ex: -0.4%). As the ECB states that APPs are flexible in size, composition and duration, new changes may be introduced in the future if the ECB considers necessary.

Table 2 Eurosystem net purchases under current asset purchase programs (€ million)

Month	Flow				Stock			
	ABSPP	CBPP3	PSPP	Total (monthly)	ABSPP	CBPP3	PSPP	Total (cumulative)
Oct 14 / Feb 15	3,463	51,262	-	-	3,463	51,262	-	54,725
Mar 15	1,160	12,587	47,383	61,130	4,624	63,606	47,356	115,586
Apr 15	1,162	11,464	47,701	60,327	5,785	75,070	95,056	175,911
May 15	1,420	10,039	51,622	63,087	7,205	85,108	146,679	238,999
Jun 15	1,590	10,215	51,442	63,247	8,796	94,997	197,530	301,323
Jul 15	944	9,006	51,360	61,310	9,740	104,003	248,889	362,632
Aug 15	1,347	7,459	42,826	51,632	11,087	111,462	291,715	414,264
Sep 15	1,928	10,110	51,008	63,046	13,015	121,151	341,462	475,628
Oct 15	1,563	9,963	52,175	63,731	14,577	131,144	393,637	539,358
Nov 15	624	6,889	55,105	62,598	15,201	138,013	448,742	601,956
Dec 15	144	5,803	44,309	50,256	15,322	143,340	491,215	649,877
Jan 16	2,264	7,197	52,956	62,417	17,586	150,537	544,171	712,294
Feb 16	985	7,784	53,358	61,127	18,571	158,321	597,529	774,421
Mar 16	421	7,819	53,059	61,299	18,994	165,638	648,022	832,654

P.S: Quarter end adjustments (€ million): ABSPP +1 (Jun 15), -23 (Dec 15), +1 (Mar 16); CBPP -54 (Dec 14), -190 (Mar 15), -326 (Jun 15), -422 (Sep 15), -476 (Dec 15), -503 (Mar 16); PSPP: -27 (Mar 15), -592 (Jun 15), -1261 (Sep 15), -1836 (Dec 15), -2565 (Mar 16). Source: ECB.

3.5 Effects of the asset purchase programs

To begin our analysis, we present a table with the net amount of bonds acquired by the Eurosystem under the current asset purchase programs, from October 2014 until March 2016. Observing the flow of purchases, we can see that since the Eurosystem began the PSPP in March 2015, the € 60 billion monthly target of balance sheet expansion has been reached (except in August and December 2015, but bond purchases were compensated by ECB in other months, so as to keep the monthly amount of purchases around the mean of € 60 billion).

In terms of the stock of purchases, we notice the significant amount of bonds bought by the PSPP: in one year, it has purchased an unsterilized sum of € 648 billion, much more than the amount bought by the SMP through sterilized purchases during two years. Considering all asset purchases since October 2014, a cumulative amount of € 832.6 billion has been bought until March 2016. Together with the TLTROs, this implies that the ECB is on its way to promote a net expansion of its balance sheet of over €1 trillion, to a size of at least € 3 trillion in assets (level observed in early 2012).

Chart 2 Euro area - Sovereign bond Yields -10 years (%)

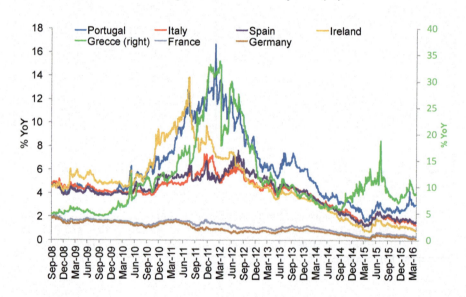

Source: Bloomberg.

Now we continue our analysis focusing on the asset purchase programs effects on important macroeconomic indicators:[4] sovereign yields, exchange rate, credit, output and inflation. Considering the initial period of the APPs,

---

[4] The analysis also includes the effects of TLTROs, as their implementation is being done in parallel with APPs.

most of those indicators had positive responses to the programs, except for sovereign yields and the euro exchange rate after May 2015, due to intra-Euro (e.g.: financial volatility in bond markets, political uncertainty in Greece) and extra-euro area factors (i.e.: price of oil, US and China economies).

3.5.1 Sovereign yields

Sovereign bonds' yields, which had risen significantly between 2010 and 2012, began to decrease since the introduction of ECB's "verbal intervention" strategy in the second half of 2012. The set of initiatives announced in September 2014 and especially the PSPP announcement in January 2015 gave new impetus to this downward trend, as it can be seen on chart 2 (with the exception of Greece, whose yields were under pressure since October 2014 because of doubts over the renewal of financial aid from the Troika). The reduction in yields is important for the periphery, once it diminishes the cost of financing their sovereign debt, and increases their ability to adjust their fiscal accounts, since they have been struggling in recent years to reduce their deficit and debt levels.

Nevertheless, yields also dropped in core countries, which were already in very low levels. In particular, there was a reduced availability of German bonds in the market, since it was the security more often purchased by the Eurosystem (because of the higher German share on ECB's capital key), and the German Finance Agency did not change substantially its issuing schedule after the announcement of the PSPP, keeping its objective of not increasing the country's debt ratio. In the end of April 2015, the German yield curve had negative yields up to maturities of 7 years, and the 10 year bund was hovering around 0.07%. In the date of April 29, the 10 year bund yield jumped from 0.16% to 0.28%, and in the first week of May it was trading near 0.58%. Analysts explained this sudden volatility (which received the name of "bund tantrum") by the following factors: (i) Macroeconomic data, which implied higher growth and inflation expectations for the euro area (e.g.: in the end of April 2015, release of first euro area HICP out of deflation after four months, coupled with higher oil prices); (ii) German bond yields in record low levels took several institutional investors to undershoot their benchmark return rates, which lead some ETFs, mutual, insurance and pension funds to sell those securities on the market at the same time. This sudden reduction in German bonds' demand lowered their prices and increased their term premiums and yields.

In the following months, German and euro area sovereign yields have experienced periods of higher volatility. When uncertainty rose (i.e. June and beginning of July 2015, with the problems in Greece), euro area's yields restored their previous diverging trend: core yields decreased with risk aversion, while peripheral yields increased with contagion fears, albeit still at much lower levels than back in 2011/2012. Also, in days when economic data pointed to higher future inflation, all sovereign yields rose due to higher inflation expectations. Nevertheless, the continuation of the PSPP implies lower yields in general during the program's implementation.

Even with the episodes of bond market volatility between May and June 2015, yields' levels remain historically low. During the implementation of the PSPP, yields of several countries were in negative territory, including mid-term maturities (e.g. Germany up to 9 years), some even below the deposit rate, which the ECB determined as the lower bound for its purchases. Some of the concerns related to the low yield's level are: (i) With the costs imposed by negative deposit rates on bank's excess reserves, banks would have lower profitability and may have problems on their balance sheets. Low profitability can also undermine the balance sheets of institutional investors, such as pension funds; (ii) Possible losses incurred by savers, as they see their income in bank deposits shrink, and may bear the costs of negative deposit rates if banks pass them on to customers; (iii) Extremely low yield levels could feed new asset bubbles, raising financial stability problems.

With regard to those critics, the ECB has its own justifications. In terms of the issues in banks' balance sheets, it states that the banking supervisory framework already had a huge improvement since 2008, and remains vigilant for any excesses, standing ready to act if there is an unwarranted tightening of financial conditions or change in the inflation outlook. As for the potential losses for savers, it states that due to competition , banks have not passed any extra costs related to negative interest rates to customers, but the ECB will continue monitoring this indicator. When it comes to worries about a new asset bubble, it states that the non-financial private sector is still highly indebted, and any new "releveraging" would be gradual. In broader terms, the ECB argues that low yields are due to the extraordinary financial conditions, and that the programs are justified because inflation expectations have not resumed their sustained path towards ECB's objective.

Nevertheless, in the episode of "bund tantrum", important players in the market that were linked to it (e.g.: insurance, pension, mutual and exchange-traded funds) are not under ECB's supervision authority. The "bund tantrum" experience and the possible problems in those agents' balance sheets associated to low interest rates suggest that financial supervision should continue to be strengthened. This is true not only in the banking sector (completing the banking union) but also in other EU financial markets authorities (securities-ESMA; insurance and pension - EIOPA). Those authorities could have more enforcement powers, in order to harmonize rules and avoid that sudden movements of institutional investors provoke sharp volatility, disrupting financial markets and the real economy. This topic could be included in the ongoing discussions regarding the "Capital Markets Union" - which intends to create deeper, more integrated capital markets in the EU, and the Markets in Financial Instruments II Directive (Mifid II)- which aims to introduce a single rulebook for financial services in the EU.

3.5.2 Exchange rate

The ECB does not have an official exchange rate policy, as the euro has a flexible exchange rate. However, the APPs can play a significant role on the euro exchange rate. In particular, an increase in APPs is usually associated to a depreciation of the euro in currency markets. Maintaining the euro at a more depreciated level is desired for the monetary union at this stage, as it enhances the competitiveness of its exports (which helps in the recovery of GDP) and brings a positive effect for inflation, by increasing the prices of imported goods.

The APPs effect on the exchange rate cannot be observed clearly if we just take into account the rate euro versus dollar. The reason behind it is the end of the QE program by the Fed in October 2014 and the outlook of monetary policy normalization in USA during 2015 onwards. The "Fed effect" led to the appreciation of the dollar against most global currencies (including the euro) between the end of 2014 and the beginning of 2015. Thus, the APPs effect amplified the euro devaluation in a global movement of dollar strengthening. However, whenever the USA disclosed weaker output data and the Fed gave signs it could delay its first interest rate hike, several global currencies (including the euro) partly recovered their losses against the dollar. Nevertheless, with the outlook of normalization of interest rates in the USA and the continuation of APPs in the euro area, many analysts project that the euro may devaluate further against the dollar in the course of 2016.

Chart 3 Euro nominal (NEER) and real (REER) effective exchange rate

Source: ECB.

Therefore, in order to better gauge the effects of the APPs on the euro exchange rate, we observe the evolution of the euro against the basket of 19 currencies which are most relevant to euro area's trade,[5] measured through the effective exchange rate. The chart 3 expresses the evolution of nominal (NEER) and real (REER) effective exchange rates from September 2008 to March 2016. The chart shows that, from January to April 2015, the euro's NEER and REER had a significant depreciation. The latter was even more

---

[5] Australia, Canada, Denmark, Hong Kong, Japan, Norway, Singapore, Korea, Sweden, Switzerland, United Kingdom, USA, Bulgaria, Czech Republic, Hungary, Poland, Romania, Croatia and China.

intense than the former, due to the low level of inflation in the euro area at the beginning of 2015. Since then, those rates took a more volatile path.

Between May and September 2015, NEER and REER's drops were partially interrupted, once "safe haven" flows with uncertainties in Greece (until June 2015) and China (devaluation of the renminbi in August 2015) contributed to a relative appreciation of the euro. In October and November 2015, the euro resumed depreciating against the basket of currencies. However, between December 2015 and February 2016, the NEER and REER appreciated again, as currency markets evaluated the stimulus measures disclosed by the ECB in December 2015 as timid. Only in March 2016, with the announcement of a broader package of stimulus measures by the ECB, the NEER and REER began depreciating again.

3.5.3 Credit

With regard to credit, euro area data area points to a gradual recovery after the implementation of the APPs, as it can be seen on chart 4.

Chart 4 Euro area – Loans to non-financial private sector – Growth Rate (% YoY)

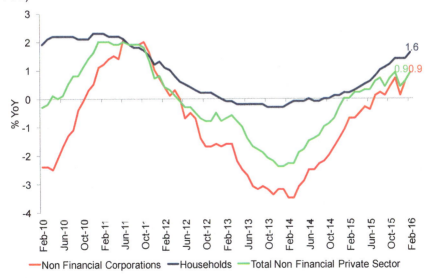

P.S.: Data seasonally adjusted, loans adjusted for sales and securitization. Total non-financial private sector included non- financial corporations, households, insurance corporations and pension funds.
Source: ECB.

Loans to the non-financial private sector had declining annual rates of growth since the end of 2011, which became negative in 2012, and only returned to positive territory in March 2015. This growth trend continued with some oscillation, up to 0.9% in February 2016. Loans to non-financial corporations experienced a sharp fall in annual growth rates since end-2011, presenting negative rates until June 2015, growing up to 0.9% in February 2016. On the other hand, loans to households traced a more benign path, not experiencing such a sharp fall such as non-financial corporations. Loans to households growth rates entered in a positive territory since November 2014, up to 1.6% in February 2016.

Further information regarding current conditions and future credit expectations in the euro area can be obtained in the quarterly ECB's Bank Lending Surveys. In general terms, the surveys during the course of 2015 and in January 2016 showed that, in terms of credit supply, there was a reduction in loan restrictions imposed by banks over non-financial companies and households. In terms of credit demand, there was an increase for non-financial companies and households.

Notwithstanding, it´s important to highlight that credit conditions are still heterogeneous inside the euro area, either among countries (higher credit spreads in the periphery than in the core) or within each country (small and medium enterprises – SMEs – with funding costs higher than large non-financial companies).

3.5.4 Output

The transmission of monetary policy effects to the real economy usually occurs with a lag. Despite that, initial output indicators released since APPs implementation point in a favorable direction. In quarterly terms, after the beginning of the APPs, euro area's GDP accelerated (0.4% QoQ in Q4 2014, compared to 0.1% in Q2 and 0.3% in Q3 2014). In 2015, the expansion continued in Q1 (0.5%), with a slight reduction in Q2 (0.4%),

Q3(0.3%) and Q4 (0.3%). According to the February 2016 European Commission forecasts, euro area might keep a growth rate around 0.5% over the following quarters, as it can be seen on chart 5. However, each country has its own characteristics, implying in different growth rates for each nation. For instance, since Q4 2014, Spain was the only of the four largest euro area countries which managed to increase domestic consumption, investment and net exports at the same time.

Chart 5 Euro Area GDP Growth: 2014-2016 (% QoQ)

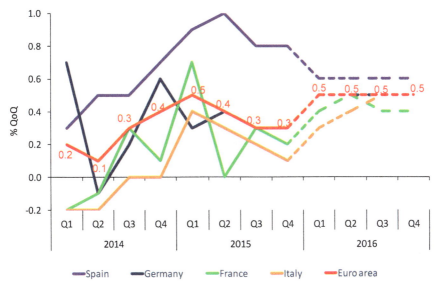

P.S. Bold lines are actual values (up to 2015 Q4). Dotted lines are forecasts (2016 Q1 onwards).
Source: European Commission (2016).

On annual terms, after recording a lower growth in 2014 (0.9% YoY), the Eurozone grew 1.5% in 2015. The European Commission February 2016 forecasts project a GDP growth of 1.7% in 2016. Beside the more accommodative monetary policy, other factors that have supported or will support the monetary union's growth are: private consumption (drop in energy prices increased real household income and boosted consumer confidence) and a more neutral fiscal stance (differing from the tightening that prevailed in last years). Despite the weaker exchange rate in historical terms (that helped net exports growth in the beginning of 2015), the slowdown of foreign demand in important emerging markets (e.g.: China, Russia) may cast some doubts over euro area's net exports growth on the next quarters. In other words, indicators point more to a domestic-led than a foreign-led recovery in the zone.

Even the unemployment rate, which is one of the indicators with slower response and presents a chronic problem in the periphery, has begun to fall too. After being stagnant at 11.5% during six months in 2014, euro area's rate started a downward trend in December 2014 (11.4%), falling to 10.3% in February 2016.

3.5.5 Inflation

When it comes to inflation, after the APPs implementation the HICP headline and core indexes increased, albeit at modest rates.. After posting negative annual growth between December 2014 and March 2015, it registered no change in April and 0.3% YoY in May, as negative effects of energy prices moderated, slowing to -0.1% in September, as negative energy price effects regained strength. Then, after some months in positive territory, deflation reappeared in February (-0.2%) and March 2016 (-0.1%). The core index increased from 0.6% YoY in March to 1.1% in October 2015, oscillating lower in the following months, up to 1% YoY in March 2016. This increase was mainly related to non-energy industrial goods (good proxy for domestic demand), which had been registering negative inflation rates from the end of 2014 until the beginning of 2015. After the implementation of the PSPP, these prices rose from 0% YoY in March 2015 to 0.7% in March 2016 .

Chart 6 Euro area – Medium/Long Term Inflation expectations (inflation swaps)

Source: Bloomberg.

In terms of inflation projections, the March 2016 ECB forecasts point that headline HICP should present an average in the year of 2016 of 0.1% YoY, just a tick up the 2015 average (0% YoY), still low due to downward effects of energy prices. However, the institution projected the HICP at an average of 1.3% in 2017 and 1.6% in 2018. Those projections are based on the assumptions that inflation would pick up further due to higher energy prices, increasing employment/domestic demand and monetary accommodation measures.

As for long-term inflation expectations, they still remain subdued. The 5Y5Y inflation swap rate indicator increased from around 1.50% YoY in January 2015 to a maximum 1.86% in July 2015. Since then, it established a downward trend, with some oscillations. It was at the end of March 2016 around 1.40%, in a level below the registered in the announcement of the PSPP in January 2015. When we observe inflation swap contracts for maturities from 1 to 10 years (chart 6), we see they have also increased from January to June 2015, then lost steam until August, and began a very modest recovery between September and December 2015. However, swaps fell again during the first quarter of 2016. This shows that the latest recoveries were short lived, and inflation expectations remain well below ECB's objective

4. Conclusions

This chapter described the path experienced by the euro area economy after the 2008 crisis, with a special focus on ECB's unconventional monetary policies. The rapid response from the authorities after the collapse of Lehman Brothers in September 2008 avoided that the US financial crash had more drastic consequences on the monetary union's financial system. However, this episode has turned financial and credit conditions in the euro area more restrictive, feeding into a crisis that became more acute after 2009. It's important to mention that the Euro crisis had earlier roots within the zone itself, originated in core-periphery divergences which lead to serious imbalances in the banking system and the balance of payments of peripheral countries.

Since then, a number of conventional and unconventional measures were taken by the ECB. Some of the actions taken in 2011 (such as the benchmark interest rate hikes in April and June 2011, the SMP and the three-year LTROs) received strong criticism for not fighting adequately or even aggravating the situation of the banking and sovereign crisis, and fostering financial contagion among countries. This crisis only began to show signs of softening in the second half of 2012, with the implementation of the "verbal intervention" strategy by the ECB (e.g.: OMT), together with other actions by the EU (permanent stabilization fund - ESM and banking union project). However, in 2013 and 2014 the output continued to present a sluggish recovery, and fears of deflation began to increase towards the end of 2014. Therefore, the ECB implemented new stimulus programs in September 2014 (TLTROs, CBPP 3, ABSPP), which were complemented by a massive public sector bond purchase program (PSPP), announced in January 2015 and implemented from March 2015 onwards.

When we undertake an analysis of these recent ECB programs on macroeconomic indicators, we observe that sovereign yields and the euro exchange rate presented initial positive effects (e.g.: up to April 2015, yields fell and the euro depreciated, what would reduce debt service costs for countries, improve net exports and later raise inflation). Since May 2015, this trend was partially interrupted and those indicators became more volatile, due to reasons related to the own euro area (e.g. bond market financial volatility, tensions in Greece) and other countries (i.e. uncertainties surrounding monetary tightening timing in the USA and in Chinese economy). Other macro indicators usually take longer to present favorable effects, but have already presented positive outcomes: credit (reduction of restrictions in credit supply and increased demand for credit to the real economy, mainly households), output (relative increase in growth rates and reduction in unemployment) and inflation (recovery in core HICP). However, headline inflation and medium term inflation expectations are still at very low levels, well away from ECB's objective of below but close 2%. That's why the ECB in the December 2015 and March 2016 meetings decided to take additional stimulus measures, and stated that it is prepared to undertake further modifications on APPs' size, composition and duration if necessary, in order to achieve its objective.

Despite the initial positive effects, the ECB has received a number of criticisms over the programs, to which the institution has presented its justifications. Nevertheless, it should be borne in mind that these ECB programs are no unique solution to the various problems currently experienced by the euro area. From the point of view of private agents (non-financial companies and households), their debt levels are still very high. It will still take several years for the deleveraging process to be completed, and thus the credit recovery may be slow. In addition, funding costs remain unequal, either in terms of countries (higher in the periphery than in the core), or among agents (higher to households and small businesses than to larger companies).

From the point of view of public accounts, most countries remain with high levels of fiscal deficit and public debt. At times when ECB's PSPP manage to reduce sovereign yields, they tend to lower countries' cost of debt service. Nevertheless, critics to the PSPP state that it stimulates moral hazard, by postponing the "necessary" fiscal adjustments in countries. On the other hand, other voices argue that what euro area countries need in fact is to avoid pro-cyclicality in fiscal policies (stricter austerity, deeper recessions). Instead, they should have more flexibility in meeting their fiscal targets, and increase public investment to resume growth. This controversy is closely related to the intricate monetary union's political framework, both inside countries, and within the euro area/EU. The case of Greece is emblematic to show how the political game is complex within a union that has a common currency, but different sovereign countries with distinct development levels and independent fiscal policies. This turns the decision-making mechanisms extremely complicated, and in several times slower than financial market reactions.

Summing up, unconventional monetary policies are necessary – and they have shown some efficacy in the euro area – but they are not sufficient to solve a crisis with very complex and multiple roots. To restore growth in a sustained path, euro area should also try to complement its monetary policy measures with the following actions: (i) Adopting a more coordinated fiscal policy among its countries, with a common budget institution ("Euro Treasury") that could pool funds collected through euro area's common securities or taxes, and use these resources to foster public and private investments (while each country would retain its sovereignty in its own fiscal issues); (ii) Allowing a higher degree of fiscal flexibility and being countercyclical when appropriate, to avoid deepening recessions; (iii) Actions towards reducing regional economic asymmetries, such as an increase in the role of the European Investment Bank and other national development banks in offering support for key areas (infrastructure, innovation, SMEs, jobs creation), mainly in the periphery; (iv) Conducting institutional reforms in the countries and the EU, to increase integration and supervision in bank/capital markets and foster productivity, to enhance countries' resilience to financial shocks and improve their competitiveness.

References

Arestis, P. (2015) "Current and Future European Central Bank Monetary Policy." *Brazilian Keynesian Review* 1(1), pp. 4-17.

Beirne, J. et al (2011) "The Impact of the Eurosystem's Covered Bond Purchase Programme on the Primary and Secondary Markets." *Occasional Paper Series No 122*, Frankfurt: European Central Bank (ECB).

Bibow, J. (2012) "The Euro Debt Crisis and Germany's Euro Trilemma." *Working Paper 721*, Annandale-on-Hudson, NY: Levy Institute of Bard College.

Brenke, K. (2009) "Real Wages in Germany: Numerous Years of Decline." *DIW Weekly Report* 28 (5). Berlin: German Institute for Economic Research.

Doran, D. et al (2013) "Was the Securities Markets Programme Effective in Stabilizing Irish Yields?" *Research Technical Paper* 7. Dublin: Central Bank of Ireland.

European Commission (2016) "European Economic Forecast – Winter 2016." *Institutional Paper* 020. Brussels: European Commission (EC).

Helm, L. (2012) *The ECB's securities markets programme: An analysis of economics, law and central bank independence*. Best Master Thesis, Department of Interdisciplinary Studies. Brugge: College d'Europe.

Lane, P. (2012) "The European Sovereign Debt Crisis." *Journal of Economic Perspectives* 26(3): pp. 49-68.

Merler, S. (2014) *Fact: T.L.T.R.O. is Too Low to Resuscitate Optimism*. Brussels: Bruegel http://www.bruegel.org/nc/blog/detail/article/1436-fact-tltro-is-too-low-to-resuscitate-optimism

Miranda, J. C. (2014) "Três Ensaios Sobre a Integração da União Europeia." In Calixtre, A. et al, *Presente e Futuro do Desenvolvimento Brasileiro*. Brasília: Instituto de Pesquisa Economica Aplicada (IPEA) 14, pp. 543-594.

Pattipeilohy, C. et al (2013) "Unconventional Monetary Policy of the ECB During the Financial Crisis: An Assessment and New Evidence." *DNB Working Paper No 381*. Amsterdam: The Netherlandsche Bank.

Chapter 5

Greece: conditions and strategies for economic recovery*

Dimitri B. Papadimitriou, Michalis Nikiforos and Gennaro Zezza

1. Introduction

Members of Greece's newly elected government have been at the negotiation table with the European elite since taking office in late January of this year. The process has been slow, and at the time of this writing no agreement has been reached. Both sides have dug in their heels by insisting that some issues are nonnegotiable, including the level of the primary budget surplus (more austerity is needed to achieve it), additional labor market flexibility, and restructuring the public pension system - the "red lines" that the government promised, pre-election, it would not cross. The focus now is on crafting creative language in an agreement that satisfies both sides by ending austerity while enabling Greece to achieve the fiscal discipline required to service its public debt and to make its economy even more competitive.

Notwithstanding the economic ruin of the past six years, the dogma of expansionary austerity lives on. Sooner or later, an agreement will be struck - the longer it takes, of course, the more difficult to achieve the goals of output growth and primary fiscal surplus. Greece has practically run out of money, while its banking system, with a steady deposit outflow and an increasing number of nonperforming loans, is teetering on the verge of collapse. How long this negotiation process will take is anybody's guess, although June 30 has been assumed to be the drop-dead date. In the meantime, as we will show, conditions have not improved as yet, and all

---

* We wish to thank the participants to the WEA Conference on *The European crisis* for useful comments. This contribution has appeared in the Levy Institute *Strategic Analysis report series*, May 2015.

bets are on increased tourism activity. The current year, therefore, will most likely end in either a negative or a very small increase in GDP. Last year's small primary surplus might be difficult to repeat this year, and in all likelihood employment growth is stuck in neutral.

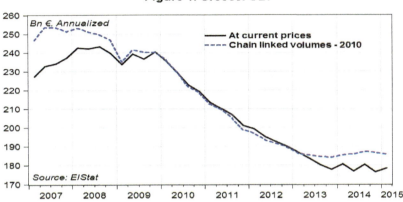

Figure 1. Greece. GDP

In what follows, we first review many aspects of the Greek economy's performance using the latest data available, and then run simulations of various alternative scenarios for the next three years, including a "pessimistic" scenario should "the institutions" (the new name for "the troika") manage to succeed in getting their way. But let us begin at the beginning.

Estimates of real output for the Greek economy, published by the Hellenic Statistical Authority (ElStat), showed some signs of recovery up to 2014Q3, after six long years of uninterrupted fall in output, even though the fourth quarter of 2014 and preliminary estimates for the first quarter of this year show a reversal that, if it continues in the second quarter, will indicate the economy has slipped back into recession (Figure 1).

Real output, at the end of 2014, was below its 2000 level, marking a more than 26 percent drop from its peak in 2007, while an even larger fall (30%) in employment has been recorded. More than one million workers have lost their jobs relative to the previous peak in 2008, with an increase of 800,000 unemployed - the total now stands above 1.2 million - while the active population is shrinking, as workers leave the country in search of better opportunities abroad. Can the positive signs of 2014 be sustained, putting the economy, finally, on the road to recovery? Can the new government expect markets to create jobs at a sufficient pace and tax revenues to increase? As we will show, unless an appropriate plan to rescue the Greek economy is quickly implemented, the answer is no.

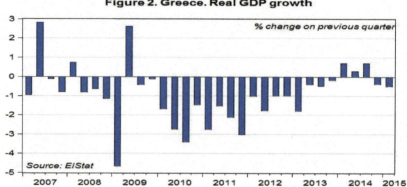

Figure 2. Greece. Real GDP growth

2. Real and nominal output

While a recession ends when real GDP increases, it is hard to believe that the Greek economy is indeed recovering, even after three consecutive quarters of increased output.[1] Indeed, as Figure 2 documents, despite some growth in the tourism sector, total real output has fallen again, in both the last quarter of 2014 and the first quarter of 2015. One reason for our disbelief is the prolonged fall in nominal output, which in the last quarter of 2014 was still 0.8 percent below its level in the same quarter of the previous year, and the fall in the first quarter of 2015 was even larger in comparison to the same quarter in 2014. The difference between the positive growth in real output and the negative growth in nominal output is due to falling prices, as measured by the GDP deflator and its determinants.

---

[1] Real GDP, measured as chain-linked volumes with reference year 2010, increased by 0.3, 1.5 and 1.3 percent in the last three quarters of 2014 (ElStat GDP Table 13.1).

In Figure 3, we report the details of nominal value added in the main sectors of the Greek economy. It can be clearly seen that the only recovering sector is the one related to tourism:[2] from its low of €38.8 billion in 2013, value added increased to €41.7 billion in 2014Q4. In real terms, value added in this sector increased by 6 percent in 2014. Other sectors continued to fall, with construction registering the largest drop in real terms (negative 16 percent!), and manufacturing down by 2 percent at the end of the year.

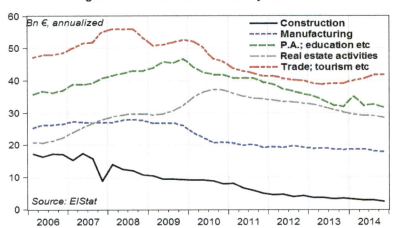

Figure 3. Greece. Value added by main sectors

3. Deflation and competitiveness

The "structural labor reforms" so violently imposed by the country's international lenders have been effective in reducing the cost of labor. The most recent measure - the index of wages published by ElStat - documents a fall of 22 percent at the end of 2014 from the peak in 2010.

In Figure 4, we report the OECD (Organization for Economic Co-operation and Development) measure of unit labor costs and an index of labor

---

[2] The sector includes "Wholesale and retail trade; repair of motor vehicles and motorcycles; transportation and storage; accommodation and food service activities". The seasonally adjusted data in Figure 3 are computed from ElStat GDP Table 10.1.

compensation. The former was down by almost 20% at the end of 2014 relative to its peak in 2010, while the latter was down by 17.8%.

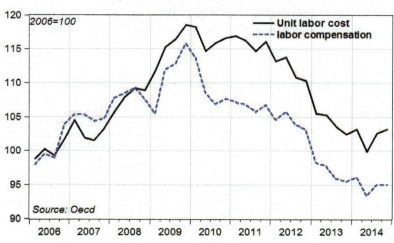

Figure 4. Greece. Labor cost indexes

These declines are not uniform, and for some sectors labor compensation has decreased even more. For instance, in the "Accommodation and food service activities" category, which includes tourism-related activities, the index of wages in the third quarter of 2014 was 40 percent below its 2008 level.

The fall in wages can also be assessed in relation to other Eurozone countries. This is shown in Table 1 using OECD data on average annual wages.[3] The data in Table 1 illustrate that Greece was the country that - starting from the second-lowest wage level in 2000 - had the best performance leading up to the 2007 crisis, with an increase of 24 percent. Notwithstanding the positive impact of this on living standards, even at their peak, wages were only 66% of comparable wages in Germany. These gains were subsequently completely erased by the crisis, pushing Greece's economy relative to Germany's back to the pre-euro-adoption days.

---

[3] Accessed on April 11, 2015.

Table 1. Selected Eurozone countries: Average annual wages (*in 2013 euro, and relative to Germany*)

	2000		2007		2013	
	€	%	€	%	€	%
France	31,383	91.9%	34,004	98.7%	35,574	99.0%
Germany	34,134	100.0%	34,465	100.0%	35,943	100.0%
Greece	18,291	53.6%	22,760	66.0%	18,495	51.5%
Italy	29,046	85.1%	29,505	85.6%	28,919	80.5%
Portugal	15,900	46.6%	16,082	46.7%	16,517	46.0%
Spain	26,015	76.2%	25,899	75.1%	26,770	74.5%

Source: OECD

If high unit labor costs resulting from high wages were one of the major problems contributing to the non competitiveness of the Greek economy, this problem has certainly been "cured" by austerity. The fallacious theory behind this approach implies that a country should, in a relatively short time, restore its competitiveness and enjoy the benefits of lower production costs, which would significantly improve its trade performance.

Figure 5. Greece. Inflation

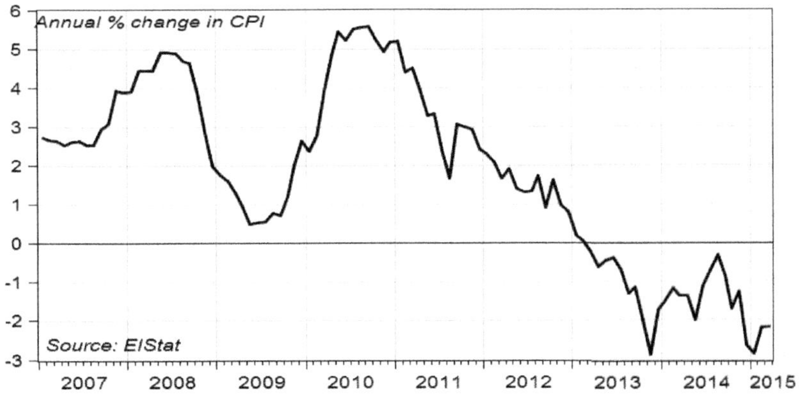

The analysis of inflation, in Figure 5, shows that prices have indeed been falling, albeit not as fast as wages. The last report on inflation issued by Elstat shows the economy continuing its deflationary trend, with the April 2015 Consumer Price Index (CPI) recording a -2.1% change, as compared to the -1.3% change in April 2014. Deflation in Greece, then, does not seem to be a temporary phenomenon: CPI has declined every month for the last 26 months. While prices for food and other necessities have not declined - to the contrary, prices have risen - the major decline in CPI is reflected in housing costs, clothing, health and education, transportation, recreation, and durable goods.

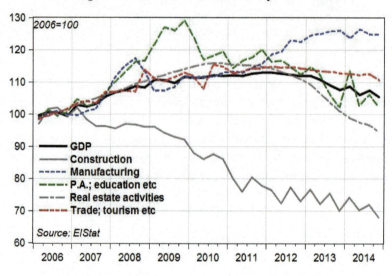

Figure 6. Greece. Price deflators by main sector

The decomposition of price dynamics casts even more doubt on the hypothesis that internal devaluation restores competitiveness. In Figure 6, we report price indices for GDP and the major components of value added. As the figure shows, prices have not followed the declining trend of wages and compensation, with the exception of the collapsed construction sector, with real value added down by 76.6% in 2014 against its pre-crisis peak in 2006. The GDP deflator is still 7% above its 2006 level and 5 percent lower than its peak at the beginning of 2012,while the deflator for the relatively small manufacturing sector[4] has trended upward, marking a 24% increase in 2014 against 2006.

---

[4] The sector is defined as "Mining and quarrying; manufacturing; electricity, gas, steam and air conditioning supply; water supply; sewerage, waste management and remediation activities".

Similarly, in Figure 7 we report the price deflator indices of the components of trade. Relative to their peak in 2012, the prices of exported goods have fallen by 9% but are still 16.7% above their 2007 level.[5] The price deflator index for services peaked in the third quarter of 2011 and has since fallen by only 2.8%, a drop not large enough to support an increase in exports through increased price competitiveness.

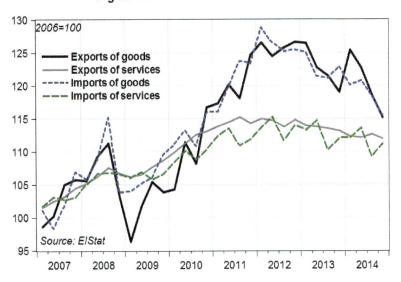

Figure 7. Greece. Price deflators for trade

We contrast these price indices with those of selected Eurozone partners in Figures 8 and 9. According to these indicators, price competitiveness for Greece, in the goods markets, continued to deteriorate until 2012, and the fall in prices has not been sufficient to bring the index in line with those of Greece's partners.

---

[5] A comparison to 2006 is not possible yet, since ElStat has reconstructed GDP series only back to 2007.

Figure 8. Eurozone countries. Price deflators for exports of goods

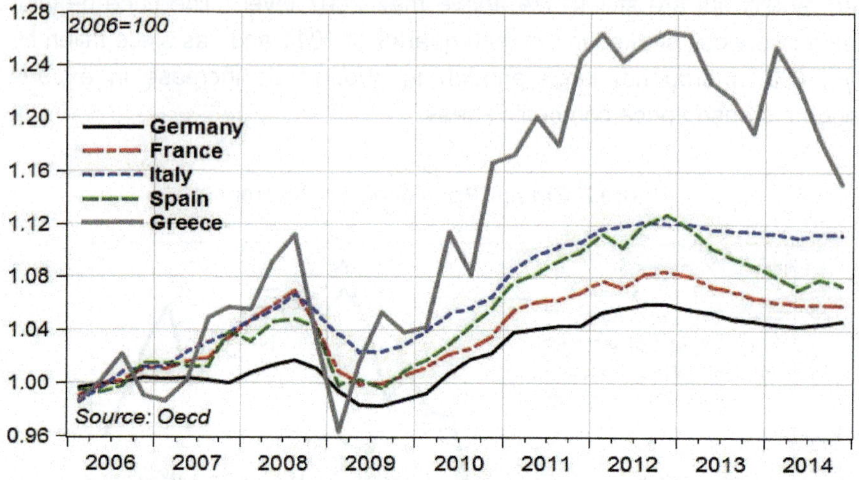

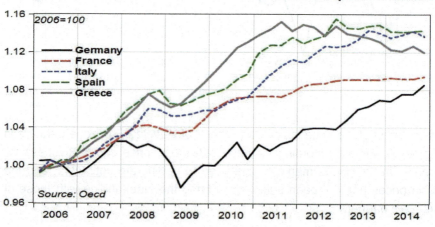

Figure 9. Eurozone countries. Price deflators for exports of services

Exports of services – which include tourism – had the worst price performance until 2012, but that performance has now somewhat recovered, albeit not to a sufficient extent to improve exports quickly through price elasticity effects. One pillar of the troika strategy was to address Greek external imbalance through "internal devaluation"; that is, a reduction in wages and unit labor costs that would increase price competitiveness. Even though this strategy has been very effective in reducing nominal and real wages (as documented above in Figure 4 and Table 1), it has thus far failed to generate a fall in prices that would sufficiently address the country's trade imbalance. Domestic prices have been prevented from falling due to the increases in indirect taxes: the ex-post indirect tax rate has gone up by 2 percentage points since the last quarter of 2013.

Recent dynamics in exports and imports seem to confirm what we have documented in our Papadimitriou et al. (2014) and elsewhere: income elasticity is more relevant for trade than price elasticity, and most of the improvement in the current account balance stems from the dramatic fall in imports from declining incomes, while the improvement in exports of goods is mainly due to changing specialization (increased activities related to oil products) and/or changing trading partners (increased trade to non-Eurozone countries). The increase in tourism is partly explained by the instability in countries like Egypt, Turkey, and others in the wider Middle East region that compete directly with Greece for tourist dollars.

And if improvement in price competitiveness has had an effect on Greek trade, it has, so far, been minor. When wages fall faster than prices, profits should rise. In Figure 10, we report two measures: the gross operating surplus of nonfinancial corporations, and their net lending relative to GDP. Greece's gross operating surplus had recovered to its pre-crisis level by the end of 2013 but fell again in 2014, likely because of increased taxation. The increase in firms' operating surplus has not translated into higher investment, which instead continues to fall. Firms may have used retained profits for deleveraging, as is shown by the strong increase in net lending in Figure 10.[6] Again, if the purpose of internal devaluation was to increase

---

[6] A precise measure of net lending is controversial. The nonfinancial accounts show net lending - defined as saving less investment - has increased substantially, from a low of 4.5% of GDP in 2009 to more than 12% of GDP at the end of 2014. The financial accounts published by the Bank of Greece - which measures net lending as the net change in financial assets - report an average *negative* value for the net lending of nonfinancial corporations. From the flows in financial accounts, it emerges that nonfinancial corporations managed to lower their liabilities (other than equities) by about €6 billion between the end of 2011 and the third quarter of 2014, while the market value of their non equity liabilities dropped from a high of 83% of GDP at the

profitability in order for investment to recover, the strategy has succeeded only in sustaining profits in the face of falling output and sales - and only up to 2013 - without any consequence for investment, as shown by the collapse of gross capital formation.

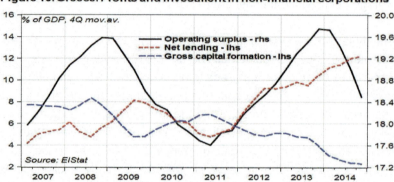

Figure 10. Greece. Profits and investment in non-financial corporations

Our final word on the internal devaluation and deflation is that the biggest contributors to the drop in prices are the construction and real estate activities sectors (Figure 6), which caused rental income in 2013 to be down 27% compared to 2006.[7] Deflation in Greece is, therefore, taking the form of a free fall in wages, with prices following suit less rapidly, generating a substantial drop in real income that has led to the collapse of domestic demand.

4. Financial assets and liabilities

The second pillar of the troika plan was the reduction in government debt as a share of GDP. This target has not yet been achieved, and the overall stock of debt, after the haircut, has returned almost to its pre-crisis (2009) level in *nominal* terms (Figure 11). Since GDP has been falling, the debt-to-GDP ratio has increased considerably, at market value, from a low of 106% of

---

end of 2013 to 70% of GDP in 2014Q3, but this is mainly due to movement in the market price of the underlying financial assets.
[7] Source: ElStat, Annual Non-financial Sector Accounts: Households, Resources.

GDP at the end of 2011 (after the haircut) to 178.5% of GDP at the end of 2014.

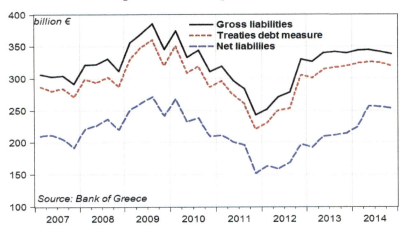

Figure 11. Greece. government debt

Source: Bank of Greece

Why has gross debt increased during the post haircut austerity period? The data from the nonfinancial accounts of the government show cumulative net government borrowing of €42 billion over the 2012–14 period, the largest part of which (€33 billion) is made up of capital transfers to the banking sector. If we take capital transfers out of the equation, the cumulative government deficit over the same period was €21.5 billion, while interest payments amounted to €22 billion. In other words, *the increase in government debt over this period was due entirely to payments to the financial sector.*

How have the successive Greek governments used the international loans? The loans obviously helped to finance the overall deficit, but a reconstruction of how international loans changed the government's net asset position, and how much funds remained in the end to help Greece recover, is of interest.

Using the data available from the flow of funds published by the Bank of Greece and the sectoral accounts published by ElStat, we have the following: We start by estimating the funds received, using the table on "Financial liabilities broken down by holding sector" and focusing on the line

"Long-term loans received from abroad". The majority of these funds have been used to reduce the existing stock of debt held abroad: line 2 in Table 2 is obtained by the change in government long-term debt securities held abroad, which has been negative since 2010. A negative change in liabilities amounts to repurchasing the existing stock of debt.[8] Another significant portion of these funds has been transferred to the domestic financial sector, either by purchasing equities (line 3 in Table 2, obtained from the data on flows of financial assets purchased by the government and issued by the domestic financial sector) or through capital transfers (line 4 in Table 2, which reports total capital transfers of the government).

Table 2. Greece: use of international loans (billion euro)

		2010	2011	2012	2013	2014	Sum
Sources of funds							
1	Long-term loans from abroad	24.3	30.0	110.0	30.8	5.6	200.8
Uses of funds							
2	Purchases of securities held abroad	19.9	24.4	44.3	8.0	7.8	104.5
3	Purchases of financial sector equities	0.2	0.9	0.0	19.0	0.0	20.2
4	Capital transfers	3.7	3.8	8.6	23.4	1.9	41.4
5	Interest payments	13.2	15.1	9.7	7.3	7.0	52.3
6	Residual = 1 − (2+3+4+5)	-12.7	-14.2	47.3	-26.9	-11.1	-17.7

Sources: ElStat; Bank of Greece

If we add the total government expenditure on interest payments (line 5), we observe that, overall, the international loans have not been sufficient to meet these expenses. It could be argued, then, that had the Greek government not recapitalized Greek banks, a major banking crisis would have had even

---

[8] A negative figure for the change in government liabilities held abroad also arises if these securities are sold to a different domestic sector, that is Greek banks.

harsher consequences for the citizens of Greece. On the other hand, these funds have not reached the Greek citizenry in any way. All debtors (households with mortgages; nonfinancial firms with loans) who have experienced a severe drop in income (for households) or sales (for firms) are now unable to meet their financial obligations, thus implying a new and possibly large fall in the value of the assets of the Greek financial sector, requiring more government intervention.

Private sector debt is still very large relative to income. Figure 12 documents the amount of long-term loans outstanding for both households and nonfinancial corporations.[9] It is feared that up to 50 percent of this debt - which totals €176 billion - may not be repaid, generating another collapse in the asset side of the balance sheet of the already shaky Greek financial sector.

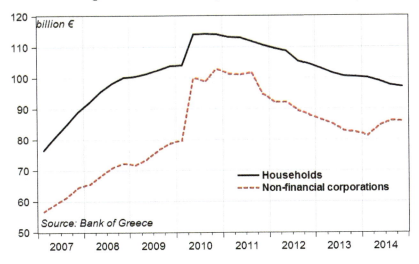

Figure 12. Greece. Long-term loans outstanding

In Papadimitriou et al (2014b), we pointed out that the nonperforming loans (NPLs) of the Greek banks are one of the biggest problems facing the Greek economy and a major symptom of the debt-deflation trap the economy finds itself in today. Data from the Bank of Greece and the European Central

---

[9] Households carried an additional €15.8 billion in short-term debt at the end of 2014; nonfinancial firms an additional €32.5 billion.

Bank(ECB) showed a staggering increase in NPLs during the crisis until the end of 2013 - the latest period for which data were then available. One year later, new data show that this trend of increasing NPLs has continued.

Data from the ECB on the gross total doubtful and nonperforming loans as a percentage of total debt instruments, loans, and advances are shown in Figure 13,[10] which indicates that NPLs increased from 3% in 2008 to 27% in the first half of 2014. In absolute terms, this means gross total doubtful and non-performing loans increased from €9.7billion in 2008 to €78 billion in the second half of 2014.

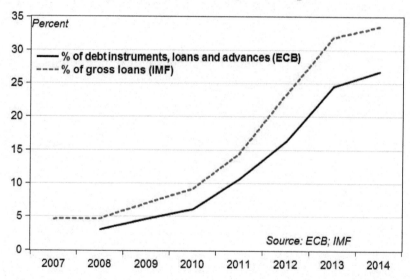

Figure 13. Greece. Non-performing loans

Figure 13 also includes data from the International Monetary Fund's (IMF) *Global Financial Stability Reports* that cover the period 2007–14. The picture that emerges is similar to that of the ECB estimate: NPLs as a percentage of total loans continued to increase during 2014, albeit at a slower pace.

Meanwhile, fear of potential bank losses has generated a dramatic fall in household deposits in Greek banks, which - although still high at €118 billion

---

[10] The data for 2014 refer to the first half of the year.

in March 2015 - dropped by more than €16 billion in the first three months of 2015 (Figure 14).

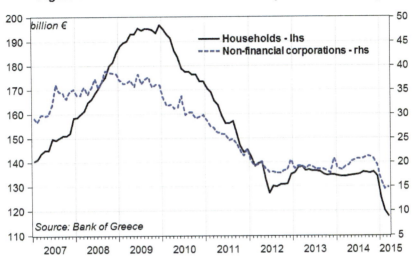

Figure 14. Greece. Non-financial sector deposits outstanding

5. Will Greece recover?

Projections of the possible paths an economy may take are always conditional on a number of assumptions that may fail to hold. The current situation in Greece is even more problematic for running projections, since the Brussels Group's failure to achieve an agreement quickly has put the economy in a state of fundamental uncertainty.[11]

Uncertainty is manifested, for instance, in the rapid fall of household deposits, as illustrated in Figure 14. The fear of extraordinary measures to obtain liquidity to fulfill payment obligations and/or fear of redenomination of euro financial assets into a new national currency led to households withdrawing in excess of €16 billion - more than 12 percent - from their bank deposits in the first three months of 2015. Unconfirmed reports show that deposit withdrawals had reached €30 billion by the end of April.

---

[11] For a good reconstruction of the current situation, see Watt (2015).

Greece: conditions and strategies for economic recovery

Almost all of Greece's public debt is held by the IMF, the ECB, and Eurozone partners (through the European Stability Mechanism), which are unwilling to rollover maturing debt as it becomes due. The last payments to the IMF in April and May on maturing debt and interest due forced the government to drain liquidity wherever it was available, with rumors of insufficient liquidity to meet ordinary government expenses. There are also rumors of lower-than-anticipated tax revenues since January 2015 contributing to the liquidity shortage. And, more probable and even more important, the ECB is warning of a deeper haircut of the government debt used as collateral for providing liquidity from its Emergency Liquidity Assistance facility.

If no agreement is reached and "the institutions" insist on debt repayment, it is inevitable that Greece will default within the Eurozone, or possibly even exit the Eurozone. This outcome would be a consequence of irrational behavior on the part of Brussels, since the costs of a Greek default would be larger than those arising from an agreement under the government's proposals. Another unlikely outcome would be for the new government to accept the previous conditions of the Memoranda of Understanding, implementing further fiscal austerity.

Since Greece has achieved a primary surplus (albeit small), and even (some of) the institutions now understand that fiscal austerity implies a further drop in GDP, forcing the government to continue cutting public employment would not be effective, and would create further strain on the already devastated Greek people.

As in Papadimitriou et al (2014a), we begin with baseline projections. We adopt an intermediate stance for our first baseline, assuming that a deal is quickly reached, one that does not require further fiscal austerity, while the tranches of existing debt coming to maturity are refinanced at prevailing ECB interest rates and interest rate payments are duly honored.

To obtain our baseline, we follow our usual strategy, which makes "neutral" assumptions on the exogenous determinants of our stock-flow consistent macroeconomic model. Growth in income and prices for Greece's trading partners is obtained from the IMF's World Economic Outlook database, and our measure of foreign demand for Greek goods and services is computed from the shares in exports of the largest of Greece's trading partners.

The exchange rate of the euro against the US dollar is assumed stable at its current (low) level; interest rates are assumed to remain stable; and inflation is projected to be negative until the end of 2015, and zero afterward. Equity and housing prices are assumed to stabilize.

Government expenditure in goods and services is assumed to grow moderately, at 1 percent in real terms, while we assume that the ex-post direct tax rate – which fell by four percentage points between the first and last quarters of 2014 – increases in 2015, regaining its 2013 level, and remains stable thereafter. Under this assumption, our model projects a further drop in real GDP of 1.4 percent in 2015, as the fall in private demand more than compensates for the increase in tourism-related activities.

Table 3. Greece: "Pessimistic" baseline projections

	2014	2015	2016	2017
Real GDP (% growth rate)	0.70	-1.40	-0.12	1.12
Government surplus/deficit (% of GDP)	-3.56	-5.46	-4.30	-3.92
Government primary surplus/deficit (% of GDP)	0.35	-1.44	-0.13	0.29
Government debt (% of GDP)	182.5	193.9	198.8	199.1
External balance (% of GDP)	3.66	-1.28	1.45	2.53
Exports of goods and services (% of GDP)	32.9	34.5	36.7	38.3
Export of services (% of GDP)	15.6	16.8	18.3	19.6
Imports of goods and services (% of GDP)	35.3	37.0	36.5	37.0
Employment (million)	3.527	3.467	3.471	3.527

The projected fall in real output by year end is due to the strong decrease in private expenditure, which is only partially offset by an increase in tourism. We should keep in mind that the private nonfinancial sector is still deleveraging, and is expected to continue doing so in our projections. As a consequence of the fall in output, the small primary surplus in government accounts reached in 2014 is eroded. We are assuming that capital transfers to the government, which were about €4 billion in 2014 and about €6 billion in 2013, revert to a smaller amount that is closer to the pre-crisis average, partially explaining the projected increase in the government deficit and the fall in the primary surplus, as shown in Table 3.

In Figure 15, we depict the projected paths of the three financial balances. The government current deficit (i.e., without considering net capital transfers) remains roughly stable. Government debt, however, keeps rising relative to GDP, and starts falling only when the improvement in revenues from tourism restores growth from 2017 onward.

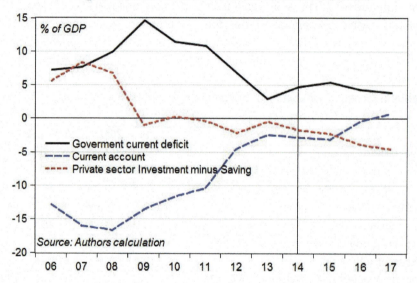

Figure 15. Greece. Baseline: main sector balances

We project the current account (without net capital transfers) to remain roughly stable in 2015, and to increase from 2016 onward, mainly due to a rise in exports of services. Again, we assume that capital transfers from abroad, which were almost €12 billion in 2014, revert to their average pre-crisis level, which explains the deterioration in the external balance reported in Table 3. Employment remains relatively stable, and so does the unemployment rate, which starts falling only in 2017.

The private sector balance in Figure 15 shows that, as a consequence of fiscal conditions and uncertainty, investment will not recover, and both households and nonfinancial corporations will continue to deleverage: as the path moves below zero, the private sector has a financial surplus, which allows for an increase in net financial assets that will most likely be used to reduce the level of debt outstanding.

In sum, our model suggests that, should Greece be allowed to roll over its existing debt but no longer receives additional external finance – and is therefore unable to pursue expansionary policies – it will suffer another year or more of recession before slowly being pulled out of the crisis by the tourism sector.

6. More optimism?

Our baseline projection in Table 3 may turn out to be too pessimistic if a good agreement with the institutions is indeed reached, the projected 10 percent increase in tourism over 2014 materializes, and restored confidence among businesspeople stimulates private investment. This implies that the existing tranches of the debt coming to maturity are refinanced at the current, favorable conditions, and we assume that, in this case, the government keeps paying interest on the existing debt.

For our "optimistic" baseline scenario, we assume that additional investment of about €1 billion takes place over the second half of 2015, and that exports of services (tourism) increase by 10 percent over what was assumed in the "pessimistic" scenario. Conditional on these assumptions, real output will grow by 0.97 percent in 2015. Our optimistic baseline projection shows an improvement in the primary deficit in 2015, which does turn into surplus beginning in 2016.

Our optimistic projections suggest that, if confidence is restored in the second half of 2015, the main effects will be felt more strongly in the following year. Real output will also grow in 2015, but not fast enough to have a significant impact on the unemployment rate. In this more optimistic baseline scenario, an additional 160,000 jobs are created by the end of the simulation period – not that many, given the current numbers of unemployed.

It is important to stress again that our results depend on the government abandoning the fiscal austerity program that is still demanded by the institutions. Conversely, should the government reduce public employment and pensions even further, real output and unemployment will be much worse than projected.

Table 4. Greece: "Optimistic" baseline projections

	2014	2015	2016	2017
Real GDP (% growth rate)	0.70	0.97	2.88	1.43
Government surplus/deficit (% of GDP)	-3.56	-4.67	-2.44	-1.87
Government primary surplus/deficit (% of GDP)	0.35	-0.74	1.48	2.01
Government debt (% of GDP)	182.5	188.6	185.9	183.8
External balance (% of GDP)	3.66	-0.21	2.83	3.82
Exports of goods and services (% of GDP)	32.9	35.3	38.2	39.9
Export of services (% of GDP)	15.6	18.1	20.9	22.2
Imports of goods and services (% of GDP)	35.3	36.8	36.7	37.3
Employment (million)	3.527	3.491	3.563	3.640

7. Scenario 1: the Geuro proposal

We next simulate our model to estimate the impact of introducing alternative financing instruments, which are compatible with keeping the euro as legal currency. We are, of course, cognizant of the government's rejection of such arrangements, but offer them in light of recent reporting in the popular press that they have been considered by the ECB, the IMF, and even Germany's strongman, Wolfgang Schäuble - all of which have, predictably, denied such claims.

The first option we consider is an update of our proposal, outlined in Papadimitriou, Nikiforos, and Zezza (2014a), of issuing zero-coupon bonds, for which we adopt the label "Geuro" (as proposed in Mayer 2012). Such bonds would bear no interest, and would be both perpetual (no repayment of principal, no redemption, and no increase in debt) and transferable. For all practical purposes, Geuros would be used as money, but the government would not re-denominate existing financial assets and liabilities into Geuros, nor would it require private transactions to be settled in Geuros.[12]

Geuros should be convertible in only one direction, from euro to Geuro, to avoid speculative attacks, limit their use to the domestic market, and curb the possibility of transfers to euro deposits outside the country. Informal discussions with ECB officials have made it clear that issuing Geuros would be a fiscal policy decision: it would not interfere with ECB monetary policy, and would therefore be compatible with keeping the euro as legal currency.
Geuros should be issued for two purposes: (1) to restore liquidity in the domestic economy, where euro liquidity is drying up because of the government's need to honor its commitments with foreign creditors, for fear of capital losses and/or extraordinary taxation measures on the part of those who still hold financial assets; and (2) to provide liquidity for additional government expenditure to sustain employment and restore confidence in a recovery of the economy among private investors.

The amount of Geuro liquidity to be issued should be very carefully determined to control the risk of inflation and the pressures for immediate depreciation of the Geuro against its nominal value. (The preferred institution charged with the responsibility of issuing Geuros is the Greek central bank or another independent financial authority.) For these reasons, Geuros would be accepted, *pari passu*, by the government for tax payments, for up to 20% of all private sector obligations to the government - that is, for direct and indirect taxes – as well as social contributions.

From the latest data on the nonfinancial accounts of the general government, we observe that, in 2014, the government received €22 billion in "Taxes on products," €16.8 billion in "Taxes on income and wealth," and €24 billion in "Social contributions". Letting taxpayers use Geuros for up to 20% of their obligations implies that up to 12.6 billion Geuros could be demanded and used each year only to be paid back to the government.

---

[12] A similar proposal, for electronic Tax Anticipation Notes, is put forward in Andresen and Parenteau (2015).

Greece: conditions and strategies for economic recovery

From the same source, we further observe that, in 2014, the government paid €21 billion in "Compensation of employees" and €33.7 billion as social benefits. In our scenario, we assume that 30 percent of such payments will be made in Geuros, starting in the third quarter of 2015, for the equivalent of €16.4 billion. If this were the only use of Geuros, there would be no impact on the economy, since the smaller payments in euro from the government would be matched by smaller revenues in euro and the Geuros issued would be entirely destroyed, as they would be used as tax payments in the same year. As stated above, the creation of the Geuro is meaningful if and only if it can finance additional expenditure and provide additional liquidity to the nonfinancial sector.

One way to increase liquidity through the issuance of Geuros would be to reimburse the domestic banking sector for its loans outstanding to the government, which totaled €4 billion in short-term loans at the end of 2014 and €6.8 billion in long-term loans (excluding loans from the central bank), for a total of roughly €10.8 billion. Increasing the liquidity of Greek banks, albeit in Geuros, would help increase the circulation of Geuros through borrowing by the nonfinancial sector. This additional emission of Geuros would improve the balance sheet of the financial sector but would not provide the needed stimulus to aggregate demand that Greece needs unless it were reemployed in the form of lending for private sector expenditures, both for consumption and for investment.

We therefore propose, as in Papadimitriou, Nikiforos, and Zezza (2014a), to use Geuro emission to finance a program of direct job creation of the employer-of-last-resort (ELR) type (Table 5). (The general details of such proposals are provided in Antonopoulos et al, 2014) In summary, the government would provide, for the production of public goods, a job at a minimum wage to anyone willing and able to work. The wage level should be low enough to make private employment more attractive, yet high enough to ensure a decent standard of living.

Assuming, to begin with, a monthly gross wage based on the (post-troika) established monthly minimum of €586 for 550,000 workers implies annual payments of about €7.5 billion, where the annual program cost includes both direct and indirect costs (benefits and social contributions of workers), intermediate consumption of goods and services, and direct and indirect taxes. In this scenario, we assume that the program is gradually implemented, starting in the third quarter of 2015, to create approximately 100,000 additional jobs per quarter for the next two years.

Table 5. Greece – Geuro scenario

	2014	2015	2016	2017
Real GDP (% growth rate)	0.70	3.68	5.93	1.44
Government total surplus/deficit (% of GDP)	-3.56	-5.95	-4.73	-4.12
Government total primary surplus/deficit (% of GDP)	0.35	-2.11	-0.95	-0.30
Government total debt (% of GDP)	182.5	185.4	180.3	180.5
External balance (% of GDP)	3.66	-0.57	1.31	1.99
Exports of goods and services (% of GDP)	32.9	34.5	36.3	37.9
Export of services (% of GDP)	15.6	17.7	19.8	21.1
Imports of goods and services (% of GDP)	35.3	36.3	36.2	37.0
Employment (million)	3.527	3.690	4.063	4.459
Government surplus/deficit in Geuro (% of GDP)	0	-2.81	-3.5	-3.2
Government surplus/deficit in Euro (% of GDP)	-3.56	-3.13	-1.25	-0.88
Government primary surplus/deficit in Euro (% of GDP)	0.35	0.70	2.53	2.94
Government debt in euro (% of GDP)	182.5	182.6	174.1	171.2

Since the government will be "saving" euro on pensions and wages of existing public sector employees, who will receive 30 percent of their compensation in Geuros, there is no need to finance the ELR program entirely in Geuros. We propose that up to 50 percent of ELR wages would be paid in euro and 50 percent in Geuros, for an additional 7.5 billion euro-equivalent stimulus to the economy per year.

We simulate our proposal on top of the "optimistic" baseline reported in Table 4. According to our model, the stimulus will be effective in restarting the economy, with real GDP growing considerably in 2015 and even more strongly in 2016, then slowing down in 2017, when the need for additional ELR jobs is lessened by the recovery in the private sector and the ELR program is tapered. The government can also choose to finance investment in key sectors that is either export-oriented or aimed at substituting the importation of goods with those domestically produced.

As expected, the stimulus to domestic demand implies a deterioration in the current account balance that is worse than in our "optimistic" baseline, but the expected increase in revenues from tourism is still sufficient to keep the current account in a surplus position.

The sum of government expenditure in both euro and Geuros results in a higher government deficit, as expected. However, with the given choice of the share of expenditure paid in Geuros, and the maximum share of taxes that can be paid in Geuros, we expect a sensible improvement in the government's euro accounts, which tend to balance by the end of the simulation period, while the primary surplus in euro as a share of GDP increases from 2015 onward. As a consequence, government debt outstanding as a share of GDP will start falling quickly.

When first proposed (see Papadimitriou, Nikiforos, and Zezza, 2014a), this alternative financing arrangement was attacked as a transitory stage in Greece's ultimate exit from the euro. This, of course, misses the point of the system's restricted parallel nature and the commitment of the government, if it were to be implemented, not to re-denominate any assets in Geuros.

Furthermore, it would not be a permanent structure, but in place until such time as the Greek economy was growing at sufficient levels, especially in net exports so as to increase euro inflows and correspondingly decrease the amount of Geuros in circulation, and in turn decrease Geuro tax receipts in favor of euro receipts. Above all, the Geuro program must be well designed and the supply of Geuros very carefully controlled – by an independent agency accountable to the Greek Parliament – to resist inflationary pressures.

8. Scenario 2: tax certificates proposal

As an alternative to the introduction of a parallel financial system, another proposal has been advanced that is also based on the creation of an alternative financing mechanism: fiscal credit certificates (FCCs). There are several variants of this proposal. We will simulate the variant proposed by Cattaneo and Zibordi (2014) for the Italian economy,[13] adapted to the Greek situation.

As proposed, FCCs could initially be transferred electronically to the bank bond accounts of recipients, and could later also be issued in paper form. The certificates could be used to pay direct, indirect, and property taxes, including social contributions, after a holding period of 24 months for their nominal value (say, €100). It could also be established that, should they be used later than 24 months, the nominal value would increase by a given interest rate.

It is expected that the recipients of FCCs, which would need liquidity in euros to increase their expenditure immediately, would sell FCCs to whoever needed to pay taxes in the future and had liquidity in euro. FCCs would obviously be sold at a predetermined discount against their nominal value, where the discount would tend to zero as they approached maturity.

The main differences between FCCs and the Geuro are: (1) FCCs would not immediately be used as a parallel currency, although nothing would prevent private payments in FCCs, with mutual consent; and (2) Geuros could be used immediately for tax payments, while FCCs could only be used to pay taxes at maturity. The reason for delaying the immediate use of FCCs would be to let the economy grow with the fiscal stimulus for some time, generating larger tax revenues in euro to offset the drop in euro revenues that would arise when the FCCs came to maturity.

FCCs have been designed with properties that will make them more palatable to the Eurozone institutions, as well as to citizens who might be unnerved by the introduction of a parallel financial system - acting as new currency – for its possible implications for inflation and/or the devaluation of existing financial assets.

Since FCCs cannot be used immediately for private sector payments or tax

---

[13] Cattaneo and Zibordi (2014) in Italian. For details in English, see Cattaneo (2013). See also Pilkington and Mosler (2012) for an earlier proposal for tax-backed bonds.

payments, introducing them as part of the compensation of existing public sector employees or for pension payments – as in the Geuro proposal – would amount to a cut in such sources of income, since the recipients would need to sell FCCs at a discount in exchange for liquidity in euro. We therefore assume that FCCs are issued mainly to increase public expenditure, financing 50 percent of the ELR program described above, with the remaining 50% funded in euro.

This implies FCC emissions of about €1,875 million per quarter, starting in the third quarter of 2015. We assume the euro-equivalent value of this program to be the same as in the Geuro scenario, but that FCCs will be sold at a predetermined discount of, say, 25% when the program starts, 10% in 2016, and 5% in 2017 as their maturity nears.

Table 6. Greece. Fiscal Credit Certificates scenario

	2014	2015	2016	2017
Real GDP (% growth rate)	0.70	3.00	6.01	1.75
Government total surplus/deficit (% of GDP)	-3.56	-5.63	-4.53	-4.03
Government total primary surplus/deficit (% of GDP)	0.35	-1.78	-0.74	-0.21
Government total debt – including FCCs (% of GDP)	182.5	186.2	180.7	180.3
External balance (% of GDP)	3.66	-0.48	1.52	2.12
Exports of goods and services (% of GDP)	32.9	34.7	36.5	38.0
Export of services (% of GDP)	15.6	17.8	19.9	21.2
Imports of goods and services (% of GDP)	35.3	36.4	36.2	37.0
Employment (mn)	3.527	3.600	4.023	4.571
Government surplus/deficit in euro (% of GDP)	-3.56	-3.55	-0.60	-2.11
Government primary surplus/deficit in Euro (% of GDP)	0.35	0.30	3.19	1.70
Government debt in euro (% of GDP)	182.5	184.1	174.8	172.6

Results of model simulations for this proposal are reported in Table 6. Again, we keep the same assumptions as in our "optimistic" baseline (Table 4) and add in the FCC stimulus. We expect FCCs to be issued for the whole of the simulation period, and, as stated, those issued in 2015 will be used for tax payments in 2017, thereby reducing euro revenues for the government in that year.

An additional proposal from the Italian proponents of FCCs is that they are transferred to exporting firms, and as this would be equivalent to a reduction in tax payments, the impact on competitiveness should be similar to that of a decrease in labor costs and should therefore help boost exports and improve the current account balance.

We believe the proposal to be of interest but preferred not to evaluate it, as its realistic impact on goods exports is difficult to establish for the Greek economy, where such exports are small relative to exports of services.

9. Can Greece use a parallel currency to pay back existing government debt?

The major concern of the Greek government in the past weeks has been how to repay debt as it becomes due, with no access to further external funding. In Figure 16, we report the tranches of government debt coming to maturity in the remaining months of 2015 (€2.153 billion, still in the chart, were repaid to the European Investment bank and to holders of Greek treasury bills in May). More than €25 billion in debt will reach maturity in 2015, and in our estimate of the impact of introducing the Geuro, the immediate improvement in government accounts denominated in euro will not be sufficient for this purpose. Moreover, should the government use additional euro liquidity to extinguish foreign debt, with no access to additional external finance, it is hard to believe that confidence will be restored - the assumed precondition for our scenarios - and that enough liquidity will be available for generating an economic recovery.

Should the government be forced to meet its existing obligations, one possibility would be to introduce an extraordinary tax on deposits, as the Italian government did in 1992, applying a tax of 0.6 percent on average bank balances. This tax was reimbursed to deposit holders when the government liquidity crisis was over. Using the same percentage, the Greek government would obtain less than €1 billion - not enough to finance debt repayment in 2015. Italy's extraordinary tax was highly unpopular, and applying a similar policy in Greece with a higher tax rate may prove politically unsustainable.

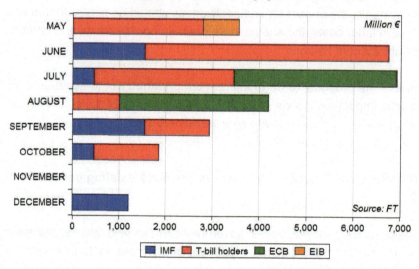

Figure 16. Greece. Debt payments in 2015

The only alternative to the government defaulting on its forthcoming debt payments lies in refinancing, and - as we have tried to show - under these conditions the government would slowly achieve an overall surplus in euro, which could be used after 2017 to begin repaying its debt. But, more important, the Greek economy would at last see GDP and income growing.

10. Conclusions

In this chapter we have argued that Greece may be on the road to recovery, provided some conditions are met. However, the most important problem, which needs to be addressed immediately, is the state of fundamental uncertainty about the near- and medium-term future. This depends on the outcome of the negotiations between the new SYRIZA government, the IMF, and Greece's Eurozone partners. If the institutional members of the Brussels Group are indeed pushing Greece toward defaulting on its debt and keeping to a path of austerity for fiscal policy and the labor market - as De Grauwe (2015) argues - then Greece will experience a further recessionary period, as private investors will remain reluctant to start new businesses in a country where the prospects for profitability are low and very volatile. In addition, households and business are still deleveraging on their existing debt, and the recent surge in tourism-related activities will not, according to our model, be sufficient to jump-start a recovery in 2015.

If, on the other hand, the Greek government gains access to refinancing its existing debt at the existing, very low interest rates, and uncertainty is at least partially lifted, we argue that investment will come back, generating sufficient growth in the second half of 2015 to more than offset the turbulent first months of the new government. In this case, government debt as a percentage of GDP will fall from 2016 onward. In this "optimistic" baseline scenario we assume that the government will meet all of its financial obligations against its creditors. However, our simulation shows that, without further policies, recovery will be slow, in the face of the humanitarian crisis and the high level of unemployment Greece is currently enduring.

We have therefore discussed two proposals to fund a program of direct job creation; neither proposal requires access to liquidity in euro, and both are compatible with the EU treaties and the current rules regulating monetary authorities. The first proposal, which updates Papadimitriou, Nikiforos and Zezza (2014a), focuses on the issuance of a nonconvertible parallel currency - the Geuro - that the government would accept, *pari passu*, in fulfillment of tax obligations. Introducing the Geuro would allow the government to finance much-needed job creation, and by restoring liquidity should help stabilize expectation and foster private investment.

Our model simulation shows that such a program would allow Greece to achieve a higher growth rate more quickly, and create a substantial number of new jobs – albeit at a minimum wage - while the level of debt relative to GDP would fall faster. The government deficit denominated in euro would fall while a deficit in Geuros would arise, but the potential inflationary impact of this additional liquidity would be negligible. A fiscal impulse may also be provided through the emission of fiscal credit certificates, non-interest-bearing bonds that are accepted for tax payment at maturity, which is assumed to be two years. In this case, FCCs would not be used as currency, but rather sold at a discount to obtain liquidity. Our simulation shows that, again, an expansionary fiscal policy financed through FCC emission would be effective in sustaining growth and job creation, while keeping government accounts in euro in line with the requests of the institutions. It is important to stress that our model shows that the expected improvement in revenues from tourism would be sufficient to finance the increase in imports arising from an expansion in domestic demand. To strengthen this result, export-oriented policies would also be necessary, to reduce the vulnerability of a country dependent mainly on tourism for balancing its external account.

In this chapter we have not discussed the possibility of Greece exiting the euro system as a result of failing to achieve a reasonable agreement with Brussels. As discussed in our previous paper (Papadimitriou, Nikiforos and Zezza, 2014a), we broadly agree with Rachman (2015): a Grexit would generate further short-term costs for the country, possibly for up to 24 months after exit. It would imply that the government had defaulted on its debt and required new external funding to finance needed imports until a new, devalued currency increased export revenues enough to bring the current account into balance. But, on the other hand, it would restore the ability of the government to pursue policies aimed at the well-being of its citizens rather than its international creditors.

References

Andresen, T. and Parenteau R. W. (2015) *A Detailed Program Proposal for Creating a Parallel Currency in Greece*. Available via http://rwer.wordpress.com/2015/03/28/a-detailed-program-proposal-for-creating-a-parallel-currency-in-greece/

Antonopoulos, R., Adam S., Kim K., Masterson T. and Papadimitriou D. B. (2014) "Responding to the Unemployment Challenge: A Job Guarantee Proposal for Greece." *Research Project Report*. Annandale-on-Hudson, N.Y.: Levy Economics Institute of Bard College. June.

Cattaneo, M. (2013) *Tax Credit Certificates*. Available via http://bastaconleurocrisi.blogspot.it/2013/09/tax-credit-certificates-certificati-di.html

Cattaneo, M. and Zibordi, G. (2014) *La soluzione per l'euro*. Milano: Hoepli.

De Grauwe, P. (2015) "Are Creditors Pushing Greece Deliberately Into Default?" *Social Europe*, April 28. Available via http://www.socialeurope.eu/2015/04/are-creditors-pushing-greece- deliberately-into-default/

Mayer, T. (2012) "Der Geuro: Eine Parallel währungfür Griechenland?" *Deutsche Bank Research. Briefing on European Integration*, Frankfurt am Main, May 23.

Papadimitriou, D. B., Nikiforos, M. and Zezza, G. (2014a) "Prospects and Policies for the Greek Economy." *Strategic Analysis*. Annandale-on-Hudson, N.Y.: Levy Economics Institute of Bard College. February.

Papadimitriou, D. B., Nikiforos, M. and Zezza, G. (2014b) "Will Tourism Save Greece?" *Strategic Analysis*. Annandale-on-Hudson, N.Y.: Levy Economics Institute of Bard College. August.

Pilkington, P. and Mosler, W. (2012) "Tax-backed Bonds - A National Solution to the European Debt Crisis." *Policy Note* 2012/4. Annandale-on-Hudson, N.Y.: Levy Economics Institute of Bard College. March.

Rachman, G. (2015) "Grexit May Be the Best End for a Bad Marriage." *Financial Times*, May 4.

Watt, A. (2015) "The Greek Stand-Off: A Proper Sense of Perspective Is Urgently Needed." *Social Europe*, April 16.

Data Sources

Bank of Greece: www.bankofgreece.gr Last accessed May 2015.

ElStat (Hellenic Statistical Authority): www.statistic.gr Last accessed May 2015.

IMF *World Economic Outlook Database*. Last accessed April 2015.

OECD: www.stats.oecd.org Last accessed April 2014.

Chapter 6
Economic policy and political power in European crises
Gerson P. Lima

1. Introduction

A crisis may be defined as a situation of excess supply that comes about after an important investment in increasing the production capacity is done and the expected new demand collapses. A financial crisis is consequence of financial capital supply excess, especially money supply excess, leading to high risk operations and financial capital losses internally and worldwide; the economic problem is to look for where the money excess comes from and close the source.

Economics deals with money and money is associated with political power; economic events may thus be analyzed considering the political power interests and its capacity of imposing decisions that benefit its members but contradict economic logics. Moreover, the political power may also impose a convenient economic doctrine as if it where theory and create economists that despise real world facts and abide by faith, especially on what money is essential, the monetary policy. Thus, some new approaches are exposed as a basis for the presentation of the main theme and the conclusion.

Some important monetary notions are here critically reviewed aiming to demonstrate that monetary policy does not deliver its target of price stability and it is observed that inflation control is essential to the political power since inflation is a great problem to financial capitalists. Monetary policy however is also a source of inflation through the interest rent from the public debt that supposedly exists to avoid inflation.

Anyway, the political power extended its control to the fiscal policy which is said to be inflationary. It is then argued that fiscal policy without debt is the right instrument to promote production and income growth and demonstrated that the money stock thus created, contrary to what happens in the monetary policy case, tends to a theoretical equilibrium status. It is inadequate to blame fiscal policy for inflation.

Fiscal policy has been more a theory than a real world fact for the monetary policy has a tendency towards creating public debt crises whose solution must be provided by the fiscal policy on the opposite direction. It is then presented a short commentary on the reversed fiscal policy to remind that committing the public to paying interests or give public assets up may be a goal of the political power.

These notions are used to develop the analysis on the economic policy and the crises in the European Union. Evidences allow for the observation that EU has two crises to fix; one is the general crisis touching almost all countries where monetary policy commands the economy, and the other is specific for such general crisis may dismantle the European Union.

Conclusions are that state-members local money emission to make countries' fiscal policy may be the solution but even if it is actually a good idea to be accepted it must be interesting to the political power and preserve democracy.

2. Political power and economics

No matter the government's system, money emission is a privilege of the ruling political power. The opposite holds; those who have the power of printing money have, or acquire the political power and thus assume the power to command the economy for their own sake. Constitutions of democratic countries pretend to follow Abraham Lincoln's statement (1863) that governments must be of the people, by the people and for the people. If so, then in democratic countries printing money would be people's monopoly and money should be printed to the people's sake. But this is not what actually happens.

Economic policy and political power in European crises

The first goal of those who intend to gain the political power without armed revolution is to convince people that governments should never print money. This seems to be easy task for in many if not all democratic countries congresses transferred the central government monopoly of money printing to "independent" central banks. These central banks are independent from the government and the people, but they are not independent public institutions for they are controlled by private bankers, directly and ideologically. This is neither Marxist theory nor one more conspiracy theory. Actually, in democratic countries the power of printing money was "voluntarily" given to profit seeking central bankers, and this power has been used to reinforce their political power internally and abroad, always looking for rent, and seldom for employment and democratic income distribution.

On the matter Michael Hudson states that "The financial sector has the same objective as military conquest: to gain control of land and basic infrastructure, and collect tribute. To update von Clausewitz, finance has become war by other means. It is not necessary to conquer a country or even to own its land, natural resources and infrastructure, if its economic surplus can be taken financially. What formerly took blood and arms is now obtained by debt leverage" (Hudson, 2015, 5).

There is no ethical economic theory that could adhere to such reality. So, the mainstream economics must be dogma, not science. The political power forged a convenient doctrine, the monetary policy, which "justify" the means and disguise the ends of the economic policy. Monetary policy became then the mainstream economics and has "been dominating the profession for about three decades" (Grim, 2013).

An empirical support to the hypothesis that the political power commands the economy is given by Hager (2013). To begin with he states that "In 1887 Henry Carter Adams produced a study demonstrating that the ownership of government bonds was heavily concentrated in the hands of a 'bond-holding class' that lent to and, in Adams's view, controlled the government like dominant shareholders control a corporation. The interests of this bond-holding class clashed with the interests of the masses, whose burdensome taxes financed the interest payments on government bonds". And that "Anchored within a 'capital as power' approach, the research indicates a staggering pattern of concentration in the ownership of US public debt in the hands of the top one per cent of US households over the past three decades. Accordingly, the bond-holding class is still alive and well in contemporary US capitalism" (Hager, 2013, Abstract). Hager therefore observes that "In the past three decades the public debt has come to serve as an institution of power working in the interests of the top one per cent... Though much has changed since Adams's time, the analysis presented here indicates that there is indeed still a powerful bond-holding class in the US, one whose power has augmented rapidly over the past three decades" (Hager, 2013, 22).

Page et al (2013) realized a comprehensive survey on the policy preferences of wealthy Americans and their possible influence on economic policy and democracy. About the top 1% of US wealth-holders they inform that "We find that they are extremely active politically and that they are much more conservative than the American public as a whole with respect to important policies concerning taxation, economic regulation, and especially social welfare programs" (Page et al, 2013, Abstract). The survey allow them to conclude that "We suggest that these distinctive policy preferences may help account for why certain public policies in the United States appear to deviate from what the majority of US citizens wants the government to do. If this is so, it raises serious issues for democratic theory" (Page et al, 2013, Abstract).

The economic science should not neglect the existence of the political power for it has the power to market a doctrine that justify its members' interests – and realize them. For instance, monetary policy abide by the paradigm that "government should never print money" and people think that if government could print money it would do it only for the sake of privileged public servants. Actually there is a political power that prints money for its members' sake, but governments have no political power to print money.

3. Monetary policy commands the economy

The Fundamental Accounting Identity discloses a very important relation connecting the three sectors of the economy. Changing its order it may be written:

$$\{(FE + INT) - T\} = \{Sp - Ip\} - CAB$$

The left term, if positive, is the public deficit produced in the government sector, which will always match the sum of excess savings over investments $\{Sp - Ip\}$ coming from the private sector plus or less the foreign sector's current account deficit or surplus (CAB). The accounting formula shows that money flows among sectors in such a way that if one sector produced a deficit at least one out the other two created a surplus. The excess of expenditures of one sector implies an excess of revenues in some or both other sectors. Altogether, the summation of all three balances must be zero. The financial market is the medium through which money flows from one sector to the others. As an intermediate, the financial market produces nothing real, it just catalyses the production process. So, it does not enter the Fundamental Accounting Identity. All the same, the monetary policy is also absent for it only establishes how some money will flow among sectors, particularly from the other sectors to the government. This means that in accounting terms neither the financial and monetary market are economic sector nor are they synchronized with the rest of the economy.

The public deficit is associated with the governmental fiscal policy decisions on the expenses FE and tax rates. The current account deficit is identified with the foreign relations policy decisions, especially decisions concerning the exchange rate. Fiscal policy and foreign relations decisions influence the interest rate and all other economic endogenous variables and no other decision making centre would be required. However, the interest rate has been accepted as an exclusive concern of the monetary policy; so, instead of two, the basic economic policy instruments have been three: the fiscal, the exchange rate and the monetary policies.

These apparatuses are tied together, in such a way that decisions on one of them impart consequences on the other two. Only one can command, the others must consent and survive with the consequences, for good or for evil. If monetary policy prevails then the exchange rate will fluctuate in accordance to the interest rate and not the international trade. For instance, the exporting sector may follow a vanishing trend caused by a continuous process of national currency appreciation through monetary policy actions. Worse, if monetary policy prevails then the fiscal policy objective will reduce to generating savings through permanent and increasing primary surpluses to pay the ever expanding interest expenditure. If monetary policy prevails then the other two main economic policy instruments become also monetary policy instruments for they must be used on behalf of monetary targets set by the political power.

4. Actually, what is monetary policy?

Inflation is the continuous growth of prices, a dynamic variable. A single variation of an economic exogenous variable cannot create dynamics; a single new value of an exogenous variable, say the fiscal expenditure, causes new values to some endogenous variables but does not impart to them an autonomous movement; it is a matter of comparative statics. What produces inflation is a continuous variation of some exogenous variable, for instance the always increasing credit supply stemming from the always increasing stock of money printed by central banks to pay interests on the public debt. Anyway, from the political power standpoint inflation is a huge concern for it works like a tax on financial capital and must be kept at the least level politically and technically possible.

Not coincidentally, mainstream monetary economics assume two basic statements aiming at firing inflation. First, the monetary policy paradigm: government should never print money. The idea seems to be to indebt people and collect interest rent but preventing government from printing money does not prevent government from spending and spending variation is the cause of price changes. Perhaps the real target of this statement is to avoid fiscal policy expansionary plans presented by occasional out of control politicians. Second, inflation must be stabilized through monetary tools, especially open market operations to sustain the interest rate fixed by the central bank aiming to maintaining the inflation rate below the inflation rate targeted by the central bank. About inflation, the experiment made by Lima (2015a) on the United States aggregate supply curve (1960-2007) brought about the equation:

$$Pde = 4.6259 + 0.03520*FE + 12.2312*MW + 0.334376*ER + 0.08377*INT$$

In this equation Pde is the estimate of the theoretical equilibrium series[1] of the Consumer Price Index, FE is the federal fiscal expenditure, MW is the federal minimum wage, ER is the exchange rate and INT is the federal expenditure on interest upon the federal public held debt. It may be observed that the public debt is omitted, in such a way that the INT coefficient carries a bias given by its relation to the public debt. This means that INT carries the effect of the monetary policy on the price index and that in this experiment monetary policy had increasing effect on prices. The weights of the explanatory economic policy instruments over prices as indicated by their elasticities at 2007 are 0.4002 to FE, 0.3265 to MW, 0.0961 to ER and 0.1561 to INT. In this experiment the GDP equation obtained was:

$$GDPde = -197.8225 + 6.36696*FE + 15.5759*ER - 0.58002*INT$$

In this equation the public debt is also omitted; its effect over the GDP is included in the INT's coefficient. Respective elasticities at 2007 are 0.96672 to FE, 0.00605 to ER and -0.01443 to INT. The reduced equation of GDPde and Pde is the US aggregate supply curve for that sample. One conclusion is that "Signs of INT, negative in the GDP equation and positive in the P equation, allow for the deduction that the monetary policy expanded the aggregate demand, through credit, but the shift so attained was less than the expansion required to compensate the contraction the monetary policy imparted to the aggregate supply. The conclusion is thus that in the United States of 1960-2007 monetary policy measured by the public debt and its

---

[1] The reduced equilibrium equation simulates a situation in which all exogenous variables stopped varying at the moment t and it is given time enough to the exogenous variables work out their full effect on the endogenous variable, thus producing the "laboratory" or "theoretical" "equilibrium" values of any endogenous variable at each moment t and the theoretical equilibrium series of each endogenous variable. Supply and demand is not an equilibrating device; actually there is no equilibrium in economics (Lima, 2015a, 12).

interest charge caused unemployment to grow and price to rise" (Lima, 2015a, 18). Thomas Palley associates the US monetary policy with an American paradigm and his analysis allow him to state that, "One flaw in this paradigm was the neo-liberal growth model adopted after 1980 that relied on debt and asset price inflation to drive demand in place of wage growth" (Palley, 2009, Abstract).

Simultaneous aggregate demand expansions and aggregate supply contractions impart different and unpredictable effects on GDP and prices. Among others, researches by Balke and Emery (1994), Barth III and Ramey (2002) and Gaiotti and Secchi (2004) indicated that monetary policy caused prices to climb, but this evidence is classified as "puzzle". About this puzzle, it is especially worrisome the statement by Michael Dueker: "Once people in the economy come to believe in the price puzzle – that interest rate hikes are inflationary – how do monetary policymakers persuade people to believe again in the determinacy regime, wherein interest rate hikes would reduce inflation? The lesson policymakers seem to have learned is to avoid this trap in the first place by remaining active inflation fighters in order to preserve people's beliefs in determinacy" (Dueker, 2006). However, the Pde equation above suggests that, contrary to mainstream monetarist statements monetary policy alone cannot fight inflation; actually monetary policy causes inflation. Elasticities of the exogenous variables suggests that if monetary policy prevails the "technically right" ways to reduce prices are the fiscal policy on the wrong direction and minimum wage cuts, what means people impoverishment.

Inflation is a phenomenon that may be explained by the real world supply and demand analysis; consequently, mainstream monetarist economic doctrine must deny supply and demand analysis and this was done indirectly by offering an unreal hence unsustainable supply and demand neoclassical doctrine that misled researchers and gave room to the idea that prices are determined by the money stock and the inflation rate by the unemployment level. Of course these variables are related with each other but not as direct causality. The Phillips curve is just a relation that comes about when the aggregate demand varies while the aggregate supply remains fixed and it is not money itself that determines prices but the growing flow of expenses or higher production costs; inflation is not an exclusively monetary phenomenon.

About open market, when a NCB sells a Treasury bond in exchange of euro it puts away the money then collected; this money is destroyed. Of course, the Treasury bond was sold since there is market demand for Treasury bonds and financial agents decided to buy it. On the opposite open market operation, when buying Treasury bonds central banks print money at the order of Treasury bonds holders; NCB can limit but cannot refuse to buy Treasury bonds held by the public. Therefore, Treasury bonds are money and the NCBs open market operations make them a kind of financial fund that safely provides remuneration to idle financial capital with near 100% liquidity. The political power monetary statement that governments should not print money makes no sense for "its" central banks print money to give to "their" bondholders.

NCBs redeem Treasury bonds printing money to pay the principal – and the accrued interest. The principal is just a return of the money previously collected, but the money printed to pay interest is new and un-backed money that increases the stock of financial capital. The private money "wealth" stemming from the accumulation of the interest rent on the public debt always grows thus constantly increasing credit supply and expanding the demand for financial assets at a rate that is higher than the assets supply expansion. Therefore growing excess of money supply leads to riskier financial operations in the internal market and abroad. Moreover, demand for credit has been an eternal characteristic of people. If borrower's income grows less than the money supply, the need of credit grows but people's capacity to paying loans back reduces the effective demand for credit. Money supply excess and high risk financial operations certainly lead to a financial crisis. It seems that the best way to avoid public and private over-borrowing is preventing un-backed money printing and thus credit excess supply.

Central banks are said to reduce liquidity, for instance the liquidity they created when buying Treasury bonds, through selling Treasury bonds operations. However, when central banks sell a Treasury bond they are in fact assuming to pay interest in a future date that is not up to them to set.

Therefore, the money stock is always scheduled not only to be restored but to increase in some moment in the future. The money supply is always autonomously escalating by the amount of money issued to pay interests on the public debt. There happens then a financial asset inflation which will eventually spill over the consumer price index directly or indirectly through credit. Possibly the central bank has no power to control the money and hence credit supplies. Moreover, despite monetary measures and primary surpluses, the probability of public debt to follow an explosive trend cannot be despised, as demonstrated in Lima (2015b): "The estimate of the US federal tax revenue points to a positive effect of the interest rent on the US tax receipts that is insufficient to compensate the simultaneous negative effect of the public debt itself. Thus, considering that these variables are mutually dependent, the conclusion is that the combined result is negative. Therefore, at least in the period 1960-2007 the US public held debt was autonomously following an explosive trend. The immediate consequence is that the un-backed money issued by central banks without auditing to pay interest on Treasury bonds followed the same trend to infinity" (Lima, 2015b, 12). The conclusion is that what has tamed inflation is not the monetary policy of raising production costs; it seems that the success of price control has been assured by a repressed fiscal policy.

Summing up, evidences suggest that actually monetary policy was created not to improve people's day life but to give to the financial political power the control over government and thus the economic policy – and raise profits. However, greed led to un-backed money emission to pay interests on the public debt and consequently to money supply excess. One important point to which has not been given suitable attention is that in any case the money created to pay interests on public debt is un-backed. The only real stuff that can back money is production, what means human labor, what means people. The money's back is the man; the higher the importance given to money the lower the value given to men and society. So, non-inflationary money emission must be associated with employment creation.

5. Fiscal policy does not cause inflation

Supply and demand has been marketed by mainstream economics supporters as an equilibrating device that provides the maximum result both to rational consumers and profit maximizing producers in a perfect foreseen world. If this were true then everybody would be happy and the political power could do whatever they want.

When we look at supply and demand as a device that transforms the exogenous events and political decisions in price and production real world facts, fiscal policy may be seriously analyzed. The fiscal policy is the instrument to provide employment to the unemployed; so it must provide demand for the existing but unsalable production and for the new production needed to hire actual unemployed workers and newcomers. The fiscal policy is materialized through governmental purchases of products and services that expand the existing aggregate demand. It may be seen as a social financial investment in expanding production; once employed the ex-unemployed workers' income grows, they have more to spend buying from others and the aggregate demand expands once more thus providing an expansion of the tax receipts; the workers so hired are the asset of this social financial investment made and managed by the government. This investment may be done with new money issuing.

However, the political power supporters keep insistently marketing the lemma that government cannot print money for this emission is the cause of the inflation that deteriorates workers' income. To be mainstream monetarists economists must abide by this lemma without realizing that there is money printing to pay interests on the public debt. The resistance to fiscal policy is thus exuberant. Notwithstanding, fiscal policy to create as much employment as required to eliminate unemployment should not properly be said inflationary.

Actually, starting at a theoretical position of zero public balance an expansion of the government fiscal expenditures paid with money issuing by a really public central bank shifts the aggregate demand curve to the right while the aggregate supply curve is not immediately touched. The multiplier effect pushes the aggregate demand once more in the same direction and the new theoretical equilibrium point will be far away above and to the right, meaning that both employment and price level increased. But the worker's income also raised and that is why new prices are higher. What happens is that having more income people climb the Maslow pyramid and can now demand products that they before considered superfluous for they had no money to buy them, and that is good news. This is not inflation; it is development.

Of course fiscal policy makes apparent a positive relation between money emission and prices levels but for inflation to come out new money emission must be endless. At the theoretical full employment status aggregate demand stops shifting, there are no more money emission and prices stop climbing. Contrary to the monetary policy model of promoting aggregate demand expansion, the money stock created by the fiscal policy tends to a theoretical point of equilibrium.

Figure 1 – Effect of a single fiscal policy expansion

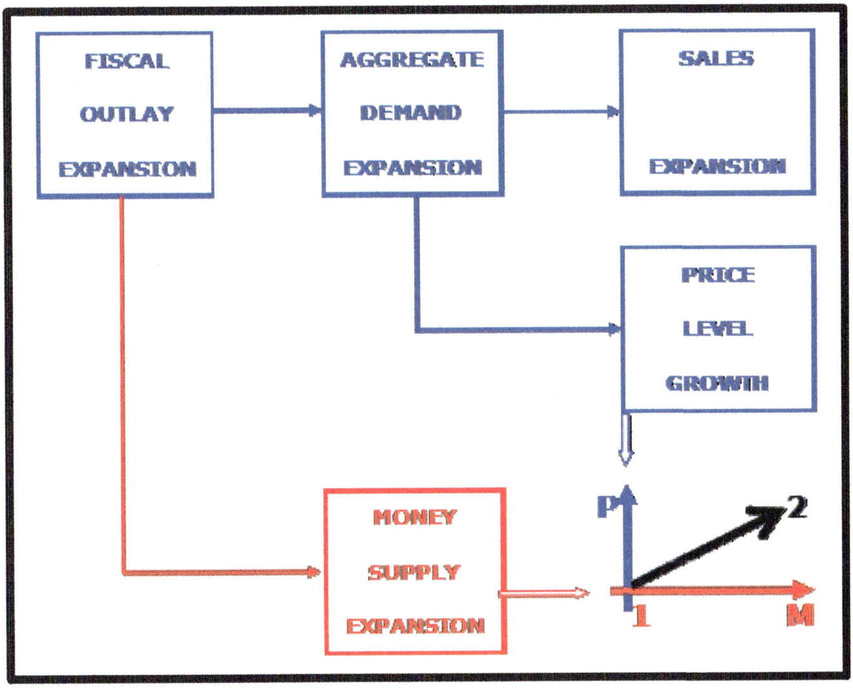

Source: Author's elaboration.

Economic policy and political power in European crises

What follows is a demonstration that, being backed by production, in the case of fiscal policy the stock of money issued by a really public central bank converges to a theoretical equilibrium amount. Suppose a democratic country where government is the political power and Constitution prevents federal government from borrowing money, both internally and abroad. There will then be no monetary policy, no public debt, no open market, no public interests expenses and the central bank would be really public. It is hard to imagine all that but if democracy prevails somewhere, then there it is a real possibility. In this ethical economic order, the monetary base would be composed exclusively by transactions on the real side of the economy: governmental fiscal policy and current account transactions. Money would be created only in cases of public deficits and current account surpluses, and vice versa. This currency may be named "primary money". Imagine that there is a legal enforcement for the really public central bank to make a deposit in the Treasury's account in an amount determined by the annual budget law.[2] For that not to look too odd, take it as the price government imposes to private banks in exchange for their license to exclusively serve the private sector of the economy. Moreover, banks make more profits from the economic expansion associated with fiscal policy and for banks money "production" comes at low cost out of thin air. The accounting formula below describes the time performance of the primary money stock:

$$M = M_{-1} + (FE - T) + CAB \qquad (1)$$

where M is the stock of primary money at the end of the present period, M_{-1} is the stock of primary money at the end of the previous period, FE represents the fiscal expenditure, T is the total government revenue and CAB is the current account balance, defined as surplus. If public budget and current account were balanced, then money stock would be invariant. CAB is an endogenous variable; it is a function of FE and a set of other exogenous variables that explains primary money stock M, for instance in the form:

$$CAB = \alpha_0 + \alpha_1 FE + \alpha_2 OV_1$$

---

[2] This is absolutely not to say that central bank could print money to pay for all government expenses, and then eliminate taxes, for in this case the stock of money would increase limitlessly. All the same, it is not being suggested that the Treasury could lend money to the public.

where OV_1 refers to "Other exogenous Variables" that may influence T values, for instance foreign income, which has been here omitted to keep simplicity.

It is assumed that, if positive, greater (FE − T) leads to greater M and simultaneously to greater aggregate demand and consequently to greater sales, prices and GDP levels and sometime later to greater tax receipts T. So, a combined hypothesis is that larger revenue T will be associated with greater stock of primary money M through GDP:

$$dT/dM = dT/dGDP \times dGDP/dM > 0$$

Tax receipts may thus be expressed by an equation like:

$$T = \beta_0 + \beta_1 M + \beta_2 OV_2 \qquad (2)$$

where OV_2 refers to other set of "Other exogenous Variables" that may influence T values but are here omitted to keep simplicity and $\beta_1 (=dT/dM)$ is expected to be positive. Replacing then the government revenue T given by (2) in the accounting formula (1), this one becomes a finite difference equation that describes the time behavior of the primary money stock:

$$M = M_{-1} + FE - \beta_0 - \beta_1 M - \beta_2 OV_2 + \alpha_0 + \alpha_1 FE + \alpha_2 OV_1$$

Collecting terms and re-ordering, it comes:

$$(1 + \beta_1) M - M_{-1} = (\alpha_0 - \beta_0) + (\alpha_2 OV_1 - \beta_2 OV_2) + (1 + \alpha_1) FE \qquad (3)$$

So re-arranged, it becomes clear that the particular solution for this difference equation, or the theoretical equilibrium value of the primary money stock M*, is given by:

$$M^* = 1/(1 + \beta_1)[(\alpha_0 - \beta_0) + (\alpha_2 OV_1 - \beta_2 OV_2) + (1 + \alpha_1) FE]$$

The theoretical equilibrium level M* of the primary money is a function of the fiscal expense FE and the other exogenous variables in OV_1 and OV_2. While

OV_1 and OV_2 stay invariants and expenses expand more than the tax revenue, the consequent deficit will immediately be incorporated to the stock of money in circulation on the real side of the economy. First government spends then public have money to spend, multiply production and pay taxes. On the other hand, the complementary solution of equation (3), which is the trend of M, or the condition for the equilibrium level M* be attained, is:

$$0 < [1/(1 + \beta_1)] < 1$$

To be fulfilled, this condition requires that, simultaneously, β_1 be positive ($\beta_1 > 0$) and greater than unity with negative signal ($\beta_1 > -1$). Given the former, the latter is redundant. Thus, the necessary and sufficient condition for money stock to be in equilibrium in the absence of fiscal expenditures variations is that β_1 be positive. This implies that, for equilibrium to be theoretically attained, the hypothesis must hold: money backed by production and tax revenue are positively associated with each other. For this hypothesis to be observed in real life it is required that a) fiscal expenses cause government deficit, b) this deficit is paid with new interest-free money issued out of thin air by the really public central bank, c) this new money is used multiple times by people to buy more things produced by people, and d) the expanded production causes tax revenue to increase.

The falsification of this theorem requires that at least one out of three statements be true: (i) more realized new purchases do not expand nominal GDP, (ii) a public deficit does not increase the primary money stock, and (iii) more production reduces tax revenue. Taken as given that there is neither empirical nor theoretical support to none of these statements, the conclusion is that there is no reason to reject the hypothesis that money printed by a really public central bank, if backed by production, is positively correlated to tax revenue.

In a democratic fiscal policy government is the political power on duty that prints money out of thin air and puts it in circulation in the real world buying goods and services. Production takes time; thus, new but decreasing emissions will probably be required. While production grows tax collection increases and the money spent returns to government in parcels; meanwhile some amounts of the printed money will remain with the people for more money is needed to run a wealthier economy. Of course prices in a wealthier economy are greater than otherwise, but this effect is unavoidable for it reflects people climbing the Maslow Pyramid. In case of problems or sectoral imbalances fine tuning may be done through tax rates and expenses reallocation.

The limit of this economic policy is the availability and productivity of natural resources, working-age people included and always reminding that technology may increase resources' productivity. Technology may also create new and more convenient products, probably more expensive, to the people in higher standards of life. Anyway, the future is unknown and therefore the limit of the fiscal policy seems to be unforeseeable. However, in the real world the political power deeply entrenched the monetary policy that enslaves the fiscal policy and thus where mainstream monetarist economics dominates fiscal policy remains a matter of economic theory without practice.

6. Reversed fiscal policy

Public deficits have been massive, in large part due to interest upon the public debt. Accordingly, public debts, few exceptions apart, follow upward trends both in value and in proportion to GDP and explosive trajectories should not to be discarded. Consequently, the stock of the central bank's un-backed money emission to pay interest also grows and inflation tends to accelerate and jeopardize the value of financial capital. Central banks however blame fiscal policy for the debt growth and impose the only solution they know to tame public debt, the primary surplus.

Despite the fact that the primary surplus cannot reduce the public debt trend to infinity (Lima, 2015b, 11), there is a great pressure on governments to reduce their expenses and hike taxes. Primary surplus works like a reversed fiscal policy and so results obtained are the contrary to those fiscal policy produces. It has been causing people's impoverishment, income and wealth concentrations and risks government defaults. At this point another "solution" is proposed by bondholders: privatization of public assets.

This situation may be not lack of economic knowledge but strategy of the political power to enlarge its members' wealth. Governments must collect tax and spend less in services to taxpayers to create a surplus sufficient to pay interest; if deficit is always kept at zero then the public debt and bondholders rent may grow forever. When lending banks do not engage in creating demand for their client's products, supporting them in realizing profits and paying the loans back, investing to realize profits and higher wages are borrower's problems. Central banks follow in relation to governments the same principles a commercial bank follow in relation to its clients; besides not expanding demand properly, interest upon public debt must be paid by taxpayers and default obliges relinquishment of the collateral: roads, ports, airports, oil reserves, services and whatever else that provides monopolistic profits.

Another evidence of the political power command over the economy is the real fact that the interest rent created by the monetary policy must be paid by the fiscal policy, that is, by taxpayers. The political power created and marketed the idea of public debt thus committing the public to paying interests or give public assets up. On the subject Michael Hudson mentions a contemporaneous example of the Finance as Warfare: "It can be seen most recently in the demands by the European Union, European Central Bank and IMF (the "troika") to force Greece and Cyprus to pay their foreign debts by selling whatever land, oil and gas rights, ports and infrastructure remain in their public domain. What is privatized will become an opportunity to extract monopoly "tollbooth" rents" (Hudson, 2015, 14). Following Hudson, crises are part relevant of the Financial Power's arsenal.

7. Economic policy and the European Union crises

The European Union faces two crises, a general and a specific and both are caused by the monetary policy. The general crisis is the same that touches many countries and the last started with the reckless American monetary policy that created an uncontrolled process of expanding money supply through money printing to pay interest on the US federal public debt. The specific European crisis was triggered by the general one and refers to the fact that the EU monetary policy, though more liberal than the American one, is European, being equally applied to countries with different endurances to support it.

As everywhere else the EU monetary policy states that inflation is the only economic and social problem and establishes that fighting inflation is the absolute priority of the ESCB and NCB´s actions. Accordingly, the Statute of the European System of Central Banks and of The European Central Bank, Chapter II, Objectives And Tasks of the ESCB, Article 2, imposes the following Objectives:

> "In accordance with Article 127(1) and Article 282(2) of the Treaty on the Functioning of the European Union, *the primary objective of the ESCB shall be to maintain price stability. Without prejudice to the objective of price stability, it shall support* the general economic policies in the Union with a view to contributing to the achievement of the objectives of the Union as laid down in Article 3 of the Treaty on European Union. The ESCB shall act in accordance with the principle of an open market economy with free competition, favoring an efficient allocation of resources, and in compliance with the principles set out in Article 119 of the Treaty on the Functioning of the European Union" (European Union, 2012, C 326/97, emphasis added).

As ever happens, also in the European Union the political power prevails and the monetary policy commands the fiscal policy. This command is justified by the European Commission, for instance, in the Economic Papers 470 (November, 2012): "This paper analyses the potential of simple fiscal policy rules to stabilise cyclical fluctuations and reduce the welfare cost of supply and demand shocks in monetary union. The focus is on the stabilization of asymmetric shocks at the level of small member states, which are not stabilized by the reaction of the common monetary policy to area-wide variables" (Vogel et al, 2012). Accordingly, the European Union created a permanent follow-up of their economic rules to member countries. In other words, implementation of the EU's economic rules is organized annually in a cycle, known as the "European Semester", which is the EU's annual cycle of economic policy guidance and surveillance.

Economic policy and political power in European crises

European specific crisis stems from the impossibility of some small country-members to satisfy the ECB requirements and EU fiscal rules, especially during the recurrent general financial crisis when EU aggregate demand drops and ESCB despite demand contraction asks for more primary surpluses. Monetary policy must be the same to the entire EU, but not all countries have sufficient resources to pay, without impoverishing people, the due interest rent to support the common monetary policy. This crisis may therefore lead to small countries sovereign debt crises that can challenge the Union.

But situation may get worse still for the European Commission projects: "A fiscal stabilization function for the euro area" intending to reinforce the monetary policy:

> "There are many ways for a currency union to progress towards a Fiscal Union. Yet, while the degree to which currency unions have common budgetary instruments differs, all mature Monetary Unions have put in place a common macroeconomic stabilization function to better deal with shocks that cannot be managed at the national level alone. This would be a natural development for the euro area in the longer term (Stage 2) and under the conditions explained above, i.e. as the culmination of a process of convergence and further pooling of decision-making on national budgets. The objective of automatic stabilization at the euro area level would not be to actively fine-tune the economic cycle at euro area level. Instead, it should improve the cushioning of large macroeconomic shocks and thereby *make EMU overall more resilient*" (European Commission, 2015, 14, emphasis added).

If the monetary policy keeps running the economy such common fiscal policy cannot eliminate the economic crises of countries' unions; probably it will make things worse.

Evidences and crises suggest that the economic policy world around will not change significantly as a consequence of technical recommendations;

political power, monetary policy and crises seem to be there a forever. Notwithstanding, real world researches must be conducted aiming to technically support political disputes to make amendments that alleviate the social effects of main known monetary socially negative consequences. A solution seems to be the local, complementary or parallel, money emission allowing country-members to make fiscal policy. Known proposals blend sovereign money emission and monetary policy, but accepting monetary policy principles implies serious restrictions to fiscal policy.

Interesting exception, Hillinger's proposal looks applicable: "Under my proposal, the Euro could be maintained, while giving to the individual countries the possibility of a flexible anti-cyclical fiscal policy, a possibility that they now lack" (Hillinger, 2015, 162). He seems however to be too optimistic when stating that "Under my proposal, the Greek government could quickly and very substantially increase domestic demand, which was its principal campaign promise and it could do so without the need for agreement on the part of some external authority" (Hillinger, 2015, 162). Mainstream economists from the world around will oppose the idea arguing that such fiscal policy is inflationary and will disturb the common monetary policy.

On the matter Häring reminds us that,

> "Another important ingredient for a successful career is how convenient your subject of study and your results are for powerful interests in society. Economics, like all social sciences, is a product of the prevailing economic and political conditions and has a role to fulfill. If the interests of the powerful change, so does economics" (Häring, 2015).

So, if economists find a macroeconomic problem, its solution is not only technical; it must be interesting to the political power and preserve democracy.

8. Conclusions

Financial and economic crises are not exclusively economic problems that real world economists are prepared to fix; they are political problems. Evidences and crises suggest that the economic policy world around will not change significantly as a consequence of technical recommendations; if the political power does not change some ideas, monetary policy and crises seem to be there a forever. Notwithstanding, real world researches must be conducted aiming to technically support political disputes on amendments that may by pass or change the monetary policy and alleviate its main negative economic and social consequences: unemployment and income concentration. Maybe the state-members own money emission to make local fiscal policy could help European Union in realizing its economic and social ends. But even if Hillinger's proposal or any other economic policy convinces decision makers that it makes the poor less poor and the rich richer, it must pass the test of the political power convenience without destroying democracy.

References

Balke, N. S. and Emery, K. M. (1994) "Understanding the Price Puzzle." *Economic and Financial Policy Review, Federal Reserve Bank of Dallas*, [Online] Jan-Mar. Available via https://ideas.repec.org/a/fip/fedder/y1994iqivp15-26.html. [Accessed 17/7/2015].

Barth III, M. J. and Ramey, V. A. (2002) "The Cost Channel of Monetary Transmission." *NBER Macroeconomics Annual 2001*. MIT Press, [Online] 16, January. Available via http://www.nber.org/chapters/c11066. [Accessed 12/7/2015].

Dueker, M. J. (2006) "The Price Puzzle: An Update and a Lesson." *Economic SYNOPSES, The Federal Reserve Bank of Saint Louis* [Online] 24. Available via https://research.stlouisfed.org/publications/economic-synopses/2006/10/02/the-price-puzzle-an-update-and-a-lesson/ [Accessed 5/9/2015].

European Commission (2015) *Completing Europe's Economic and Monetary Union*. Available via
http://www.europarl.europa.eu/the-president/en/press/press_release_speeches/press_release/press_release-2015/press_release-2015-june/html/completing-europe-s-economic-and-monetary-union [Accessed 18/7/2015].

European Union (2012) "On the Statute of the European System of Central Banks and of The European Central Bank." *Official Journal of the European Union*, March 3. Available via http://www.ecb.int/ecb/legal/pdf/c_08320100330en_ecb_statute.pdf [Accessed 17/7/2015].

Gaiotti E. and Secchi, A. (2004) "Is there a cost channel of monetary policy transmission?" *Bank of Italy, Department of Economics Working Paper 525.* Available via https://ideas.repec.org/p/bdi/wptemi/td_525_04.html [Accessed 4/8/2015].

Grim, R. (2013) "Priceless: How The Federal Reserve Bought The Economics Profession." *The Huffington Post*. May 13. Available via http://www.huffingtonpost.com/2009/09/07/priceless-how-the-federal_n_278805.html.[Accessed 2/7/12015].

Hager, S. B. (2013) "What Happened to the Bondholding Class? Public Debt, Power and the Top One Per Cent." *New Political Economy*, April 16. Available via http://bnarchives.yorku.ca/356/ [Accessed 14/3/2015].

Häring, N. (2015) "Economics as Superstructure." Presentation at the seminar "Economics and Power" on 23 March, House of Lords, London. *Real-World Economics Review* March 26. Available via https://rwer.wordpress.com/2015/03/26/economics-as-superstructure/ [Accessed 14/7/2015].

Hillinger, C. (2015) "From TREXIT to GREXIT? – Quo vadis hellas?" *Real-World Economics Review* 70 (20) February, pp. 161-163. Available via http://www.paecon.net/PAEReview/issue70/Hillinger70.pdf [Accessed 20/4/2015].

Hudson, M. (2015) *Finance as warfare*. World Economics Association, WEA Books. Available via http://www.worldeconomicsassociation.org/books [Accessed 20/8/2015].

Lima, G. P. (2015a) *Supply and Demand Is Not a Neoclassical Concern*. Available via http://mpra.ub.uni-muenchen.de/63135/ [Accessed 14/9/2015].

Lima, G. P. (2015b) *Public Debt Is Economic Nonsense. Ideas towards a new international financial architecture?* World Economics Association Conferences. 15 May – 20 July, 2015. Available via http://www.worldeconomicsassociation.org/conferences/past-conferences/ [Accessed 14/9/2015].

Page, B. I., Bartels, L. M. and Seawright, J. (2013) "Democracy and the Policy Preferences of Wealthy Americans." *Perspectives on Politics* 11 (1) March pp. 51-73. Russell Sage Foundation. Available via http://www.russellsage.org/research/reports/wealthy-americans-political-preferences [Accessed 14/9/2014].

Palley, T. I. (2009) "America's Exhausted Paradigm: Macroeconomic Causes of the Financial Crisis and Great Recession." *Institute for International Political Economy Working Paper 02*. Berlin. Available via http://www.econstor.eu/bitstream/10419/59308/1/718077881.pdf?origin=publication_detail [Accessed 21/6/2015].

Vogel, L., Roeger, W. and Herz, B. (2012) "The performance of simple fiscal policy rules in monetary union." European Commission *Economic and Financial Affairs Economic Papers*, Summary for non-specialists, 470, November. Available via http://ec.europa.eu/economy_finance/publications/economic_paper/2012/pdf/ecp470_summary_en.pdf [Accessed 26/7/2015].

The European crisis

Chapter 7
At the root of economic fluctuations: theoretical framework and empirical evidences
Carmelo Ferlito

1. Introduction: on the inevitability of economic fluctuations

The economic crisis that erupted in 2007 was presented, when it burst in the summer of that year, with bank and stock market collapses, as a typical financial crisis. This presentation was followed by numerous attacks on the free market and the capitalist system; sometime ideologically targeted yet often incapable of grasping the true nature of the crisis. Subsequently, the emphasis shifted to the question of public indebtedness and, in 2013, to the single European currency, with the clear intention on the part of certain Governments to return to the possibility of devaluing a national currency in order to obtain short term export advantages.

Nowadays, the great depression is still and mostly labeled as the 2008 financial crisis.[1] Our analysis, on the other hand, will show that: 1) the crisis cannot be called neither financial, nor fiscal, nor even one of currency; 2) the crisis is more generally economic in nature and caused by systematic modifications of the structure of production and the allocation of employment resources.

The crisis drove Sachs (2010, 20) to conclude that "classic Keynesians are singing their swan song" and that "faced by a public debt crisis, the time has come to abandon short-term theories and prioritize the long-term investments needed to ensure a solid recovery". However, the great depression did not bury Keynesian economists; led by Krugman (2008),

---

[1] Not only the crisis is not financial, but economic; it started to emerge in 2007. See Ferlito (2007).

post-Keynesian analyses did not miss the chance for asking for more government intervention, consumption stimuli and relaxation of public budget constraints;[2] for many of them, moreover, it was occasion to ask for further financial regulation. On the opposite side, Austrian economists took occasion to revive the Austrian Business Cycle Theory (ABCT) and to point the finger against the distortive action played by government intervention and in particular by central banks.[3] Neoclassical economists, instead, suffered more than the others, apparently unable to deal with the events and focusing on proposing further interest rate cuts. Some of them brought out interesting reflections, questioning the mainstream approach and trying to incorporate heterodox elements in their analyses; it is the case, i.e., of Borio (2012) and Calvo (2013). Leijonhufvud (2009), illuminating as usual, presented an analysis that tried to learn from Keynes, the Austrians and Hyman Minsky.

The most interesting fact emerging from the post-crisis economic debate is maybe that, while neoclassical mainstream is suffering, old heterodox schools are trying to revive themselves and face a growing consensus. Under this perspective it emerges that the Hayek/Keynes debate is far to be defunct.[4] Disciples of the two great economists are still on the fighting ring. Keynesians blame the free market while Austrians believe that without government induced monetary distortions crises would not arise.

According to our vision, instead, the first point to stress is that economic crises do not demonstrate the end of the capitalist economic system; on the contrary, they testify its vitality. In Ferlito (2013, 30) and in Ferlito (2014a) we tried to demonstrate that capitalism without fluctuations does not exist.[5] Indeed, we find ourselves in good company when believing that the cycle is

---

[2] See, i.e., Roncaglia (2010).
[3] Among the others, see Salerno (2012), Hülsmann (2013) and Ferlito (2013).
[4] See Ferlito (2015).
[5] Huerta de Soto (1998, 468) points out that «one of the more curious points on which a certain agreement exists [between Marxian and Austrian analysis] relates precisely to the theory of the crises and recessions which systematically ravage the capitalist system».

the real form of economic development in a capitalistic system.[6] Marx was the first to realize this.[7]

The same awareness is to be seen in Schumpeter's vision, influenced by Spiethoff (1925, 112), who concludes that "the cyclical upswings and downswings are the evolutionary forms of the highly developed capitalist economy and their antithetic stimuli condition its progress". In turn, the Austrian economist influenced his student Paolo Sylos Labini,[8] and similar considerations can be found in Lachmann (1956, 110-112). Realizing that the cyclic form is typical of capitalist development, and is also echoed in the words of another Italian economist, Marco Fanno (1931, 248-249).

Supported by the testimony of such economists, we shall bring out the motivations which drove us to the same conclusions. The core of our analysis will be the accent on the role of expectations, time preferences and innovation mechanisms. We will build our theory on the pillar of the ABCT; however, as we shall demonstrate, Mises's approach, supporting the thesis that crises happen only when monetary authorities intervene on the money supply, needs to be overcome. Austrian tradition, in fact, distinguishes between sustainable and unsustainable booms; only in the latter situation crises arise. Instead, we will argue that depressions always follow booms; the difference is only in intensity and duration.

In order to support our view, we shall abandon Mises's view and use instead Hayek's perspective as starting point. Such perspective will be then integrated with key elements coming from Schumpeter and Lachmann.

2. Methodological intermezzo: why economic theory failed in forecasting the crisis

We believe that modern macroeconomics failed to understand economic fluctuations because it is prisoner of a static paradigm (general economic

---

[6] Ferlito (2011, 96).
[7] Rothbard (1969, 13).
[8] See Sylos Labini (1954, 12-14) and Sylos Labini (1984, 37 and 89).

equilibrium), founded on econometric predictions. However, crises cannot be understood with the equilibrium framework.

First of all, it is thus necessary to define the nature of the object of investigation. Indeed, method is imposed by the object. This does not mean surrendering to indistinct methodological relativism, but acknowledging that the phenomena of reality are complex and varied in nature. The problem of business cycles is, of course, a dynamic one. As in all economic theory, it should relate to reality, to living human beings, dynamically acting in a specific time and space framework. The centre of economic analysis, in our view, is therefore human action. Dealing with real people is very different from dealing with phenomena in physics or chemistry or natural sciences in general.

In this context, it is evident that the proper perspective for studying dynamic economic phenomena is subjective. The first fact to be noted as regards studying individuals and their actions is that every gesture is guided by a principle of finality. As we shall see in the following paragraphs, it is the purpose (expectation) that determines the action. Economists are thus faced by qualitatively very well defined elements: man and reality. They should be inspired by these elements, should allow themselves to be astonished by what happens.

The essence of an economist's work lies in observation of reality, without seeking to put it in a cage. Observation of reality helps identify certain dynamic trends that represent constants in human action. For example, as we have seen, the human action has a finalistic nature. That is not to say, as in the rationalist terms of the general equilibrium theory, that every subject maximizes units of utility in accordance with mathematical models. This is not what happens in reality. It is true, however, as a dynamic trend, that man acts to achieve goals.[9] This sees the onset of relationships with the surroundings, people, things and complex society in general. Economists may certainly analyze everything that individuals do within the dynamics of enterprise in the search to attain their objectives.

---

[9] Fragments of what he believed to be his most general happiness.

This definition may seem extraneous to more familiar concepts in economics such as prices, interest rates, profit and loss, etc. But this is not the case. As we will see later, when defining their goals, people also choose the means for achieving them. In doing so, the attainment of other goals is waived and this becomes the cost of the action. If the goal is reached within the desired terms, and the satisfaction achieved is superior to the waiver, then the outcome is positive. Prices, in numerical terms, are merely a brief representation of subjective assessments and their variegated universe. In the course of their actions, individuals meet each other and, unconsciously, their assessments of ends and means meet in turn and start an unending journey of mediation. The market comes into being as a spontaneous institution, a place for relationships, where the individual choice over means and ends is challenged through inter-relationships. The system of prices emerges in this process as the mediated (objective) result of the combination of subjective assessments. This system of values allows those involved to make rational economic calculations and verify, over time, whether they are attaining their goals or not.

It is possible to study these dynamics but without any pretense of planning and inclusion of attitudes within strict and formal models. Explanations are possible, only they must be of a qualitative nature. And achieving this requires the right set of tools. In conclusion, the business of the economic scientist is possible if the search of functional relations is replaced by the desire to really understand how reality works, abandoning every constructivist temptation determined by pseudo-scientific dazzle or the possibility of perfect planning.

3. Human action, time and expectations

As we already mentioned, at the very heart of economic theory we must place human action. Two essential phenomena surround it: expectations and time. Expectations are indeed at the very root of any economic process. They are the element guiding men toward action. Action is always *purposeful* action. We act in order to achieve goals, which are set according to our expectations. The next step is that, in order to achieve the desired goals, human beings need to implement plans, choosing the means they believe to be appropriate in order to reach ends. What we call *market process* is nothing more than the interactions of human beings busy implementing plans to achieve goals. One thing must be noted. Mainstream economics treats ends and means as given; moreover, knowledge is often considered perfect and unchangeable. What happens in reality, instead, is that the content of available information is always changing and the market is precisely the place where the exchange of knowledge happens. In the flow of real time, thus, ends/means framework and the linked plans can be revised.

Consumers, entrepreneur–producers and resource owners are the players in the market; the latter, in turn, is where their interacting decisions, during any period of time, take place. Every player has his own content of (limited) knowledge, tastes and expectations. Depending on their knowledge, tastes and expectations, the players set up their action decisions, or plans. Since, in order to carry out their plans, individuals need to interact, it is only through interaction and in time that content of information will be modified and eventually a revision of decisions can happen (Kirzner 1973, 10).

As defined by Kirzner (1973, 10), then, market process is built up by "this series of systematic changes in the interconnected network of market decisions". Therefore, it is not possible to conceive a market process in the realm of perfect knowledge. The process arises precisely because of the initial ignorance of market participants and the natural uncertainty of human action. And the process can only happen during the flow of real time. With no market ignorance and no review of plans, there is no process at all. As explained by Kirzner, since from one period of market ignorance to the next one, ignorance has been somewhat reduced, market participants realize that not only they should implement more attractive opportunities but also that such attractiveness needs to be judged in comparison with the opportunities offered by competitors. This is the competitive process. When the incentive to offer more attractive opportunities stops, such process stops too. In a situation of market equilibrium, such as the one described by the neoclassical theory of perfect competition, there is no more room for competition at all.

At the root of economic fluctuations

It now becomes necessary to explain what we mean when we talk about *real time*. At first sight, it may seem that contemporary economic theory has included time in its historical calculations based on historic series, econometric functions and stylized models. However, such a perception of time, while perhaps being useful in the study of physical sciences, is rather unsuitable for the discovery and surprise dynamics typical of human action. It is what we may define as Newtonian time.

The Newtonian conception of time is spatialized; that is, its passage is represented or symbolized by "movements" along a line. Different dates are then portrayed as a succession of line segments (discrete time) or points (continuous time). In either case, time is fully analogized to space, and what is true of the latter becomes true of the former. O'Driscoll and Rizzo (1985, 82-85) emphasize that time conceived in this way has three main characteristics: homogeneity, mathematical continuity and causal inertia. Homogeneity means that different temporal moments are simply points in space, a temporal position; nothing may happen between one moment and another. This means that homogeneous time is fundamentally static. Mathematical continuity, on the other hand, implies that time is simply a sequence of moments, which may even be different, but no change can take place endogenously. Since time is a sequence of static situations, each change must be exogenous. Causal inertia, lastly, means that nothing happens with the flow of time. There is no learning, there is no change in knowledge or adjustment of expectations. The system itself must already contain all the elements needed for it to function. It is evident such a concept lends itself poorly to representing unpredictable and dynamic human actions.

What interests us, on the other hand, is *real* time, a "dynamically continuous flow of novel experiences. [...] We cannot experience the passage of time except as a flow: something new must happen, or real time will cease to be" (O'Driscoll and Rizzo 1985, 89). As described by O'Driscoll and Rizzo (1985, 89-91), the characteristics of real time are precisely opposite to those of Newtonian time. They are: dynamic continuity, heterogeneity and causal efficacy. If we consider dynamic continuity, time must consist of *memory* and *expectations*; i.e. it is *structurally* related moments, past and future, through the perceptions of the individual; one cannot imagine a present without memory of the past and expectations for the future; inasmuch, all the moments in the flow of time are intimately linked and reciprocally influenced. Heterogeneity, on the other hand, means that in each successive moment the individual's perception has of the facts may be, and in fact is, different: the past, once it has occurred, becomes memory, enhancing the present and thereby also changing perception of the future; therefore, the perception of things changes from moment to moment, thereby making the characteristics of a given moment in time radically different from those of the previous moment. The direct consequence of heterogeneity is causal efficacy; the flow of time modifies knowledge, awareness and information, thereby expanding the creative potential of human action. Yet this is possible precisely because of acquisitions made "beforehand" in time.

We can now introduce two more elements crucial to our analysis. They are *time preferences* and the *inter-temporal structure of production*. According to the law of time preference, "other things being equal, humans always place present goods higher than future goods on their scales of value" (Huerta de Soto, 2000, 50); starting from this assumption, the Austrian School comes to a definition of interest rate radically opposed to that of the dominant theory ('cost of money'). We may define "the interest rate [as] the market price of present goods in terms of future goods" (Huerta de Soto 2000, 50-51). It is therefore limiting and wrong to define the interest rate as *the cost of money*.

The law of time preference does not apply only to the capital market. It should be extended to the entire economic system, where the natural rate is consequently that rate *of equilibrium* which reflects the *temporal preferences* of economic agents. It is thus possible to define an interest rate for the economic system, which measures the more general structure of time preferences. As regards consumers, it defines the relationship between consumption and saving. In the case of entrepreneurs linked to investments, it measures the propensity towards the future, the desire to undertake long-term projects in the investment goods sector that makes the production structure more roundabout and the production period longer, compared to investments in consumer goods and investments having a faster realization cycle.

In a *future-oriented* system, consumers are more savings-oriented, thereby encouraging the accumulation of loanable funds that can be used by entrepreneurs in long-term projects. A *present-oriented* society, in contrast, has a greater propensity towards consumption on the consumer side, while investors do not lengthen the production process. Situations of equilibrium may exist in a system with a high time preference as on the contrary. It is not the sum of one of the aggregates that defines this equilibrium but the possibility for time preferences to come together through the free exercise of the entrepreneurial function that each person enacts in relationships with other people in the process of satisfying needs of various kinds.

The level of equilibrium for a combination of time preferences is measured by the natural interest rate, which in turn corresponds to a well-defined structure of the production process. The key element that, by fuelling a modification of the inter-temporal structure of production, generates a cycle of expansion and crisis is given by a change in level of the natural rate. According to the traditional Austrian perspective, if the mutation of the natural interest rate reflects a change in time preferences, this generates a positive expansive cycle, which will not be followed by a painful crisis (and we will seek to demonstrate, on the other hand, that a readjustment crisis is inevitable). Conversely, if the rate – rather than settling in response to interaction on the free market of entrepreneurial action of different individuals – is set by central planning authorities which follow precepts of monetary policy or political motivations, the expansive cycle that will be followed by monetary expansion will generate a crisis. In fact, there will have been no change in the natural rate and no change in time preferences; the change generated in the structure of production will be the outcome of a false signal, the manipulation generated by monetary authorities.

To summarize: expectations generate action plan, who are carried out in time and eventually revised in order to cope with modified information, which, in turn, can force expectations to change. Expectations define also the time preference of an economic system; action plans set the intertemporal structure of the production process, which, as a process, is subject to a continuous revision. In any moment, the time preference of the system is a measured by what the Austrian tradition, following Wicksell, calls the *natural* interest rate, defined as the price of present goods in terms of future goods. The natural interest rate, therefore, is generated by expectations too.

The European crisis

Expectations are consequently the hallmark of a society made of real players which, starting precisely from them, form their own plans for the future, meeting and modifying knowledge and the plans themselves. This generates the *kaleidic society* (Shackle 1972, 76-79), "a society in which sooner or later unexpected change is bound to upset existing patterns, a society 'interspersing its moments or intervals of order, assurance and beauty with sudden disintegration and a cascade into a new pattern'" (Lachmann 1976, 54). The *kaleidoscopic world* is a world where change is constant.

In a kaleidoscopic society, moreover, "the equilibrating forces, operating slowly, especially where much of the capital equipment is durable and specific, are always overtaken by unexpected change before they have done their work, and the results of their operation disrupted before they can bear fruit. [...] Equilibrium of the economic system as a whole will thus never be reached" (Lachmann 1976, 60-61).

From what we have seen so far we can conclude that expectations are not something "up in the clouds", to be treated as exogenous data; without them, there is no economic activity as such; it is starting from expectations that every decision is taken with the intention of making a profit or achieving personal satisfaction. However, these attempts emerge in a context of imperfect knowledge and an unexpected and unpredictable future (Lachmann 1982). *Uncertainty* is a key element in the economic process; we cannot even imagine that opportunities for profit will arise outside a context of uncertainty and disequilibrium (Rizzo 1979, 10). In fact, without uncertainty, all occasions for profit would have already been exhausted; in an uncertain context, on the other hand, entrepreneurs who make the best forecasts or people who, for various reasons, best fulfill their expectations and plans, enjoy an advantage created precisely by the fact of knowing better how to move in such a context, how to "imagine the future better".

The main features of true uncertainty "are the inherent instability of all possible outcomes resulting from a course of action, and the complete endogeneity of the uncertainty" (O'Driscoll and Rizzo 1985, 100). In as much, if uncertainty is endogenous to the system, an intrinsic feature, it cannot but originate a constantly changing system, in which human action is essentially guided by expectations: expectations determined by preferences, that in turn generate any kind of action. Such action is intrinsically uncertain: nothing, *a priori*, ensures that such expectations will be realized.

The accumulation of knowledge merely changes the uncertainty (O'Driscoll and Rizzo 1985, 102-103). The information content is not complete, only larger. Aspects affecting the pursuit of action have changed but are not complete. The outlines on the horizon, and consequently the uncertainty in relation to the complete form, are different. It is therefore clear that the theoretical bridge between preferences and action is made of expectations: desires as regards the future and the scenarios awaiting us take place, determining our possibility for action.

It is evident that expectations cannot be considered, as in neoclassical theory, as a static element fixed at the beginning of the match and then unchangeable until the final result is achieved. On the contrary, since human action is a dynamic process that unfolds over time, the set of information available to players constantly changes, bringing about a continual modification of expectations, objectives and plans.

4. At the roots of economic fluctuations: the intertemporal structure of preferences

Economic fluctuations are related with the modification of the intertemporal structure of preferences. At any given time, a time preference structure (summarized in the natural interest rate) is matched by a production structure, i.e. a heterogeneous set of combinations of production factors, organized by human creative and entrepreneurial action in order to carry out processes that, over time, generate an output. This output should meet a demand defined by the structure of time preferences. This structure is reflected in an interest rate that, in turn, expresses the magnitude of the preference of economic agents for present goods compared to future goods.

The central point is the distortion of the production structure defined by the system of preferences (Hayek 1929, 123), and the reasons behind such a modification. The system of time preferences is determined by the expectations of players on the market who, following their own expectations, seek to implement plans to achieve them. In a free market system, this mechanism of action takes place through the meeting of different subjects who in the process acquire new information and change their expectations. We are therefore witnessing a gradual and continuous process of re-adaptation of plans, in a natural effort to ensure that their realization "meets" the realization of the plans of others.

4.1 The unsustainable boom

The typical situation taken in account by the ABCT (Mises) is when a natural rate is flanked by a monetary rate set by a central authority. In this scenario, the signal role played by the monetary rate overpowers that of the equilibrium rate, because it is immediately publicized and more visible to the players on the market: it "anticipates" the discovery mechanism typical of the market, it creates a wall between supply a demand. The monetary rate, inasmuch, becomes one of the essential engines driving profit expectations and the subsequent formation of plans. A difference between the natural rate and the monetary rate, by disorienting certain agents, may therefore modify the structure of production but without this change reflecting a parallel change in time preferences. Or, another possibility is that the monetary rate may not follow a unilateral change in preferences, thereby interfering with the process of adaptation by the economic system whose own preferences have not changed.

Let us now assume starting from a situation of equilibrium, a hypothetical starting point '0'. We have a natural rate that reflects the meeting of time preferences and a production structure organized accordingly. Let's also suppose that the monetary rate set by central authorities is the same as the equilibrium rate. In this scenario, a disequilibrium between monetary rate and equilibrium value, whereby the former is at a value lower than the second, thereby prompting entrepreneurs to lengthen the production process, may arise in two ways. The first and most immediately intuitive hypothesis is that the central authorities cut the monetary rate in the belief that lowering the interest rate sets in motion an expansion cycle without negative repercussions. In such a scenario, central bank is misleading the profit expectations of entrepreneurs, wrongly informing them that new resources are available for investments.

Therefore, entrepreneurs consider it is more convenient to invest in long-term projects; however their choices are wrongly guided by a false signal, which, in "hiding" the natural rate, does not allow the system to activate the necessary counter-measures to the resurgence of natural tendencies towards equilibrium typical of a regime of freedom of entrepreneurial action. Entrepreneurs, following interest rate manipulation, become more future-oriented, although more savings are not generated; consequently, available resources are fictitious and time preferences are changed unilaterally, leading to a disequilibrium in inter-temporal preferences; future-oriented investors and present-oriented consumers (or not as future-oriented as entrepreneurs). A change in time preferences always happens unilaterally, but when only the natural interest rate plays a role this change can be communicated to the other side of the market. The monetary interest rates do not allow the natural one to play is information transmission role.

Yet the situation whereby the monetary interest rate is below the natural rate may also occur without the intervention of central banks. In fact, the natural rate can be pushed upwards by expanding profit expectations. Entrepreneurial action, while always seeking results, may be also determined by so-called *sentiment*, the inkling that certain initiatives might be profitable. In this situation, entrepreneurs become future-oriented, raising the interest rate level and pushing demand for funds to begin the longer-term production processes.

It is an apparently unimportant difference in exposition which leads one to this view that the Monetary Theory can lay claim to an endogenous position. The situation in which the money rate of interest is below the natural rate need not, by any means, originate in a deliberate lowering of the rate of interest by the banks. The same effect can be obviously produced by an improvement in the expectations of profit or by a diminution in the rate of saving, which may drive the "natural rate" (at which the demand for and the supply of savings are equal) above its previous level; while the banks refrain from raising their rate of interest to a proportionate extent, but continue to lend at the previous rate, and thus enable a greater demand for loans to be satisfied than would be possible by the exclusive use of the available supply of savings (Hayek 1929, 147).

There can be many kinds of reasons for this. New inventions or discoveries, the opening up of new markets, or even bad harvests, the appearance of entrepreneurs of genius who originate "new combinations" (Schumpeter), a fall in wage rates due to heavy immigration; and the destruction of great blocks of capital by a natural catastrophe or many others. We have already seen that none of these reasons is in itself sufficient to account for an *excessive* increase of investing activity, which necessarily engenders a subsequent crisis; but that they can lead to this result only through the increase in the means of credit which they inaugurate (Hayek 1929, 168). Even in this case, however, preferences change unilaterally.

If, in the presence of a monetary rate, central banks do not realign the latter towards the equilibrium level in order also to encourage savers themselves to become more future-oriented by increasing saving amounts, the structure of preferences will remain disproportionate and the new inter-temporal production structure will reflect such an imbalance. In this case, therefore, expectations change before the intervention of central banks. In this case, it is not monetary manipulation that plays the key role capable of altering the system of preferences by dis-coordinating plans and the structure of production. In the first situation, the crucial role is given by the manner and direction in which monetary expansion influence expectations. In the second case, on the other hand, expectations themselves divert the system away from equilibrium.

Changing expectations, caused by (case 1) or the cause of (case 2) a monetary rate below its natural level, is – on closer inspection – a natural part of the entrepreneurial instinct emphasized by Schumpeter. The analysis of the entrepreneurial role (innovation) as a fundamental element in initiating an expansion cycle, implemented in an organic way by Schumpeter, is entirely coherent with our analysis. We are explicitly discussing the concept of expectations: entrepreneurs see opportunities for profit and take advantage of them, i.e. they have positive expectations, or, otherwise, they are future-oriented and ready to make the production process more roundabout. Some are prepared to take risks on real innovations that can create a competitive advantage for them. Others merely imitating on the wave of enthusiasm. Still others by launching poorly grounded economic initiatives.

Let's return now to our analysis and the disequilibrium between natural and monetary rates. The situation consideration therefore encourages the onset of major investments in production assets, or capital goods, whereby the economy becomes, in general, more capital-intensive, i.e. the production period is extended (Hayek 1931, 35-36). The cardinal point of the theory is the difference created between entrepreneurial decisions and consumer choices (Hayek 1933, 143-148). The funds available for investments initially do not correspond to the amount of savings. In fact, an artificially low monetary rate corresponds, on the capital market, to a higher availability of money because it translates into lower interest payable on investments.

In general it is probably true to say that most investments are made in the expectation that the supply of capital will for some time continue at the present level. Or, in other words, entrepreneurs regard the present supply of capital and the present rate of interest as a symptom that approximately the same situation will continue to exist for some time (Hayek 1933, 142).

What Hayek says is true, and the central role of expectations is resumed. Yet, all the more, the indicator on which entrepreneurs base their choices actually does not reflect any current propensity among consumers to save (Hayek 1933, 144). In this way, the proportion in which producers decide to differentiate production between products for the immediate future and those for the longer term (inter-temporal production structure) does not reflect the way in which consumers intend to divide their income between savings and consumption (Hayek 1933, 144-145). It is evident that sooner or later a disequilibrium in time preferences, which is reflected in the inter-temporal production structure, will arise and the typical form will be the frustration of the expectations of one of the two groups (Lachmann 1943, 69 and Hayek 1933, 145).

So, while entrepreneurs invest in new processes for the production of capital goods, savers are frustrated in their desire to consume, because what they want is not being produced. The *forced saving*[10] phenomenon thereby comes about, i.e. – as a consequence of the fact that production resources were diverted from sectors close to consumers – there is a gradual reduction in the production of consumer goods and therefore an involuntary limitation of consumption (Kurz 2003, 191 and Hayek 1933, 145-146).

The entrepreneurial impetus towards new investments, on the other hand, initially involves an increase in raw material prices and consequently of the capital goods produced with them.[11] And the impetus becomes particularly violent when the wave of the first innovative entrepreneurs is joined by the pressure of imitators described by Schumpeter, who grasp profit opportunities only in a second stage and attempt to benefit by following the "fashion". On a closer look, imitative speculation waves are typical of every boom stage described in history.

At the same time, demand for labor increases, and is attracted towards the new investments, with relative wages: this leads in turn encourages demand for consumer goods and prices in this sector also increases. And it is therefore evident that the increase in non-monetary income will not be matched by an increase in real incomes, because of the inflationary effect exerted by unsatisfied demand for consumer goods.

This increased intensity of the demand for consumers' goods need have no unfavorable effect on investment activity so long as the funds available for investment purposes are sufficiently increased by further credit expansion to claim, in the face of the increasing competition from the consumers' goods industries, such increasing shares of the total available resources as are required to complete the new processes already under way (Hayek 1933, 147).

Nevertheless, in order to be sustained, this process requires credit expansion without respite – which would bring about a cumulative increase in prices that sooner or later would exceed every limit. The conflict seems to

---

[10] See Hayek (1932). See also Huerta de Soto (1998, 409-413).
[11] It is evident that this upsurge, during the expansion phase of the cycle, causes the prices of raw materials and capital goods to increase more than the prices of consumer goods (Hayek 1939, 29).

be evident when demand for consumer goods exceeds the funds available for investment in terms of absolute value. At this point, the interest rate cannot but rise, frustrating demand for capital goods precisely when their price has also risen.[12] A considerable part of the new plant installed, designed to produce other capital goods, remains unused since the further investments required to complete production processes cannot be made (Hayek 1933, 148). As a result, in an advanced stage of the boom, growth in demand for consumer goods brings down demand for capital goods (Hayek 1939, 31).

As we have seen, such a situation may actually occur even without monetary manipulation but as a result of growing profit expectations which, since the monetary rate is not allowed to rebalance itself with the natural level, cannot find counterparts in realignment with the value of the savings. Inasmuch, the economy is unable to sustain production oriented over and above its possibilities. Sooner or later, it is realized that an increase in wages is cancelled by growing inflation. In addition, demand for capital goods runs out, taking with it the over-production in the particular sector and it is here where problems arise. Many economic initiatives set up through excessive reliance on credit cannot be completed, although the debts still have to be paid. Many companies have to be expelled from the system. Capital is scarce and banks raise interest rates. A period of adjustment and return to equilibrium begins, only it has aspects of a depression.

4.2 The sustainable boom

According to the traditional version of the ABCT, the wave dynamics typical of capitalism would be sustainable if, in typical situations of bright expectations, players were free to learn through interaction with each other and allow their choices to be judged on the market. Without the interference of a monetary rate, players would be forced to seek, on the market, to what extent their expectations are in line with those of other agents and therefore this would allow plans to be accomplished. The natural rate, although unknown as a magnitude, is dynamically given by time preferences, thereby

---

[12] As the rate of interest increases, the rate of profit declines (Hayek 1939, 31).

generating a production structure consistent with such preferences. The system would move and settle continuously.

In this way, every change in the structure of production would be the adaptation to a change in time preferences, a dynamic adaptation: if profit expectations rise, pushing the natural rate upwards, the new production structure cannot begin to change until the new natural rate also convinces consumers to change their attitudes; at the same time, it is likely that not all the intense demand for new investments will be "met" by new savings, so that the natural rate will tend to stabilise at a lower point than the initial expansionist impetus generated by entrepreneurial expectations. Demand and supply mechanism will generate, through information transmission, the new price able to link expectations of investors and consumers.

As can be seen, the situation is very different if there is a monetary rate capable of disguising the real strength of natural rate. And it is precisely the discrepancy generated between the natural and monetary value of the interest rate that tells us how long and painful cyclical dynamics will be (Hayek 1929, 183).

In a system where there is no central bank, there is no monetary interest rate imposed by central authorities. In such as system, in which an effective free market would operate, there would simply be the natural equilibrium rate, capable of measuring the structure of time preferences. This means that price system as information transmission mechanism can actually work. What happens in the event of a unilateral modification on time preferences, such as an increase in the savings rate? This is the situation in which consumers become more future-oriented. It is thereby evident that a conflict arises between the time preferences of consumers and those of investors.

Yet this also means that the equilibrium rate moves downwards, in an attempt also to orient the plans of entrepreneurs towards the future, who would therefore be encouraged to change the structure of the production process, starting with investments in more capital-intensive goods: the new lower interest rate is "informing" investors that new resources are available for long-term investments. These investments will be financed precisely with the new savings. The new equilibrium rate, the only signal for players on the market, allows entrepreneurs to modify their expectations and plans; it informs them that new resources are available and that investments can be implemented profitably. The entrepreneurial instinct, typically Schumpeterian and also emphasized by Spiethoff, thereby allows the re-adaptation of expectations in order to harmonize time preferences.

Consequently, without the interference of the central bank, the natural equilibrium rate (a price generated by the interaction of supply and demand and not imposed by central banks) allows the production structure to adapt to the new system of time preferences. The profit expectations of entrepreneurs, encouraged by the lower rate of interest, are not frustrated because they find a counterpart in the different attitude among consumers, who are now less oriented towards immediate consumption. In this case, the elongation of the productive structure, the expansion cycle, is sustainable because the free interaction of players does not encounter interference and plans can be adapted. This does not mean that, in the process of adaptation, errors are not encountered or that certain expectations will be frustrated. Preferences adaptation is a process that takes place in *real* time, not instantly.

However, conditions exist whereby free transmission of information helps one to learn from mistakes and rearrange plans in line with the new situation. And the scenario itself will be continually changing. The re-adaptation process does not take place "once and for all"; it is a continuous and never tamed process. Nonetheless, it can be implemented in a balanced manner only if the natural rate, generate by the demand-supply interaction, the only signal (price) for the players, i.e. if divergent signals are not introduced from the outside which may wrongly guide decisions and make the discoordination of preferences perpetual, thereby preventing the free inter-temporal coordination mechanism of plans.

In short, a growth path is generated when time preferences change on a global scale. And this is only possible, according to the Austrian theory, if the central element measuring time preferences – the interest rate – is free to set itself on the market through the interaction of individuals freely exerting their entrepreneurial function in the process of meeting their needs.

4.3 Is sustainable boom actually sustainable?

In all the cases analyzed so far, we could notice how the boom is always generated by a moving toward the future of the intertemporal structure of the preferences. Changing expectations can occur from the consumer side or from the entrepreneur side. What matters is that the result is a lengthening of the structure of the production: more roundabout production processes are started by entrepreneurs. These new investment are what are called innovations in the Schumpeterian approach; they generate *development*,[13] or the "spontaneous and discontinuous changes in the channel of the circular flow and [the] disturbances of the centre of equilibrium" (Schumpeter 1911, 65).

It is time to implant some Schumpeterian elements into the theory we sketched so far. This will help us to understand why economic crises are unavoidable. Let us assume that we set off from a situation of perfect static equilibrium in which assumptions of perfect competition, constant population, lack of savings and everything needed to meet the requirements of the circular flow hold true (Schumpeter 1964, 132-133).[14] It is also assumed that, in the capitalist society model, there will always be the possibility of new combinations and people capable and willing to implement them (their motivation is the prospect of profit).

> "Some people, then, conceive and work out with varying promptness plans for innovations associated with varying anticipations of profits, and set about struggling with the obstacles incident to doing a new and unfamiliar thing [...] we suppose that he founds a new firm, constructs a new plant, and orders new equipment from existing firms. The requisite funds he borrows from a bank. On the balance acquired by so doing he draws, either in order to hand the checks to other people who furnish him with goods and

---

[13] Development in Schumpeter's point of view must be absolutely distinguished from growth, which can also occur even a stationary condition, in being distinguished by the absence of structural changes. In this regard, see also Lachmann (1940, 271).
[14] Schumpeter (1964, 29-38) calls such a situation of equilibrium the 'theoretical standard'.

> services, or in order to get currency with which to pay for these supplies. [...] he withdraws, by his bids for producers' goods, the quantities of them he needs from the uses which they served before. Then other entrepreneurs follow, after them still others in increasing number, in the path of innovation, which becomes progressively smoothed for successors by accumulating experience and vanishing obstacles" (Schumpeter 1964, 133-134).

What we note from the foregoing excerpt? Firstly, Schumpeter assumes that entrepreneurs immediately spend their deposits, except for a minimum reserve. Secondly, since there are no unused resources at the outset (given the circular flow hypothesis), the prices of production factors will increase, as well as monetary incomes and the interest rate. Thirdly, revenue will also increase, in line with the expenditure by entrepreneurs in investment goods, alongside those of workers, momentarily employed with higher wages, and those of everyone receiving all those higher payments (Schumpeter 1964, 134). However, up to this point, it is legitimate to assume that there has not yet been an increase in production (Schumpeter 1964, 135). This is what happens until the plant of the first entrepreneur begins to run:

> "Then the scene begins to change. The new commodities – let us say, new consumers' goods – flow into the market. They are, since everything turns out according to expectation, readily taken up at exactly those prices at which the entrepreneur expected to sell them. [...] A stream of receipts will hence flow into the entrepreneur's account, at a rate sufficient to repay, during the lifetime of the plant and equipment originally acquired, the total debt incurred plus interest, and to leave a profit for the entrepreneur. [...] the new firms, getting successively into working order and throwing their products into the market of consumers' goods, increase the total output of consumers' goods [...]" (Schumpeter 1964, 136).

Such new goods, according to Schumpeter, enter the market too quickly to be absorbed smoothly. In particular, the old enterprises and the pursuers have several possible scenarios before them, but there is no fixed rule: some become part of the new scenarios, others close because they are unable to adapt, others still seek rationalization (Schumpeter 1964, 137-138). However, the competitive advantage of the driving company tends to fade, since, as the products progressively come on to the market and the debt repayments quantitatively increase in importance, entrepreneurial activity tends to diminish to the point of disappearing altogether (Schumpeter 1964, 138). As soon as entrepreneurial impetus loses steam, pulling the system away from its previous area of equilibrium, the system embarks on a struggle towards a new equilibrium. The initial outline of a cyclic pattern can be seen (Schumpeter 1964, 142).

Each of those two phases is characterized by a definite succession of phenomena. The reader need only recall what they are in order to make the discovery that they are precisely the phenomenon which he associates with "prosperity" and "recession": our model reproduces, by its mere working, that very sequence of events which we observe in the course of those fluctuations in economic life which have come to be called business cycles and which, translated into the language of diagrams, present the picture of an undulating or wavelike movement in absolute figures or rates of change (Schumpeter 1964, 142).

The following is the reasoning that leads to the second approximation of the cycle. If innovations are incorporated into new plant and equipment, spending on consumer goods will increase at least as fast as spending on capital goods. Both will expand starting from those points in the system where they exerted the first impact and will create that set of economic situations which we call prosperity.

Two phenomena arise here: firstly, old businesses will react to this situation and, second, a number of them *will speculate on it*. Those who seek to take advantage of the situation, by speculating, act on the assumption that the rates of change they observe will continue indefinitely; such an attitude anticipates prosperity, causing a *boom* (Schumpeter 1964, 150). At this point, transactions join the picture that, in order to become possible, assume an expected or effective increase in prices. This is how, in the cyclic process, a secondary wave comes into play, the effects of which overlap those of the primary wave (Schumpeter 1964, 151). The outcomes of the new wave are also more visible than the first wave.

Even in secondary prosperity, the break is induced by a turning point in the underlying process. Any state of prosperity, however ideally limited to essential primary processes, involves a period of failures that, in addition to eliminating enterprises that are obsolete beyond any chance of re-adaptation, also gives rise to a painful readjustment process of prices, quantities and values, as the framework of a new system of equilibrium progressively emerges (Schumpeter 1964, 153-154). Secondary prosperity even sees risky, fraudulent or in any case unlucky initiatives take shape that are unable to cope with the recession (entrepreneurs defined as imitators and speculators, who simply follow the situation of change). The speculative position involves many unsustainable elements, which even a minimal deterioration of the value of collateral elements will cause to fall.

Inasmuch, a great deal of the day-to-day business and investments will suffer a loss as soon as prices fall, as they undoubtedly will in view of the primary process. A portion of the debt structure will also collapse. If panic and crisis prevail in this case, further adjustments become necessary: values fall and every fall brings with it yet another fall. For a certain time, the pessimistic expectation may play a decisive role, even if it subsequently does not hold up unless substantiated by objective factors (Schumpeter 1964, 154). A cyclical pattern with four stages is consequently outlined (remember that first approximation only included prosperity and recession): prosperity, recession, depression, recovery.

For our purposes, it is vital to emphasize the characteristic element of secondary prosperity: imitations and their role in further swelling the growth process. As acknowledged by Lachmann (1986, 15), perhaps the most Schumpeterian of the Austrians, a "competitive process taking place within the market for a good consists typically of two phases, and in it the factors of innovation and imitation may be isolated as iterative elements".[15] The expansion stage of the cycle is always characterized by the elongation of the production structure – an elongation that occurs because of investments

---

[15] See also Lewin (1997, 15).

usually associated with a specific sector of assets, i.e. the one linked with growing profit expectations, in turn stimulated by a certain kind of credit policy or change in time preferences. The success of the first investments, when the liquidation process is still not on the horizon, modifies information and the expectations of many other subjects, attracting imitators who additional investments, usually financed by credit, contribute towards intensifying the magnitude of expansion.

5. The inevitability of crises: the *natural cycle*

Now we shall attempt to demonstrate how crisis is a consequence of all stages of growth and how sustainable and artificial booms are not distinguished by the onset of depression but by its intensity and duration. Inasmuch, in our view, even in the case of "healthy" expansion, the growth stage will be followed by a process of resettlement (crisis). This is because – even for sustainable development – positive profit expectations, once the cycle has been set in motion, facilitate the appearance of speculative-imitative initiatives that, at a given point, must be liquidated in order to 'normalize' the progress of growth. What distinguishes sustainable development from an artificial boom is not the emergence of a crisis; the difference lies in the *nature* of the crisis and its *intensity*.

The crucial elements in our analysis, therefore, are expectations and the imitative process. As we have seen, Hayek (1929, 147) recognized the central role of expectations as early as 1929, when he emphasized profit expectations as the driving force behind entrepreneurial preferences, with the possibility of entrepreneurs becoming more future-oriented and thus shifting the equilibrium interest rate upwards.

Profit expectations are a key element in both the Hayekian vision of sustainable growth and in the opposite case. We will use them to describe the emergence of imitations and secondary expansion, then followed by a crisis. It is now time to see how the so-called *sustainable growth* in Austrian theory turned, in our view, into the *natural cycle* (Ferlito 2014a).

At the root of economic fluctuations

In the ideal situation where the monetary rate does not exist (nor the Central Bank), a lengthening of the production period, with the emergence of capital-intensive investment processes, is in fact possible when either consumers or investors become more future-oriented. If consumers are the first to change their preferences, this will take the form of growing savings followed by a decrease in the natural rate of interest, in order to attract investors to use those resources for more roundabout investments. If, on the other hand, entrepreneurs are the first to push towards lengthening of the production structure, the natural rate will rise in order to attract savers in the same direction, thereby providing necessary resources for new investments. In both cases, the natural rate is driven by a change in the structure of temporal preferences, in turn generated by different expectations. What follows is a process of sustainable development.

The role of business expectations in generating capital-intensive investments is also emphasized by Schumpeter. We have seen earlier how Hayek referred explicitly to Schumpeter in highlighting the innovative and investment process that follows positive profit expectations. In this process of expansion, in accordance with the traditional version of the ABCT, the aspects needed to generate a crisis do not arise.

However, observation of reality leads us to emphasize, following Schumpeter and Lachmann, that the first wave of investments it is always followed by a secondary wave of imitations and speculations. As analyzed above, the pace of economic growth becomes particularly sustained when the primary wave of entrepreneurial investments is joined by a stage of secondary growth encouraged by the instincts of imitators in search of profit and driven by 'fashion'. Why are imitations inevitable? This is what we have already seen as regards Lachmann's vision of capitalist development characterized by innovation and imitation. Keeping faith with subjectivism and the role of expectations, it is easy to imagine how the success of entrepreneurial initiatives is readily followed by imitators looking for success within what at first sight always seems to be a period of growth destined never to end. The primary stage of growth is characterized by investment set in motion by a limited number of entrepreneurs – those who are able to seize opportunities that go unnoticed by most people and therefore the first to change their expectations (Schumpeterian entrepreneurs). The secondary stage is characterized by the appearance on the market of an exceptional number of imitators, driven by profit expectations arising from observing the ongoing of the boom set in motion by the first innovative entrepreneurs.

This is how we identifies the first two stages in our natural cycle: primary expansion, generated by a change in the structure of time preferences and expectations (the system becomes more future-oriented), and secondary expansion characterized by imitative investments. If, therefore, the reality of imitative speculations cannot be eliminated, it outlines the character of the growth process by emphasizing development above the initially imagined level. Like the primary wave of investments, the second wave is generated by profit expectations, particularly the expectation that the current situation will not change (Schumpeter 1939, 145). From a quantitative point of view, moreover, imitation (secondary) investments might even be greater than the first cycle of investments since they involve a larger number of individuals, whose expectations are "over-excited" by the boom (Schumpeter 1939, 146). These secondary investments will have to be liquidated through an adjustment crisis, as we shall attempt to demonstrate.

The fact that secondary wave investments necessarily bring about their liquidation, by generating a crisis, even for booms not induced artificially by discoordination between natural and monetary rates, apparently seems to be at odds with the traditional version of the Austrian theory, which does not admit crises whenever such discoordination is not at the base of the growth process. We believe, on the other hand, that – while not denying the validity of the Austrian approach – this vision should be superseded.

Let's summarize the appearance of primary expansion characterizing our natural cycle. When, given positive profit expectations, entrepreneurs become more future-oriented, the natural rate of interest rises, in order to move consumer preferences in the same direction, encouraging them to save more and thereby generate resources to meet increased demand for loanable funds by investors. The mirror-image situation arises when consumer expectations change in a more future-oriented direction; in this case, the natural rate of interest falls, informing entrepreneurs that new resources are available for investments in the longer term. Both situations, to use "Austrian" jargon, give rise to a sustainable boom.

According to this schema, given that the lengthening of the production structure derives from a change in time preferences and market operators are not deceived by a monetary rate inconsistent with the natural rate, current investments will always find available resources to complete the business projects launched. This is precisely because, without the interference of political-monetary authorities, market operators are free to "reveal themselves" to each other and readjust their scheme of preferences in conformity with the modified situation.

However, we have the distinct impression that this view does not take a fundamental fact into account: the *rhythm* of investments in *real time*. The Schumpeterian distinction between primary wave and secondary wave investments in this regard becomes critical. In fact, the initial increase in investments followed by a change in the structure of time preferences does not seem to generate any problem. Whether savings grow or the natural interest rate increases because of profit expectations, the timing of the onset of business ventures is necessarily dictated by the realignment of preferences. When savings increase, in fact, the problem does not arise precisely because the increased resources are the first cause of the reduction of the natural rate and the lengthening of the productive structure its consequence. All the more, if there is increased demand for loanable funds, new resources for investment will not be available until consumers decide to increase their propensity to save, that is, until the intentions of the two groups of players re-align again.

The matter changes when second wave of investments comes into play, generated by the imitative process. It is first and foremost a natural fact, intrinsic to the boom, regardless of its type. Indeed, as Schumpeter emphasized, innovation is never generated as a mass phenomenon; on the contrary, it arises through the initiative of certain "elect spirits" – entrepreneurs – whose essence lies precisely in being able to grasp profit opportunities where others fail to see them. Subsequently, in any case, when the expansion phenomenon is already set in motion – when an opportunity for profit has already been identified and grasped by some people – the prospect of grabbing a slice of the cake becomes tempting for many (the role of expectations). Not for those who have seized the opportunity and, having begun to invest, are now on the way towards reaping their reward; but for those who were bystanders and are now seeking to take part in the boom stage (with a time lapse compared to the primary wave).

What form does the imitative desire take? It generates new demand for loanable funds in order to insert a more roundabout production process into the expansive cycle. This means an attempt to extend the expansion process temporarily, thereby also increasing the degree of uncertainty. More time taken implies more things can happen – providing the possibility of greater productivity but also greater uncertainty. Since the value of higher order (capital) goods depends on the prospective value of the consumer goods they are expected to produce, the elapse of time, and with it the arrival of unexpected events, implies that some production plans are bound to be disappointed and thus the value of specific capital goods will be affected (Lewin 2005, 151).

And this brings us to the second stage of the natural cycle: secondary expansion. Pressure on demand for loanable funds forces the natural interest rate to rise further, in order to attract new savings to finance these investments. And this is where the role of banks joins the game to a very similar extent to that described by Schumpeter. Initially, demand for loanable funds cannot be met because preferences have not yet realigned with the new interest rate level and it is even likely that such a realignment does not actually take place.

However, the positive sentiment, the positive profit expectations, that becomes "incandescent" at the end of the primary expansion stage, also plays a role as regards the action of banks. In fact, precisely because of what happens during expansion, it is highly likely that banks make available "virtual funds" that are not backed up by real savings (as is the case during the first wave of investments), driven by expectations that the adaptation of consumer preferences (further savings) cannot but occur, precisely because of the enthusiasm generated by the boom.

On the other hand, it is more than likely that the long-awaited realignment does not come about. Even though the natural rate may increase, in view of the profit expectations arising from the request for second wave of investments (imitative), the likelihood that savings may increase is limited by two factors. The most obvious one is of course that consumers must also consume, hence their capacity for saving (and realignment) is objectively limited by the necessity to consume. In addition, in all likelihood, consumers will also be influenced by the general enthusiasm of the boom stage and consequently change their preferences in the opposite direction, i.e. by increasing their propensity for consumption. This is all the more true given the fact that real wages grow during the boom in order to attract workers into the new investment areas or to employ formerly unemployed workers. As in the conventional Austrian explanation, this leads to pressure in demand for consumer goods, with an initial phenomenon of forced savings and the production structure subsequent needs to return to present-oriented projects (consumer goods). At this point, the growth of price and wages and the pressure on prices goods of consumer goods brings about what Hayek called the "Ricardo effect": it helps explain why a prolonged boom stage driven by monetary expansion is likely to turn into a crisis.

If the credit expansion boom does not come to an end sooner for some other reason, it must come to an end when consumer product prices advance ahead of wage and resource prices. The Ricardo effect lowers real wages and encourages a shift toward labor-intensive methods of production. A lowering of the real wage of labor makes short-term (labor-intensive) projects appear to be more profitable than long-term (capital-intensive) methods of production. The Ricardo effect may account for the sudden wave of bankruptcies among the large fixed-investment projects that occurred toward the end of many nineteenth-century business cycles (Moss 2005, 8-9). So, while the first wave of investments can complete its cycle because of the real existence of prior and stable funds (without which the expansion cycle would not even have started), the second wave will be frustrated by a change in consumer preferences and a banking policy influenced by profit expectations.

The difference between sustainable growth and artificial boom, therefore, lies in the following fact: where the "defective" cycle is triggered by a discoordination between a natural rate and a monetary rate controlled by the monetary authorities, in general many of the roundabout processes of production end up being frustrated by the onset of the Hayekian phenomenon of scarcity of capital, as described above. On the other hand, for a sustainable boom (*natural cycle*) generated by a change in expectations, it is only the inevitable wave of speculative-imitative investment, backed up by a banking policy influenced by a positive sentiment, which itself will later be frustrated, wherein a crisis will be the necessary action to liquidate such faulty initiatives.

What will follow in the latter case will be a crisis (third stage of the natural cycle) but limited in terms of intensity, duration and the number of sectors involved. We could even define it as a transitory readjustment crisis, which does not eliminate the beneficial effects of the previous boom but merely liquidates business ventures launched for speculative-imitative purposes. What will not follow, instead, is a fourth stage, the depression, typical of the unsustainable cycle.

6. Our theory and the current crisis

The crisis emerged in the United States and Europe in 2007 can be described by our theory; first and above all it falls into the category of what we described as *unsustainable boom*: the production structure becomes more roundabout not because of a modification in the intertemporal structure of preferences, but because of credit policy sending wrong price signals to entrepreneurs.

The quantitative easing igniting the typical Misesian artificial boom is strongly supported by empirical evidences.[16] Table 1 in Ferlito (2010, 40-41) shows a distortive monetary policy starting to happen in 2001. From the peak reached in 2000 (6.4%), the Federal Reserve began to lower the official interest rate. We remember that at that time America was facing the difficulties created by the end of the new economy bubble and, later in 2001, by the 9/11 attack. Such an expansionary policy lasted until mid-2004 (i=1%), when, because of an inflationary dynamics, the Fed started to move in the opposite direction. However, interest rates remained below levels

---

[16] See in particular Koppl (2014, 18-40), Ahrend (2010), Young (2012) and Bocutoğlu and Ekinci (2010).

suggested by the Tailor rule until 2006. As argued in Taylor (2009), "Fed kept the funds rate below that suggested by the eponymous *Taylor rule* for 4 years".[17] Figure 1 summarizes the situation.

Figure 1: Actual federal funds rate vs. counterfactual federal funds rate

[Graph showing actual Federal funds rate vs counterfactual Federal funds rate from 2000 to 2006]

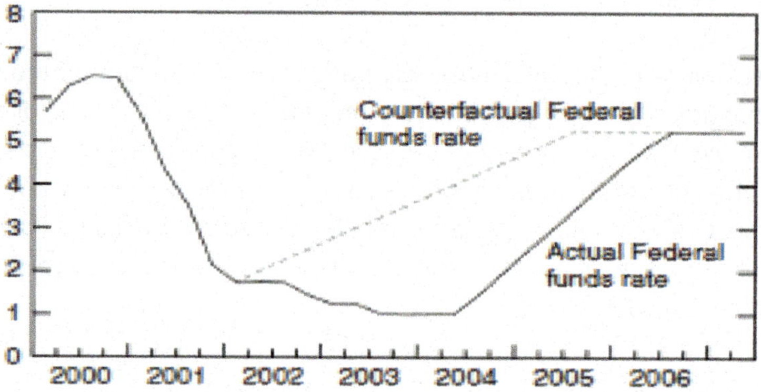

Source: Koppl (2014, 23).

The trend inverted again on July 2007 (i=5.25%), after the emergence of the subprime crisis. Since then, official interest rate never stopped to move downward, as it is well known. A similar trend is observable in the ECB interest rate policy, with some time lag and less drastic movements (Ferlito 2010, 40-41). The expansionary trend of the monetary policy is supported by statistics regarding M3 and M0 (Ferlito 2010, 43) and particularly astonishing is the 106% jump in M0 in the USA in 2009.

Data on American bank credit confirms the easy money trend of pre-crisis years. According to statistics published by the Federal Reserve of St. Louis, the USA banking system was lending 5,000 billions USD in 2000 and more

---

[17] Young (2012, 79): "The rule advised the Fed to target the short-term interest rate (the federal funds rate). This rate 'should be one-and-a-half times the inflation rate plus one-half times the GDP gap plus one' (Taylor 2009, location 519). In this case, the GDP gap is just the percent deviation of real GDP from a target, which he takes to be the trend of 2.2 per cent per year growth that held between 1984 and 1992" (Koppl 2014, 20). Detailed graph comparing actual rates and Taylor rates country by country can be found in Ahrend (2010, 6-7).

than double in 2008 (Ferlito 2010, 44). Moreover, M2 recorded a 32% growth between 2002 and 2006 (Koppl 2014, 24). As it is well known, most of the new credit was real-estate credit, financing a bubble in the housing market.

Figure 2: Real-estate/bus loans credits in the United States

Source: Bocutoğlu and Ekinci (2010, 12).

As stated in Taylor (2009), the effects of the boom and bust were amplified by several complicating factors including the use of subprime and adjustable-rate mortgages, which led to excessive risk taking. There is also evidence the excessive risk taking was encouraged by the excessively low interest rates.

Delinquency rates and foreclosure rates are inversely related to housing price inflation. These rates declined rapidly during the years housing prices rose rapidly, likely throwing mortgage-underwriting programs off track and misleading many people (quoted in Bocutoğlu and Ekinci 2010, 15).

Figure 3 Total derivative market (TDM) (trillions)

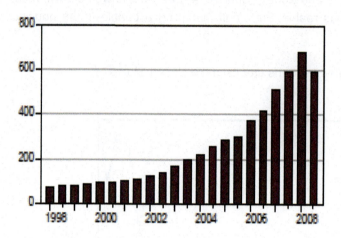

Source: Bocutoğlu and Ekinci (2010, 15).

The effect of monetary expansion is visible on the GDP trend (Ferlito 2010, 46). Europe and USA experienced good rates of GDP growth and a moderate reduction in unemployment between 2002 and 2006. However, the trend proved to be unsustainable, because driven by monetary expansions and not by a change in the intertemporal structure of preferences.

Table 1 Unemployment rate, real GDP growth, and the federal funds rate: 2002–2009

	Unemployment Rate	Real GDP Growth Rate	Federal Funds Rate
2002	5.8	1.8	1.67
2003	6.0	2.5	1.13
2004	5.5	3.6	1.35
2005	5.1	3.1	3.21
2006	4.6	2.7	4.96
2007	4.6	1.9	5.02
2008	5.8	0.0	1.93
2009	9.3	-2.6	0.16

Source: Young (2012, 80).

The European crisis

Now that we observed the monetary expansion and the effect on the GDP, it is necessary to check how the production structure and the price dynamics were distorted by such expansion. In the USA, investment in capital goods touched a lower peak in 2002, following the 2001 crisis: around 47 billions USD. Following the monetary expansions, the amount started to rise again to reach 68 billions USD in 2007, when a new downward movement began to go back to 50 billions USD in 2009.

The trend is confirmed by the price dynamics: moving upward between 2003 and 2007, starting to fall down after the emergence of the new crisis (Ferlito 2010, 45).

As it is well known, the bubble regarded in particular the property industry, so we should be able to observe an upward trend in prices of property. This is, indeed, the case: while property prices increased by 59% from the beginning of 1997 to the end of 2001, the rise in housing prices was 83% in the period from December 2001 to June 2006 (Bocutoğlu and Ekinci 2010, 10).

Figure 4 Case-Schiller Home Price Index (CS) and effective federal-funds rates (FF) for the period 1987–2010

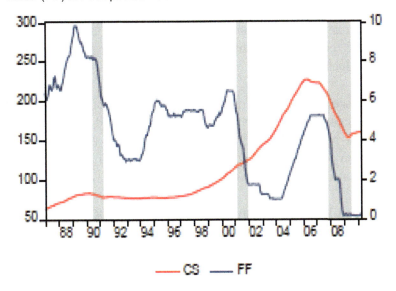

Source: Bocutoğlu and Ekinci (2010, 10).

At the root of economic fluctuations

The relation between monetary expansion and housing prices is empirically verified also for a panel of countries by Ahrend (2010, 14).

		Real House Prices	Housing Investment	Mortgage Credit	Credit to private sector	M2	Stock Market Indices
US	2001-06	Strong increase	Very strong increase (intially)*	Very strong increase	Very strong increase	Moderate increase	Moderate increase
Canada	2001-07	Very strong increase	Very strong increase	Very strong increase	Very strong increase	Strong increase	Strong increase
Denmark	2001-04	Strong increase*	Very strong increase	Very strong increase	n.a.	Very strong increase	Strong increase
Norway	2004-07	Very strong increase	Moderate increase	Very strong increase	n.a.	Strong increase	Very strong increase
Australia	2000-03	Very strong increase	Moderate decrease	n.a.	Very strong increase	Strong increase	Moderate decrease
Portugal	1998-2005	n.a.	n.a.	Strong increase	n.a.	n.a.	Strong decrease
Spain	1998-2007	Very strong increase	Very strong increase	Very strong increase	Very strong increase	n.a.	Strong increase
Greece	2000-07	Very strong increase	Very strong increase	Very strong increase	Very strong increase	n.a.	Moderate increase
Netherlands	1998-2004	Very strong increase	Moderate decrease	Strong increase	Very strong increase	n.a.	Strong decrease
Italy	1999-2006	Strong increase	Strong increase	Very strong increase	Very strong increase	n.a.	Moderate decrease
France	2001-06	Very strong increase	Very strong increase	Very strong increase	Strong increase	n.a.	Moderate increase
Ireland	1999-2007	Very strong increase	Very strong increase	Very strong increase	Very strong increase	n.a.	Moderate increase
Finland	2000-02	Very strong increase	Strong decrease	n.a.	Strong decrease	n.a.	Very strong decrease
US	1990-93	Moderate decrease	Moderate increase	Strong increase	Moderate decrease	Moderate decrease	Very strong increase
Switzerland	1985-89	Very strong increase	Very strong increase	Very strong increase	Very strong increase	Strong increase	Very strong increase
Finland	1987-89	Very strong increase (intially)*	Very strong increase	n.a.	n.a.	n.a.	Very strong decrease
UK	1987-90	Very strong increase	Very strong increase (intially)*	Very strong increase (intially)*	Very strong increase	Moderate increase	Moderate decrease

In order to understand the modifications that the production structure experienced because of the credit expansion, we shall refer to the empirical evaluation done by Young (2012:81-90). In fact, quite uniquely, the author tried to give a quantitative measure of the level of what the ABCT calls "round-aboutness": because of the monetary expansion, entrepreneurs try to expand early production stages.

However, and here we can find the reason why the boom cannot be sustained, consumers don't become more future-oriented, they do not change their time preferences and therefore they are still demanding the same consumption goods. Entrepreneurs try to make longer the production structure, while consumers want to preserve it as it is.

Young (2012) used the total industry output requirement (TIOR) in order to measure the round-aboutness of the production processes. The TIOR is, for a given industry, "the output required, both directly and indirectly, by each [other] industry to deliver a dollar of final demand of industry output to final users".

In other words, it is the amount of gross output from other industries that must be produced per dollar of a given industry's output: the ratio of total gross output to final output for an industry. This ratio will be greater than unity by definition. The critical assumption of this study is that an industry's round-aboutness is proportional to its TIOR (Young 2012, 81-82).

Austrian economics considers production process as divided into a series of stages, $i=1, \ldots, N$. The initial amount of input is called X_0. At each stage, the gross output will be X_i, where $X_i = X_{i-1} +$ (value-added)$_i$. The final gross output X_N is $X_N = \sum_{i=1}^{N} X_i$. At each stage, TIOR = X/X_N. Young (2012, 82-83) summarized this in the following table.

Table 2 Value-added, gross output, and TIOR

Stage	Value-Added	Gross Output	Total Gross Output	TIOR
1	100	100	100	1
2	10	110	220	2
3	11	121	341	2.81
4	12	133	474	3.56
5	13	146	610	4.17

Source: Young (2012, 83).

An economic system becoming more roundabout is, i.e., an economic system moving from having four stages and therefore producing 474 with a TIOR of 3.56 to recording five stages and producing 610 with TIOR=4.17. Young (2012) collected TIORs for 65 industries for the years 1998 to 2009. With such data a measure of round-aboutness was built, weighing each industry using the shares of total value added. The aim was to check if the production structure changed during the period 2002-2006. Results are shown in the below figure 5.

At the root of economic fluctuations

Figure 5 US Aggregate round-aboutness and federal funds rate, 1998–2009

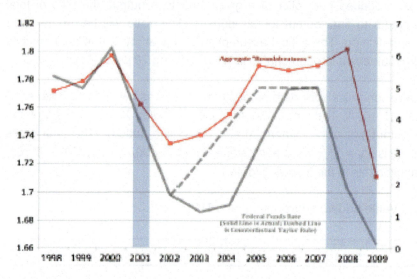

Source: Young (2012, 85).

Figure 5 shows that heading into the 2001 recession, the aggregate TIOR was falling. Then in 2002, following the recession, and precisely when the Federal Reserve embarked on an exceedingly expansionary policy (by the Taylor rule standard), the aggregate TIOR began to expand at an increasing rate. The TIOR levels off and then rises only slowly following the Fed's (belated) increases of the funds rate starting in 2004.

The 2007 to 2009 recession was then characterized by a remarkable decrease in the aggregate TIOR, indicating a contraction of the time structure of production. While the aggregate TIOR low following the 2001 recession was just under 1.74, the last observation available for the TIOR (in 2009) is about 1.71 (Young 2012, 85).

Subsequently, Young (2012, 86-87) divided industries in two group, the more roundabout (MR) and the less roundabout (LR). According to the theory described in section 4, we should expect that MR and LR registered both a growth during the artificial boom (2002-2006). But we should expect that MR industries grew earlier and at a heavier pace, while the LR industries peak should arrive later. At the same time, the growth for MR industries should turn negative earlier. This is what indeed happened.

While coming out 2002 the (average) growth rates of value-added in both MR and LR industry subsamples increased, value-added growth in MR industries accelerated markedly, peaking at about 11.7 percent in 2004. Value-added growth in LR industries also accelerated during the boom, but the acceleration was more muted and peaked later (at about 7.5 percent in 2005). MR value-added growth also contracted relatively early, turning negative in 2007. LR value-added growth remained positive until 2009. Notably, the timing of the peak in MR value-added growth coincided with the Fed beginning to increase the federal funds rate in 2004. (Young 2012, 86).

Figure 6: Value-added growth rates for most and least roundabout industries; federal funds rate, 1998–2009

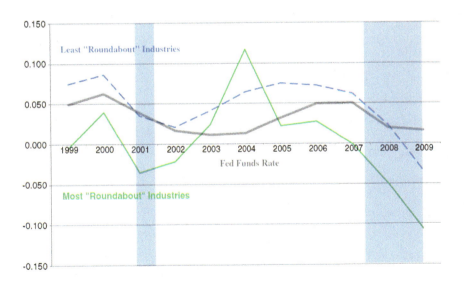

Source: Young (2012, 88).

Such a dynamics should find a counterpart in the inflationary trend. If the theory is consistent, we expect to find inflation for MR industries during the 'hottest' years of the boom (2002-2004). On the contrary, price dynamics for

At the root of economic fluctuations

LR industries should manifest less intense variations. Again, such conclusions are confirmed by Young statistical investigation.

The LR (average) industry inflation rate was relatively stable from 1999 to 2009. A slow acceleration (consistent with ABCT) did occur from 2002 through 2006, followed by a subsequent decrease in PPI inflation. For the MR industries a remarkable acceleration in PPI inflation (peaking in 2004) accompanied the corresponding nominal value-added boom (Fig. 3). Moreover, the MR inflation rate in 2004 was greater than the value-added growth rate (15.6% versus 11.7% (Young 2012, 88).

Figure 7 PPI average inflation rates for most and least roundabout industries, 1998–2009 (Young 2012:89)

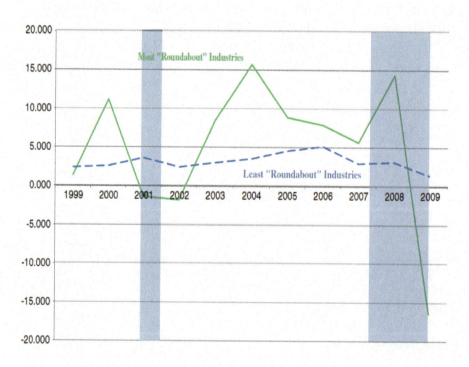

Source: Young (2012, 89).

The European crisis

Finally, we shall try to distinguish what happened with the unsustainable boom and what could had happened in case of *natural cycle*. Or, better, we should look at the two stages of the growth path (primary and secondary waves), which, according to our vision, are experienced in both cases. And, instead, we should identify crisis and depression in the unsustainable case, while in case of natural cycle the downturn movement should have been less severe.

In fact, what we claimed, following Schumpeter, is that all the booms (ignited by monetary easing or by more future-oriented expectations) are characterized by two stages: the initial growth and the speculative wave (fever). In the case of inflation induced boom we should then experience a longer a deeper crisis than in case of natural cycle.

Eurostat and Federal Reserve Bank of St. Louis support our idea that the boom should be divided into two stages.

Table 3 GDP USA (trillions of USD) and EU-15 (billions of EURO), 2001-2014

Date	GDP USA	% Δ on Y-1	GDP EU-15	% Δ on Y-1
2001-01-01	USD 10,508.10		EUR 9,082,627.20	
2002-01-01	USD 10,834.40	3.11%	EUR 9,418,817.40	3.70%
2003-01-01	USD 11,230.10	3.65%	EUR 9,750,628.90	3.52%
2004-01-01	USD 11,988.40	6.75%	EUR 9,922,512.10	1.76%
2005-01-01	USD 12,813.70	6.88%	EUR 10,395,107.00	4.76%
2006-01-01	USD 13,648.90	6.52%	EUR 10,782,958.70	3.73%
2007-01-01	USD 14,233.20	4.28%	EUR 11,361,207.80	5.36%
2008-01-01	USD 14,668.40	3.06%	EUR 11,964,559.40	5.31%
2009-01-01	USD 14,383.90	-1.94%	EUR 11,925,489.60	-0.33%
2010-01-01	USD 14,681.10	2.07%	EUR 11,303,488.80	-5.22%
2011-01-01	USD 15,238.40	3.80%	EUR 11,777,522.40	4.19%
2012-01-01	USD 15,973.90	4.83%	EUR 12,113,108.60	2.85%
2013-01-01	USD 16,440.70	2.92%	EUR 12,347,726.10	1.94%
2014-01-01	USD 16,984.30	3.31%	EUR 12,425,758.80	0.63%
2015-01-01	USD 17,649.30	3.92%	EUR 12,795,712.20	2.98%

Source: Federal Reserve Bank of St. Louis and Eurostat.

At the root of economic fluctuations

Table 3 shows that the boom started, both in America and in Europe, with growth rates between 3 and 4%. It is only in 2004 that the USA economy started to grow at an annual pace close to 7%. In Europe it is visible the same dynamics, though slightly later and at a lower pace. Growth remained around 4% for the greatest part of the expansion, while we can talk of a secondary and speculative fever only in 2006 and 2007.

What is important is that in both continents we can clearly distinguish a moment of initial expansion (first wave of the boom), stably running at around 3.5% a year, and a strong secondary boom with rates well above 6.5% in the USA and around 5.5% in the EU.

On the Western side of the Atlantic Ocean the first wave of expansion lasted only two years to give way to an early secondary wave, lasting three years, which gradually turn off (two years) before reaching the crisis. In Europe, instead, we see a primary wave lasting five years, before the entering of the secondary boom (two years) which ended directly into the crisis.

Such dynamics is confirmed by data on house pricing in the USA.

Table 4 HPI indexes, USA, 2001-2015

Year	Quarter	Purchase-Only Index (1991Q1=100)	HPI % Change Over Previous 4 Quarters	HPI % Change Over Previous Quarter
2001	1	146.57	7.66%	2.46%
2001	2	150.16	7.71%	1.68%
2001	3	152.68	7.43%	1.55%
2001	4	153.98	7.11%	1.24%
2002	1	156.13	6.04%	1.44%
2002	2	160.37	6.06%	1.69%
2002	3	163.75	6.51%	1.99%
2002	4	165.80	6.70%	1.42%
2003	1	168.18	6.47%	1.22%
2003	2	172.46	5.97%	1.22%
2003	3	176.21	5.49%	1.53%

The European crisis

Year	Quarter	Purchase-Only Index (1991Q1=100)	HPI % Change Over Previous 4 Quarters	HPI % Change Over Previous Quarter
2003	4	178.82	6.95%	2.82%
2004	1	182.18	7.31%	1.56%
2004	2	188.58	8.60%	2.43%
2004	3	193.81	11.05%	3.82%
2004	4	196.96	10.30%	2.13%
2005	1	201.10	11.11%	2.30%
2005	2	208.64	11.94%	3.19%
2005	3	214.39	11.06%	3.01%
2005	4	217.04	11.21%	2.26%
2006	1	219.51	10.44%	1.60%
2006	2	223.77	8.12%	1.03%
2006	3	224.52	5.84%	0.84%
2006	4	223.56	4.55%	1.02%
2007	1	224.02	3.30%	0.38%
2007	2	226.56	2.18%	-0.06%
2007	3	223.97	0.22%	-1.10%
2007	4	218.00	-1.07%	-0.28%
2008	1	211.79	-2.12%	-0.69%
2008	2	209.16	-4.48%	-2.47%
2008	3	204.25	-6.42%	-3.11%
2008	4	196.23	-6.99%	-0.89%
2009	1	194.09	-5.65%	0.75%
2009	2	194.64	-5.82%	-2.65%
2009	3	193.81	-5.37%	-2.65%
2009	4	191.69	-5.20%	-0.71%
2010	1	188.13	-7.03%	-1.20%
2010	2	190.92	-5.34%	-0.88%
2010	3	187.91	-1.82%	0.97%
2010	4	183.85	-1.82%	-0.71%
2011	1	178.08	-3.37%	-2.76%
2011	2	180.57	-4.15%	-1.68%
2011	3	181.65	-4.32%	0.80%

At the root of economic fluctuations

Year	Quarter	Purchase-Only Index (1991Q1=100)	HPI % Change Over Previous 4 Quarters	HPI % Change Over Previous Quarter
2011	4	179.67	-3.18%	0.47%
2012	1	179.02	-1.46%	-1.03%
2012	2	186.34	-0.13%	-0.35%
2012	3	188.65	0.36%	1.30%
2012	4	189.10	0.71%	0.82%
2013	1	191.35	2.30%	0.53%
2013	2	200.08	4.32%	1.62%
2013	3	203.92	4.69%	1.66%
2013	4	203.32	4.88%	1.00%
2014	1	204.34	5.30%	0.93%
2014	2	211.18	5.87%	2.17%
2014	3	213.65	5.76%	1.54%
2014	4	213.58	5.63%	0.87%
2015	1	215.10	5.56%	0.87%
2015	2	222.58	5.25%	1.86%

Table 4 testifies that because of the 2001 new economy crisis houses prices slowed their growth path in 2002 and 2003, recording an annual average growth around 6%. It is from 2004 that we can see, accordingly to what we could expect, the rate of annual growth speed up to 10-12%. As for the GDP we observe a moderation in 2007, after three speculative years (2004-2006). Toward the end of 2007, with the emergence of the economic crisis, housing prices started gradually to fall down, to start to rise again in the third quarter of 2012.

Our considerations about the existence of two waves in the boom is therefore confirmed by GDP and housing prices dynamics. It is more difficult, instead, to reach definitive conclusions regarding the recession. When would the downturn stop if instead of an artificially ignited expansion we had experienced a growth driven by rising profit expectations met by a growing saving rate? It is hard to say, in particular because QES did not allow the deflationary process to take the necessary course in order to definitely clear the field from the results of mal-investments (Ferlito 2014b). GDP data do not adequately testify the intensity of the crisis and the structural process of readjustment toward a new production structure consistent with the intentions of consumers and investors.

However, we can observe that the years after the crisis are characterized by slow growth and, moreover, high unemployment. Data on housing prices show the struggle in the industry that led the boom. The point in our analysis on the natural cycle is that, if such a case would occur, the system would not need to struggle to go back to the production structure typical of the years preceding the boom (long readjustment process). Instead, what the system would need to clear out would be only the results of the years of the secondary wave, the speculative one. We could imagine, thus, a shorter readjustment process affecting only a smaller number of companies; low growth performances should last for a limited period and unemployment should set at a lower level. Such conclusions are based, of course, on the hypothesis of absence of interest rate manipulations by the central banks and the banking system in general.

7. Conclusions

The analysis developed so far allows us to conclude, in a very simple way and in the wake of authoritative economists of the past, that the cyclical trend is the form that development takes in a capitalist economy.

While acknowledging the basic assumptions of the Austrian business cycle theory as valid, especially in Hayek's version, the systematic introduction of "real" expectations, acting in "real time", in the sense advocated by Ludwig Lachmann, can only lead us towards the rediscovery of secondary investment waves (imitations and speculations) on which, in particular, Schumpeter focused. In being made possible by a banking policy sensitive to and part of the general positive sentiment of an expansion stage, they precisely match that part of the growth stage that has to be liquidated through a readjustment crisis.

We therefore believe that the Austrian distinction between sustainable and unsustainable growth is valid. What we rather seek to overcome is the belief that, in the first case, the expansion stage is not followed by a crisis. On the contrary, a liquidation crisis occurs in both cases. The difference lies in the intensity and duration of the crisis. Most of the long-term entrepreneurial projects initiated by entrepreneurs will struggle to be completed in the case of a boom generated from the outset in an "unhealthy" manner. For growth set in motion in a "sustainable" manner, only the imitative and speculative initiatives will not be completed. Inasmuch, the positive effects of the first part of the expansion will not be eliminated. It is merely a question of 'clearing up'. We call this instance the *natural cycle*. In the previous case, on the other hand, reconstruction will have to begin from a pile of rubble.

What the Western world started to experience in 2007 is a typical unsustainable boom, ignited by artificial monetary expansion. Quantitative evidences support the conclusion, including the modification of the production structure. Moreover, two separate parts of the boom (the initial one and the speculative one) are clearly observable. Finally, our framework allows us to claim that crisis typical of a natural cycle would end earlier and after a less severe readjustment process.

References

Ahrend, R. (2010) "Monetary ease: a factor behind financial crises? Some evidence from OECD countries." *Economics: The Open Access, Open Assessment E-Journal* 4(12), 14 April. http://www.economics-ejournal.org/economics/journalarticles/2010-12

Bocutoğlu, E. and Ekinci, A. (2010) "Austrian Business Cycle Theory and Global Financial Crisis: Some Lessons for Macroeconomic Risk and Financial Stability." Paper presented at the ICE-TEA 2010 *The Global Economy After the Crisis: Challenges and Opportunities*, 1-3 September.
http://ersanbocutoglu.net/Custom/OdesisMc/ekinci.pdf

Borio, C. (2012) "The financial cycle and macroeconomics: What have we learnt?" *BIS Working Papers No 395*. http://www.bis.org/publ/work395.htm

Calvo, G. (2013) *Puzzling over the anatomy of crises: Liquidity and the Veil of Finance*. Background paper for the Mayekawa Lecture at the Institute for Monetary and Economic Studies Conference, Bank of Japan, Tokyo, 29-30 May.

http://www.columbia.edu/~gc2286/documents/CalvoBOJpaperMay2013REVJune282013.pdf

Fanno, M. (1931) "Production Cycles, Credit Cycles and Industrial Fluctuations." In H. Hagemann (ed.) *Business Cycle Theory. Selected Texts 1860-1939, II, Structural Theories of the Business Cycle*. Pickering and Chatto 2002, pp. 225-261.

Ferlito, C. (2007) "Bolla immobiliare: dove sono gli economisti?" *Rinascita*, 11 agosto, p. 16.

Ferlito, C. (2010) *Dentro la crisi. Combattere la crisi, difendere il mercato*, Chieti: Solfanelli.

Ferlito, C. (2011) "Sylos Labini's Unpublished Notes on Schumpeter's *Business Cycles*." *The Quarterly Journal of Austrian Economics* 14 (1), 88-129. https://mises.org/library/sylos-labinis-unpublished-notes-schumpeters-business-cycles

Ferlito, C. (2013) *Phoenix Economics. From Crisis to Renascence*, New York: Nova Publishers.

Ferlito, C. (2014a) "The Natural Cycle: Why Economic Fluctuations are Inevitable. A Schumpeterian Extension of the Austrian Business Cycle Theory." *Journal of Reviews on Global Economics* 3, 200-219. http://dx.doi.org/10.6000/1929-7092.2014.03.16

Ferlito, C. (2014b) "ECB and the fear of deflation." *The Malaysian Insider*, 14 April. http://www.themalaysianinsider.com/sideviews/article/ecb-and-the-fear-of-deflation-carmelo-ferlito

Ferlito, C. (ed.) (2015) "Hayek, Keynes and the Crisis. Analyses and Remedies." *Journal of Reviews on Global Economics* 4, Special issue 184-280.

Hayek, F. A. (1929) *Monetary Theory and the Trade Cycle*, 1966 edition. New York: Kelley.

Hayek, F. A. (1931) *Prices and Production*. 1967 edition. New York: Kelley.

Hayek, F. A. (1932) "A Note on the Development of the Doctrine of 'Forced Saving'." *Quarterly Journal of Economics* XLVII, 123-133.

Hayek, F. A. (1933) "Price Expectations, Monetary Disturbances and Malinvestments." In *Profits, Interest and Investment and Other Essays on the Theory of Industrial Fluctuations*, Augustus M. Kelley (ed.), Cliftony, 1975, 135-156.

Hayek, F. A. (1939) "Profits, interest and Investment." In F. A. von Hayek, *Profits, Interest and Investment and Other Essays on the Theory of Industrial Fluctuations*. Clifton: Augustus M. Kelley, 1975, pp. 3-71.

Huerta de Soto, J. (1998) *Money, Bank Credit, and Economic Cycles*. 2006 edition, Auburn: Ludwig von Mises Institute.

Huerta de Soto, J. (2000) *The Austrian School. Market Order and Entrepreneurial Creativity*. 2010 edition, Cheltenham and Northampton: Edward Elgar.

Hülsmann, J. G. (2013) *Krise der Inflationskultur. Geld, Finanzen und Staat in Zeiten der Kollektiven Korruption*, Munich: Finanzbuch Verlag.

Kirzner, I. M. (1973) *Competition & Entrepreneurship*, Chicago: University of Chicago Press.

Koopl, R. (2014) *From Crisis to Confidence. Macroeconomics after the Crash*, London: The Institute of Economic Affairs.

Krugman, P. (2008) *The Return of Depression Economics and the Crisis of 2008*, New York: Norton and Company.

Kurz, H. D. (2003) "Friedrich August Hayek: la teoria monetaria del sovrainvestimento." In U. Ternowetz (ed.), *Friedrich A. von Hayek e la Scuola Austriaca di Economia*, Soveria Mannelli: Rubbettino, pp. 175-207.

Lachmann, L. M. (1940) "A Reconsideration of the Austrian Theory of Industrial Fluctuations." In L. M. Lachmann, *Capital, Expectations, and the Market Process*, Kansas City: Sheed Andrews and McMeel, 1977, pp. 267-286.

Lachmann, L. M. (1943) "The Role of Expectations in Economics as a Social Science." In L. M. Lachmann, *Capital, Expectations, and the Market Process*, Kansas City: Sheed Andrews and McMeel, 1977, pp. 65-80.

Lachmann, L. M. (1956) *Capital and Its Structure*, 1978 edition, Kansas City: Sheed Andrews and McMeel.

Lachmann, L. M. (1976) "From Mises to Shackle: An Essay on Austrian Economics and the Kaleidic Society." *Journal of Economic Literature* 14 (1), 54-62.

Lachmann, L. M. (1982) "Why Expectations Matter." In S. Gloria Palermo (ed.), *Modern Austrian Economics. Archaeology of a Revival*, I, *A Multi-Directional Revival*, London: Pickering and Chatto, 2002, pp. 251-269.

Lachmann, L. M. (1986" *The Market as Economic Process*. Oxford: Basil Blackwell.

Leijonhufvud, A. (2009) "Out of the corridor: Keynes and the crisis." *Cambridge Journal of Economics* 33, 741-757.

Lewin, P. (1997) *Capital in Disequilibrium: A re-examination of the capital theory of Ludwig M. Lachmann*. Unpublished draft.
http://www.utdallas.edu/~plewin/hopentrv.pdf.

Lewin, P. (2005) "The Capital Idea and the Scope of Economics." *The Review of Austrian Economics* 18 (2), 145-167.

Moss, L. S. (2005) "The applied economics of the modern Austrian School." In J. G. Bakhaus (ed.) *Modern Applications of Austrian Thought*. London and New York: Routledge, pp. 3-19.

O'Driscoll, G. and Rizzo, M. J. (1985) *The Economics of Time and Ignorance*. 2002 edition, London and New York: Routledge.

Rizzo, M. J. (1979) "Disequilibrium and All That: An Introductory Essay." In M. J. Rizzo (ed.), *Time, Uncertainty, and Disequilibrium. Exploration of Austrian Themes*, Lexington: Heath and Company, pp. 1-18.

Roncaglia, A. (2010) *Economisti che sbagliano. Le radici culturali della crisi*, Rome and Bari: Laterza.

Rothbard, M. N. (1969) *Economic Depressions: Their Cause and Cure*, 2009 edition, Auburn: Ludwig von Mises Institute.

Sachs, J. (2010) "La terza via tra Keynes e i tagli." *Il Sole-24 Ore*, 9 June, p. 20.

Salerno, J. T. (2012) "A Reformulation of Austrian Business Cycle Theory in Light of the Financial Crisis." *The Quarterly Journal of Austrian Economics* 15 (1), 3-44.

Schumpeter, J. A. (1911) *The Theory of Economic Development*, 1983 edition, New Brunswick and London: Transaction Publishers.

Schumpeter, J. A. (1939) *Business Cycles: A Theoretical, Historical and Statistical Analysis of the Capitalist Process*, 2005 edition, Chevy Chase and Mansfield Centre: Bartleby's Books and Martino Publishing.

Schumpeter, J. A. (1964) *Business Cycles. A Theoretical, Historical and Statistical Analysis of the Capitalist Process*, 2008 abridged Edition, digital edition. Un document produit en version numérique par Didier Lagrange.

Shackle, G. L. S. (1972) *Epistemics and Economics: A Critique of Economic Doctrines*, 2009 edition, New Brunswick and London: Transaction Publishers.

Spiethoff, A. (1925) "Business Cycles." In H. Hagemann (ed.), *Business Cycle Theory. Selected Texts 1860-1939*, II, *Structural Theories of the Business Cycle*, London: Pickering and Chatto, 2002, pp. 109-205.

Sylos Labini, P. (1954) "Il problema dello sviluppo economico in Marx e Schumpeter." In P. Sylos Labini, *Problemi dello sviluppo economico*, Bari: Laterza, 1977, pp. 19-73.

Sylos Labini, P. (1984) *The Forces of Economic Growth and Decline*, Cambridge and London: MIT Press.

Taylor, J. B. (2009) *Getting off track: How government actions and interventions caused, prolonged, and worsened the financial crisis*, Stanford: Hoover Institution Press.

Young, A. T. (2012) "The time structure of production in the US, 2002-2009." *The Review of Austrian Economics* 25, 77-92.

The European crisis

Chapter 8
Unemployment around the North Atlantic, 1948-2014
Merijn Knibbe

1. Introduction

From 1948 up to around 1973 unemployment rates of over 3% were exceptional in Europe while rates of over 6% were exceptional in the USA. After the first oil crisis in 1973 rates of between 5 and 10% however became the norm, while in Europe after the fall of communism in 1991 unemployment became, in extreme cases, as high as 15 (Finland), 22 (Spain) and even over 30% (Macedonia). And this was not the end of the movement towards ever higher rates of unemployment. After the Great Financial Crisis (GFC) in 2008 such rates became more and more common as a large number of European countries like the three Baltic states, Greece, Bulgaria, Croatia, Macedonia, Kosovo and Albania saw unemployment rise to percentages of over 15, 20% and sometimes even 25% while unemployment for the entire EU and the Euro Area became as high as 11%. Neoclassical economics cannot really explain such shifts and levels. Just ahead of the GFC, Pissarides, who in 2010 received a Nobel prize for his neoclassical work on labor markets and especially unemployment, tried to do so (Pissarides, 2007). He shows a relation between high productivity growth and low unemployment in the fifties and sixties of the twentieth century. His friction model of unemployment tries to explain this relation by assuming that low unemployment before 1973 was caused by a large gap between the production of a laborer and his wage, a gap caused by the "surprise" increase of productivity and causing companies to employ additional labor (he abstracts from the government).

As he does not proof the existence of this gap and leaves the most interesting cases, like Finland and Spain, out of his small sample, his explanation for low unemployment is wanting – he simply does not try to explain why unemployment in Spain and Finland, which did not experience any out of the ordinary development of productivity, was so much higher than in other North Atlantic OECD countries. Or why unemployment in the USA was, up to 1973, higher than in Europe, between 1973 and 1991 about at par and after 1991 somewhat lower. His model and sample are simply too restricted. This idea is corroborated by Hendry and Mizon (2014) who show for the UK between 1850 and 2015 that shifts as those mentioned above are "robust" and "fundamental" and not accounted for by neoclassical models, which exclude the possibility of such shifts. It is as if the labor market is a kind of game played by supply and demand which, from time to time, suddenly moves to a higher or lower playing field.

This leads to the question if non-neoclassical explanations explain the ever higher level of unemployment. Mitchell and Muysken (2009) provide one explanation. Mitchell and Muysken argue, in their article *"Full employment abandoned: shifting sands and policy failures"* that shifts happened – because politicians enabled them to happen. Their basic economic framework is totally different from the Pissarides analysis. Pissarides explicitly states that his analysis is *"independent of decisions made in the goods market"* (it neglects the role of aggregate demand). The analysis of Mitchell and Muysken is, contrary to this, very focused on changes in aggregate demand. And while Pissarides abstracts from the government (including the Central Bank) the government takes central stage in the Mitchell and Muysken story. They argue that while up to, about, 1973 governments took responsibility for a high level of employment, especially, a low level of unemployment and adapted spending (but not just spending) to assure this while after 1973 the focus of government policy increasingly shifted to keeping inflation low while low level of unemployment became ever important and, indeed, to an extent unwanted as high unemployment was seen as an effective and sometimes even necessary way to combat high inflation.

They convincingly show the "ideological" shift in government policies and think tank reports towards what they call 'total employability' of individual unemployed instead of "total employment" in the entire economy. Instead of changing total spending to a level consistent with full employment, governments put an ever larger emphasis on improving the skills and lowering the "reservation wage" of the unemployed (the lowest wage an unemployed person will accept) as well as deregulating the labor market. One of the consequences of this shift in policies was the disappearance of all kinds of (often socially quite useful) government or subsidized jobs for less employable people, jobs which according to Muysken and Williams might not always have been monetary efficient but which did contribute to micro- and macro-economic stability and social coherence of countries. As well as to the possibility of people to "produce" an acceptable life for themselves.

An example of the change towards "employability" (not mentioned by Mitchell and Muysken) is the abolishment of the draft. This was at first not really part and parcel of the neoliberal agenda (quite some neoliberals and even libertarians opposed it) but it was very successfully promoted, on purely neoliberal grounds, by no one less than Milton Friedman, who later also played a decisive role in the committee which advised the USA government to abolish it. It is enlightening to quote him about this:

> "The case for abolishing conscription and recruiting our armed forces by voluntary methods seems to me overwhelming. We should at once raise the pay of enlisted men improve conditions of service and stimulate more efficient use of manpower by the services. We should continue to raise the pay until the number of 'true' volunteers is large enough so that the lash of compulsion can be eliminated" (Friedman, 1967).

The neoliberal agenda is clearly visible: markets everywhere. Friedman understood abolishing the draft (and, thus, relying on market forces) as an emancipating measure. But this was written in a time when unemployment was relatively low while Friedman also was a strong proponent of, if need be, aggressive monetary policy to keep high unemployment in check – in those days, when the government took care of full employment, the phrase "voluntary" was not yet empty.

Which shows that the policies described by Mitchell and Muysken must clearly be understood as the combination of Friedman deregulation and relying on market forces "everywhere" *plus* a smaller role for the state to mitigate the business cycle. Later generations of Chicago economists even rejected monetary policies aimed at lowering unemployment and doubled down on low and stable inflation as the one and overriding goal of macro-economic policy. The Eurozone can clearly be understood as the greatest "success" of this macro-economic agenda, as there is no entity which is even able to pursue fiscal policies. We will return to this below. As such, the emphasis of Mitchell and Muysken on changing ideological and institutional environment is totally warranted. There *are* fundamental differences between epochs.

But do the differences mentioned by Mitchell and Muysken suffice to explain 2008 events? Both Pissarides as well as Muysken and Williams of course do not incorporate post 2008 developments in their analysis. Also, many new kinds of labor market data have become available, which might shed more light on the questions posed by these authors. Below, we will expand the data set presented by Pissarides as well as Muysken and Williams with the post 2008 years as well as with some more countries and investigate if these analyses might be extended to the post 2008 world. First we will however look at the new "flow" data on the labor market: what do these tell us? As these data are, to many people, still quite unknown we will first have to look at these flow data in more detail, which happens in the next paragraph.

2. What do flow data tell us on the nature of low and high unemployment?

To understand the flow data on the labor market more thoroughly, a little background on why they exist has to be added. Unemployment wasn't always measured as we do it today. After the war until sometime in the eighties of the twentieth century estimates of unemployment were, in many countries, based not on surveys but upon administrative data. People inscribed by some kind of employment/social security agency were counted as 'unemployed'. In the eighties, such data were, to counter criticisms that a considerable part of the rapidly increasing numbers of unemployed people was not actually looking for work, increasingly replaced by surveys. These asked, among other things, if people were actually seeking work. This change fits with the shift from "full employment centered" to "full employability centered" public policies, with its larger emphasis on the behavior individual unemployed.

Quite some of the questions in the survey indeed focus on "instantaneous employability" – anyone who was not directly available (i.e. employable) or was not at that very moment actively seeking for a job was not counted as "unemployed". These surveys showed, on one hand, that unemployment as defined in the survey (people not having any kind of paid work, immediately available for work, seeking actively) was often indeed somewhat lower than "administrative" unemployment. On the other hand, they also enabled statisticians to define "broad" unemployment, a variable which also encompasses underemployed part time workers, people not immediately available for a job (like students which are almost graduated but which are already seeking) and "discouraged" workers, i.e. people who want a job and are immediately available but who do not bother to seek for a job. And these 'broad' data showed that (a) total unemployment, including 'broad' unemployment, was quite a bit higher than old style administrative unemployment. While (b) downward swings in the business cycle did not just lead to a rise in "official" unemployment but also to increases in the number of discouraged workers as well as part-time workers who wanted more hours – which, for one thing, shows that unemployment itself had a negative effect on employability, as defined by policymakers! And (c): in many countries (most so in Italy) broad unemployment was massive.

Eurostat (2015) shows, not even counting the underemployed part-time workers, that the "potential additional labor force" (another phrase for: "unemployed people") in the EU was no less than 4,8%-point of the labor force and i.e. almost halve as large as official unemployment. In Italy it was even, because of a very large amount of discouraged workers, as high as 13.6% of the labor force (defined as people with a job plus the official unemployed!) – a level which really changes any political or economic calculation about the output gap, the sustainability of pensions and government spending, prosperity or whatever!

Though partly consistent with the neoliberal, individualist Zeitgeist of the eighties and beyond, these survey data are still not consistent with many neoclassical models which model unemployment as a kind of pleasurable "leisure" while empirical investigations as well as common sense show, without a shadow of a doubt show that unemployed people are less happy and less healthy than the employed. This holds even more so for the results of the new flow data estimated by economists. These do not only count the unemployed but also the number of people who flow into or out of (un)employment or the labor force. These flows turn out to be rather independent of the level of unemployment. Which is fully consistent with the findings of Hendry and Mizon. When a shock increases the level of unemployment the flows might, after the shock, return to the pre-shock level and, when those levels were consistent with stable unemployment, lead to a situation with a permanently higher level of unemployment. The concept plus the results of the surveys(including data on broad unemployment),however, do square with the Harrod-Domar idea that the economy can be understood as a huge and often growing machine which needs labor, but which, until labor shortages appear and impose a limit on the growth of this machine, develops, when left to its own, more or less independent from the *level* of unemployment.

Spain might serve as an example of how these flow data can, in combination with traditional data, be used to give a more comprehensive description of the labor market. Spain is often portrayed as a country with a sclerotic labor market. The opposite is true. Spanish employment growth before 2008 was miraculous. Employment increased from 12,2 million in 1993 to 20,4 million in 2008.[1] This meant that 29% of the increase of employment in the *entire* EU in this period (+28,5 million) happened in Spain, a country with half the amount of inhabitants of Germany and only about 8% of the population of the entire EU. In some years, like 2001, employment growth in Spain even took account of over 50% of total employment growth in the EU. Despite these astonishing increases Spanish unemployment only decreased from 22% in 1993 to a still high 8% in 2008, a rate which after the 2008-2011 construction bust would increase again to 26%.The limited decline of unemployment was not caused by a sclerotic labor market but to the contrary by the dynamism of labor supply. A large influx of immigrants as well as a rapid increase in the participation rate of women had led to an

---

[1] When no other source is indicated all data come from Eurostat.

increase of the labor force which, almost, matched the increase of employment. When, in 2008, foreign private capital stopped flowing into the Spanish construction sector employment decreased again, to 17,1 million in 2013. Despite the fact that this was still 5 million higher than the 1983 level, which implies that net Spanish job growth 1993-2013 was twice the size of total German job growth in this period, this of course led to massive unemployment, not just because the number of jobs diminished but also because, at first, the female participation rate continued to increase.

When we add the 'flow' data on the Spanish labor market, i.e. the information which tells us how large gross flows into and out of employment, unemployment and the labor market were, it shows that after 2010 "job churn" in Spain was *about twice as high than in the UK*, which is known for its flexible "easy hire easy fire" labor market (Knibbe, 2015). This, again, underscores the flexibility of the Spanish labor market. High gross flows however *did not* prevent the rapid increase of unemployment. Unemployment is according to these data a kind of reservoir and it is the net amount of water which flows into or out of it which changes it level, not the gross flows. These data are however important I the sense that they make us realize that 26% unemployment means that, as people flow in and out of unemployment, much more than 26% of the entire population is affected by unemployment. The Spanish data show convincingly the dynamic, flexible nature of the Spanish labor market – but also show that despite of this unemployment went down only slowly while the extremely high rates of post 2008 unemployment affected much more people than indicated by the mere statistic (not even counting the families of the unemployed).

3. Gross and net flows of labor and hysteresis

When we look at British flow data we can tell a little more about the relation between flows on the labor market and the level of unemployment. The surprising result of this way of looking at the labor market is the enormous dynamism which these data show. In the UK there was in the first quarter of 2015 (Henshall, 2015) a net flow from inactivity to employment of 27 thousand people, but gross flows from inactivity to employment and vice versa were 573 and 546 thousand people. Gross flows were twenty times as high as the net flow (Henshall, 2015)! For the flows between inactivity and unemployment this "leverage" factor is "only" 3 to 4 (gross: 333 and 434; net 101 from inactivity to unemployment) while for the flow between unemployment and employment this "dynamism coefficient" was 2 to 3 (net flow of 169 out of unemployment to employment, gross flows of 340 and 509).

These results do not only show a more complicated labor market. It's not just about the employed and the unemployed, but also about the inactive, as we have already seen in Spain, which its fast rise of the female participation rate. They also underscore the fact that when unemployment is 10% the total amount of people which experience a spell of unemployment during a year is much higher than this 10%. When we look at the long run development of flows it shows (1) that during crises relatively small and temporary changes in the gross flows lead to large changes in unemployment. And during severe downturns, these changes are, albeit fairly short lived, not that small and lead to an explosive increase in unemployment, which, despite the temporary nature of the changes, tends to be quite sticky as, after the crisis, the flows tend to return to their previous levels. There is no catching up. If there is a return to equilibrium it is a return to equilibrium of the individual flows, not of the net results.[2]

As stated, the pattern shown by Hendry and Mizon is consistent with this idea. When the temporary increases of outflows and decreases of inflows related to a crisis do not lead to changes in the "permanent" level of inflows and outflows it becomes easy to explain the differences in levels between epochs (though we still have to explain the 'permanent' level of inflows and outflows). With this in mind, we can move on to the log run development of unemployment: does out extended dataset (more countries, more years) tell

---

[2] This metaphor is also consistent with Harrod-Domar type growth models. Considering data on broad unemployment, it can also be argued that a shift to a new 'epoch' has occurred with an even higher level of unemployment in which even the employability framework has been abandoned in change for a framework were high levels of unemployment are seen as necessary for the moral and ethical purification of political systems! See for instance Coppola (2015), for the extreme stance of Brussels based EU bureaucrats on government deficits already in the spring of 2009, when the worst of the downturn still had to come.

us something new about 'epochs' of high or low unemployment? Did, after 2008, a new epoch start?

4. The long run development of North Atlantic unemployment, 1948-2015: Core countries

Graph 1 shows the development of unemployment in a number of core western countries (plus the Netherlands) and is more or less an update of figure 2 in Mitchell and Muysken (2009) (additional years added, Australia dropped, Europe split up in four different countries). It confirms and sometimes underscores their ideas: the high post WW II level in Germany may look out of sync, but can easily be explained by domestic turmoil, an undefined political situation and the inflow of around 10 to 12 million refugees into what would become Western Germany. And the relatively fast decline of German unemployment to a consistently low rate after 1955 underscores the ideas of Mitchell and Muysken about the success of postwar economic development and policies. Mind that at the time 11% unemployment in a devastated Germany was considered to be very high, while at the present it is pretty "normal" in a non-devastated Europe! Below, we will as it was the maximum level in post war Germany as well as about the maximum level in the entire EU after 2008 as a benchmark.

It clearly seems as if Europe and, to a lesser extent, the USA after 2008 entered a new period of even higher unemployment. In Europe, economic policies have doubled down on the ideas of deregulation and employability even in the absence of an entity able to pursue contra cyclical policies. Up to the moment of writing of this article there has been, in the EU, no coherent policy response to levels of national unemployment which directly threaten the stability of nations and even the entire EU. One response has, for a time, even be to accept and encourage extremely *high* domestic interest rates in countries like Spain, Greece and Italy despite very elevated unemployment and falling levels of inflation, to impose "discipline". It has only been since the end of 2014 that a clear convergence between interest rates in southern and northern European countries is visible. Even the neoliberal textbook response to economic crises – low interest rates – was thus absent in many countries. Which is clearly consistent with the Mitchell/Muysken argument that neoliberal governments abandoned "the full employment framework" and embraced "the full employability framework". It can even be argued that they understated their case. Still, it is remarkable that after 2008 and in the "core" countries shown in graph 1 unemployment did not break historical records. Below, we will see that, in a wider perspective, this was quite unusual.

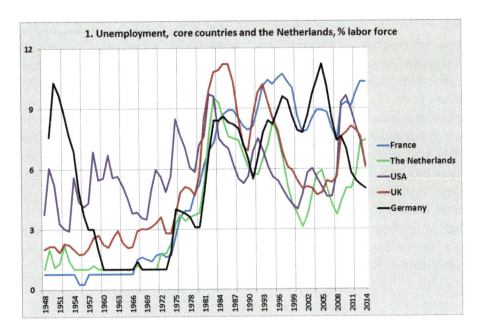

Sources: Central Bureau voor de Statistiek (Netherlands); Bureau of Labour Statistics (USA); Bank of England (UK, data increased a little to account for differences with ONS data); Villa (1995) (France: data increased to account for the fact that they are presented as a % of the entire population while all other data are a % of the labor force); Statistisches Bundesamt (Germany); Eurostat.

It is true that unemployment in the Germany, the UK and the USA is reaching lower levels again and labor markets in these countries are (especially looking at the number of vacancies) showing signs of increasing tightness. But this does not necessarily mean that the high unemployment epoch is over – broad unemployment in the UK remains elevated and, as it is well known, the USA participation rate is still remarkably low. Also low is unemployment in Germany: this might well be related to higher unemployment elsewhere in the Euro Area, as an analysis of the Eurozone Phillips Curve suggests (Knibbe, 2013). A counter-arguments is however that Germany might be moving to a new epoch in a different way, because of demographic developments.

Between 1945 and 1948 Germany experienced, unlike its neighbors, a severe baby bust, which means that the number of people going into retirement was, between around 2005 and 2013, relatively low. But at this moment the post-1948-born babies are retiring: an autonomous increase of the gross flow out of employment into inactivity. As, after 1965 the German birth rate plunged and remained exceptionally low "ever after" the "domestic" inflow in the labor market is getting lower and lower: an autonomous decline of gross inflows. Don't underestimate this effect: the number of 0 to 5 years old in Germany is less than 50% of the number of 50 to 55 year olds. This may lead to permanently lower unemployment as already shown by East Germany, which during the last ten years did not see net employment creation, but which did witness a steady decline of its very high rate (20%) of unemployment; at the time of writing the highest unemployment in Germany was not measured in one of the East German "Länder" but in Bremen. As in the case of Spain, however, mass immigration (even net of refugees) might well counter these tendencies.

5. The European experience post-1983: non-core countries

The next graphs show unemployment in "non-core countries" of Europe. They are based upon Eurostat data as Eurostat provides a more or less consistent data set about unemployment – the data are however not always totally consistent with graph 1 which was based upon data of national statistical agencies. Also, the Eurostat data only start in 1983 and for Eastern European countries even quite a bit later, which means that 1983 has to be used as the starting point. Graph 1 above however, shows that, in 1983, the shift to a new epoch with a new "equilibrium" level of unemployment (i.e. more or less matching flows into and out of (un)employment and (in)activity) had already been completed while, in a historical sense, it's also after the British "winter of discontent" of 1979 and the 1981 air traffic controllers strike in the USA, two landmarks in the advent of the neoliberal policies emphasized by Mitchell and Muysken. This means that there are good statistical reasons to use 1983 as a starting point. The series for the Eastern European countries starts somewhere in the nineties, after their shift to more market oriented societies. Before this shift, unemployment as defined in this article in these countries was around zero because of the communist job guarantee.

The countries have been clustered in six more or less homogenous groups which are shown in graphs 2 to 5 below. Graph 2 shows the "Nordics" (Sweden, Finland, Denmark, Belgium, Austria; the Netherlands can be joined to this club but Dutch data are already shown in graph 1). Finland stands out in this group, as it was the only one of these countries plus the core countries which, after its 1991 banking crisis, broke the 11% threshold (this crisis coincided with the demise of the USSR, an important trade partner of Finland). There is no sign that this high Finish unemployment was caused by an exceptional low increase of productivity, as suggested by Pissarides.

Graph 3 shows the Mediterranean countries (Portugal, Italy, Greece and yes, I do know that Portugal is not actually Mediterranean) as well as Ireland and Spain: the housing boom countries. All these countries breached the 11% threshold, often by large margins and for long periods. Italy seems to have had *relatively* low unemployment but this is a bit of a "trompe l'oeil" as this country has very high levels of 'broad unemployment' (see also below).

It is interesting to investigate the link between productivity and the rise of unemployment in Ireland and Spain. As construction is a low productivity activity, a construction bust will boost average productivity in the entire economy while at the same time increasing unemployment. Which shows that a more sectoral approach to the relation between unemployment and productivity instead of the "entire economy approach" of Pissarides is warranted, at a fundamental level this is caused by the fact that the market economy should be understood by a number of not imperfectly connected sub-economies, the disconnect between the construction economy and the rest of the economy in this case caused by the fact that construction investments are, compared with the rest of the economy, largely financed by loans instead of equity, swings of irrational optimism and the long term process involved in planning and building real estate.

Graph 4 shows "Emerging Europe countries" with high pre-2008 as well as high post 2008 unemployment (the Baltic countries, Croatia). Remarkable is the volatility of unemployment in the Baltic states. At this moment unemployment is coming down fast in a number of these countries, which is however decisively influenced by large out-migration in combination with an autonomous demographic decline of the working age population.

Graph 5 shows "Emerging Europe countries" with high pre-2008 and lower post-2008 unemployment (Slovakia, Bulgaria, Poland) as well as "Emerging Europe countries" with lowest unemployment during the entire period (Czech Republic, Romania, Slovenia – more or less).[3] Using the 11% threshold mentioned above (German unemployment in 1950 was actually not 11%, but 10,2%) the next conclusions can be drawn (see the graphs). This 11% maximum seems to have been a maximum too, for the Nordics except Finland as well as Romania, the Czech Republic and to a lesser extent Slovenia. For all other countries, the 11% almost seems like a minimum: unemployment percentages of 15 and 20% are pretty normal and in Spain and Greece the 25% threshold was even surpassed. There clearly is a kind of core-periphery dynamism going on.

The next patterns seem to exist:

i. Somewhat surprisingly, considering the severity of the 2008/2009 crisis and the double and triple dips and lackluster recovery after 2009, quite a number of countries managed to restrict the increase of unemployment after 2008 and succeeded in reaching unemployment levels which for these countries are historically (defined as: after the fall of the Berlin wall) relatively low, albeit often still elevated: Bulgaria, Slovakia and Germany while, as stated, unemployment in Romania and the Czech Republic is also relatively low. And even the Baltic countries have lower unemployment at the moment;

---

[3] I am not sure about the unemployment data of Slovenia. The Eurostat data seem to be on the low side.

The European crisis

ii. In the medium run, the relative positions of countries are remarkable stable;

iii. The very comparable patterns of Ireland and Spain stand out. These patterns were of course caused by comparable booms and inflows of capital. They have interestingly underscored the hysteresis idea. The difference in unemployment between Spain and Ireland also stayed remarkably equal, surely when we take into account that the unwinding of the real estate boom in Spain went remarkably slow;

iv. A most remarkable aspect of unemployment in Italy and Portugal is the consistent increase since the introduction of the Euro.

v. Turning to the political realm: it is clear that the emphasis of economic policy is neither on employment or employability (do Spanish and Greek children already learn German in high school?) but on fiscal discipline – when it comes to normal expenditure. Bad assets of banks and (at the end) real estate developers are however shifted to the balance sheet of governments and, hence, tax payers. The employability paradigm as described by Mitchell and Muysken at least acknowledges the importance of employment. But the new political paradigm (which, considering the structure of the EU and the ECB, is to quite an extent voted into existence by Eastern European countries with a history of lasting and extreme unemployment and extreme neoliberal reforms) seems to diminish this importance and creditors are getting the upper hand. Levels of unemployment of over 20%+ seem to be considered "normal".

That's not a hyperbole. When we look at the estimates of the "Non Accelerating Inflation Rate of Unemployment". This is the inflation rate which is considered to be consistent with the ECB inflation target. For Spain, the European Commission estimated this rate to be 26,6% for Spain for a time, which meant that the Commission in fact stated that whenever Spanish unemployment would drop below 26,6% Spain would experience galloping inflation. Totally absurd, indeed, but economics professors at German universities do seem to take this hullaballoo serious (Tong, 2015).

Unemployment around the North Atlantic, 1948-2014

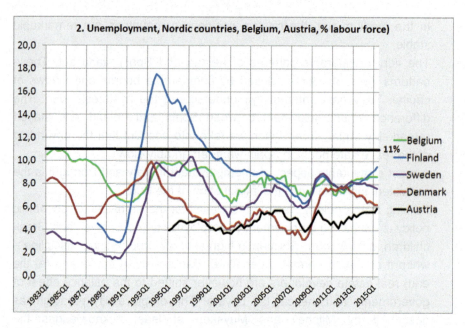

The European crisis

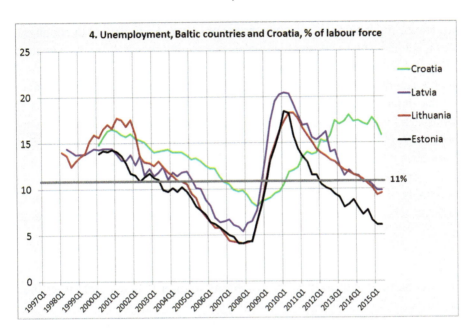

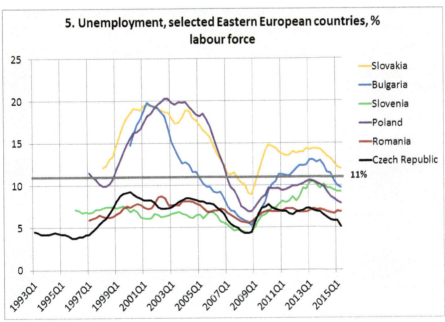

Summarizing: looking at a slightly longer period and a larger set of countries, the evidence shows a situation which is patently worse than the situation sketched by Mitchell and Muysken. Levels of above 11% of unemployment (non-existent in the Mitchell and Muysken dataset) and even of more than double have become common while (consistent with the total absence of centralized fiscal policies in the Euro Area) unemployment has become very volatile. A clear core periphery dynamism seems to exist in the sense that the above 11% rates seem to be a characteristic of non-core Eurozone and EU countries. The political response to this has been one of denial (the estimates of the NAIRU-rate!) and has to an extent even consisted of policies which aimed to increase interest rates during a time of extreme crisis.

6. How does incorporating "broad unemployment" in our data alter the picture?

Aside from the normal unemployment data Eurostat also publishes data on broad unemployment, i.e. job seekers without a job but not immediately available for work, discouraged workers and underemployed part time workers. Data for "restricted" broad unemployment (without the underemployed part time workers) are available from 2005 onwards, data for total broad unemployment (including underemployed part time workers)from 2008 onwards. These show that broad unemployment is cyclically sensitive though less so than normal unemployment (graph 7) and *has about the same level as normal unemployment.*[4]

Looking at data for individual countries, it shows that quite some countries knew or know broad unemployment levels of about 3% (graph 7). Taking this as a minimum it shows that in many countries, governments fail their

---

[4] I have used a slightly different approach than Eurostat (2015) to calculate broad unemployment as Eurostat does not add "underemployed part time workers" to unemployment because they are already counted as employed. I do. I have also adapted the in my view suspect Eurostat database data for the Netherlands in 2013 and 2014 in the database of Eurostat to the data for the Netherlands as shown in Eurostat, 2014. My hunch is that Eurostat mixed up age groups for the Netherlands in the database. Data base data for all other countries are consistent with Eurostat (2015).

citizens: adding 2% to take account of unavoidable cyclical developments gives a red line of 5%: everything above this should be considered "wasteful". In several countries levels are above 10%, twice my red line level of 5%. Let's be harsh about this: last year I encountered an elderly very well educated Slovenian couple whose son works in the Netherlands.

They were in shock about the high level of unemployment, the impossibility to find work and the people who had to leave their houses in Slovenia – a country which, according to Eastern European standards, does not even have very elevated levels of unemployment and is considered to do relatively well! They couple had expected that a capitalist regime would deliver better results than the former Yugoslav variant of socialism – but they were reconsidering their expectations. The data are consistent with the statement of Branko-Milanovic, based on macro statistics, that: "Only 1 out of 10 people living in 'transition' countries have seen a successful transition to capitalism and more democracy" (Milanovic 2015). One of the supposed successes of "really existing socialism" in Eastern Europe was low (in fact: non-existent) unemployment, which, supposedly, came at the price of low efficiency.

But to quote Alan Blinder (as cited in Mitchell and Muysken, 2008, p. 11):

> "The political revival of free-market ideology in the 1980s is, I presume, based on the market's remarkable ability to root out inefficiency. But not all inefficiencies are created equal. In particular, high unemployment represents a waste of resources so colossal that no one truly interested in efficiency can be complacent about it. It is both ironic and tragic that, in searching out ways to improve economic efficiency, we seem to have ignored the biggest inefficiency of them all."

There seems to have been a baby, in the communist bathwater. Maybe a sickly one – but still it should not have been thrown out. The data on broad unemployment show this inefficiency to be even higher than indicated by normal unemployment: for Slovenia about 6.5 %-point have to be added to an already elevated level of "normal" unemployment. And Slovenia is one of the countries with relatively low "broad" unemployment; in Italy "discouraged workers" alone are a whopping 14.4% of the active population 92015 Q3).

On a micro level even more costs have to be added. A level of, say, 16% total unemployment in Slovenia means that around 20 to 25% of the total labor force are without paid work during a time of the year. This also means that next to production foregone the regular flow of money and spending is also interrupted in many households. Hence part of the social and personal dislocation caused by people who are forced to leave their houses and, the other side of the coin, the rapidly increasing rate of non-performing loans has not only to be ascribed to the amount of "macro production foregone" but also to social and economic dislocation on the micro-level. Graph 7 shows that, in many countries, these costs are massive. Remarkably, the graph also shows that only three countries show a decline of broad unemployment between 2008 and 2015: Germany, Lithuania and Turkey. Turkey has been included to show the obvious: a growing labor force does not preclude declining unemployment. We will return to Lithuania and Germany in the last paragraph – what contributed to the decline in these countries?

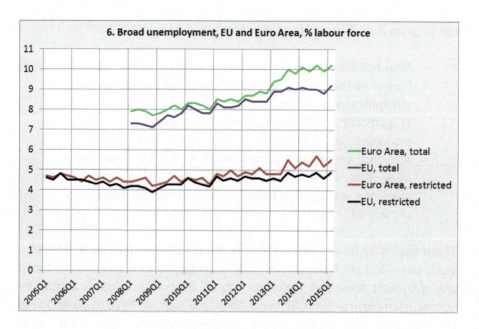

The European crisis

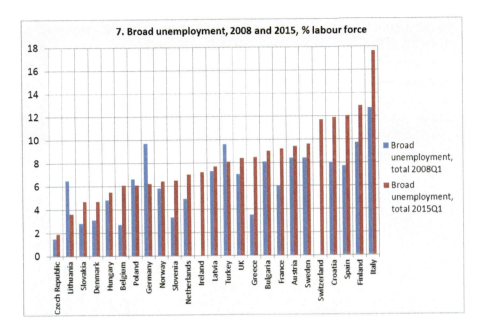

In graph 8, total unemployment (normal unemployment plus broad unemployment) is shown. Mind that not all unemployed want a full time job (a fortiori so for the underemployed part time workers and their wish for additional hours). On the other side: some want more.

What is the implication of these data? How much production is foregone. Dutch data from graph 1 show that, in 2001, just after the peak of the dot.com bubble unemployment in the Netherlands was 3.1%. Only at that level, employers started to snatch employees away from other employers and to use creative ways to attract people, a clear sign of an overheated labor market (and it is not a bad thing when this market is a little overheated, so now and then).

Let's therefore define full employment at a level of 3% of normal employment plus (see above) 3% of "broad" unemployment, i.e. a combined level of 6% unemployment (remember: quite a number of these people already have a part time job, see graph 6). This means that, at this moment, only the Czech Republic has anything like full employment.

The other countries fail their citizens – sometimes in an epic way. And, of course, the EU fails its citizens, in an epic way! The level of total unemployment in the Mediterranean countries is even almost incomprehensible. In a sense this situation was foreshadowed by East-German where, after the fall of The Wall, despite massive outmigration, massive income transfers and radical structural reforms unemployment went up to over 20% and is only coming down because the labor force is shrinking – a striking contrast with developments in West-Germany after 1950.

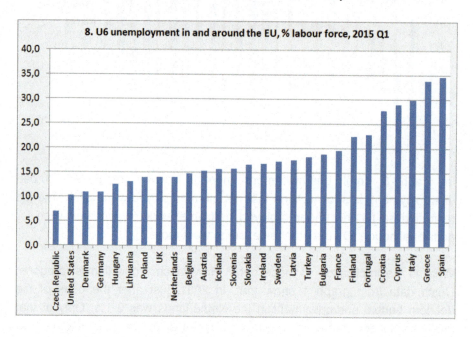

7. Towards a new epoch?

This paragraph does not set out to solve the problem sketched above in any comprehensive way. It will, however, elaborate a few of the arguments of Mitchell and Muysken. Mitchell and Muysken do not pay attention to three large differences between the "trenteglorieuses" and the post-1980 era: up to about 1975 European productivity increased much, much faster than nowadays, a catching up process after the stagnation, war and again stagnation between 1929 and, say, 1951. Private debt levels were also much lower. Populations were younger and less inclined to save. And inequality was less high than today and companies and the government had a more powerful tool to adapt their production process to increasing costs. With this in mind, we can discuss if the present situation is still aptly described by the analysis of Mitchell and Muysken and investigate if their solutions still fit the situation.

First, according to the data show above, Mitchell and Muysken (2008) understates the problem as it does not include the post 2008 data, restricts its empirics to the western "core" countries (which never saw unemployment rise above 11%) and does not pay attention to broad unemployment. Extending and broadening the data set shows that the problem is worse than they stated. Also, unemployment seems to have become even less of a policy priority than it already was, at least in the EU (aside – this might not hold for the ECB, it might even be thought that the ECB employment but also unemployment has become more important than it used to be).A 'scientific' metric of this idea is the total ridiculous nature of estimates of NAIRU by, among other institutions, the European Commission (though they did lower the 26.6% estimate for Spain to a still ludicrous 20.7% in May 2015). For on oversight of such estimates, which do not take account of the empirical downward stickiness of wages (technically: a "non-linearity") see ECB (2013).

There are however some countries which show surprisingly favorable developments. As stated above, this paper does not try to use any kind of labor accounting framework to explain these developments. But graph 9 shows that quite a number of countries show a considerable decline of the 15-64 age group. The largest declines are caused by austerity demographics: a combination of a gentle but consistent and increasing natural decline of this age group and sizeable out migration. These declines are sometimes as large as 10% (Latvia, Lithuania) – which of course explains quite a lot of the decline of unemployment (at one instant, Latvia even posted lower employment but at the same time an increase in the employment rate…). Considering that the decline in Spain took place in the 2013 and 2014 period and still continues (mainly because of the return migration of foreign workers) while it can be predicted that total net emigration in Greece and Portugal will increase we have something like the opposite of the situation of the "trenteglorieuses": the machine is not adapted to the population but the population is adapted to the machine (though we do have to admit that, in the fifties, at least the Netherlands had an active emigration policy)! Finland will at this moment, probably experience the same process. Emigration will stop sometime, but the natural decline is set to continue and to add to the decline of the inflow into the labor market. A somewhat comparable development: during the fifties and especially the sixties average work weeks declined, which had a comparable effect while quite a part of the present success of the German labor market is caused by a recent (2008-2013) decrease of the average work week, too. Supply side developments do make a difference and at least part of the favorable developments in the countries mentioned has to be explained not by any kind of success of economic policies but by people fleeing poverty and unemployment. Aside: the data also show that the demographic balance between European countries is shifting, rapidly. Finally, data on immigration and emigration in Spain, the Baltic countries and Germany show that potential EU labor mobility is much higher than generally assumed.

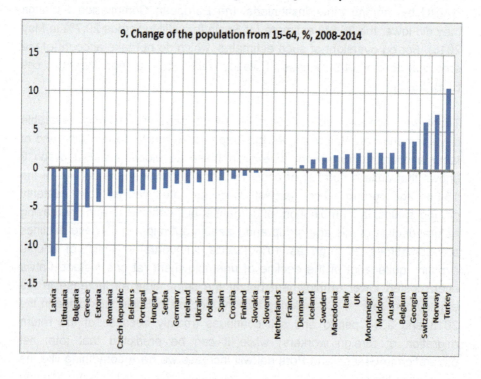

8. Conclusions

Mitchell and Muysken suggest using a combination of a printing press and a shredder, loosening the budget constraint for the government, plus a job guarantee to enable a shift to a new low unemployment epoch. About this, we can say that:

i. Money printing and relaxing the budget constraint: after 2009, the opposite happened. Budget constraints became more binding and instead of money printing governments resorted to money destruction (Cyprus!) to solve problems.[5] And government expenditure increasingly consisted of asset swaps. Greece was forced to cut pensions (i.e. transfer incomes which will be spent) and lend tens of billions of Euro to be able to refinance the banks (which will not directly lead to additional spending). Money printing in the EU will be necessary, not so much to finance government spending or a job guarantee, but by the ECB to buy the enormous amount of bad debts from the banks (while, of course, at the same time restricting asset based lending by the banks will force them to increase lending for GDP transactions);

ii. A consistent critique of a job guarantee is that there is a problem with the allocation of these jobs. When the market does not work its magic, who will decide which people will perform which guaranteed jobs. This is a good question. But in 2012 the Nobel prize for economics was awarded to Alfred Roth and Lloyd Shapley for developing algorithms which take care of the problem how to plan an efficient allocation of "items" (kidneys, study placements, jobs?) when there is no really existing market. Matching characteristics of donor kidneys to the characteristics of people needing a donor kidney is the same thing as matching characteristics of people in need of work to available guaranteed jobs. We do not always need markets (economists call the work of the Roth and Shapley "market design" but it really is "non market design"). Here, this is just a suggestion but the point is that there are efficient non-market allocation systems, too;

---

[5] Unless, as the Fed does in the USA, QE also consists of purchases of assets from pension funds and not just from MFI banks it will not directly result in an increase of M-3 money, as the banks have to transfer the new money to their amount of "reserve money", which does not count as M-3.

iii. Combining this information yields that there is quite a lot of work to do. Not doing anything might solve the problem, too, in the course of time, as the East German example shows. When there are no working age people left, the unemployment problem is solved! But this clearly is not the preferred solution. The starting point has of course to be the realization that elevated unemployment is totally inefficient as well as personally debilitating. And, sad to have to add this, it does not lead to moral and ethical improvement (discipline!, discipline!) of a country but, if anything, to the opposite. And the realization that the problem is, in the EU, massive. It is about tens of millions of additional jobs while the political surrounding has, compared with the situation described by Mitchell and Muysken, hardened. In that sense, we're indeed in a new epoch.

Demographics are, however, a countervailing power when it comes to labor supply. As the Japanese example shows, an ageing population is however also less spend thrift than a young population and a situation as the opposite of stagflation can ensue: relatively low unemployment in combination with a continuous deflationary pressure because of declining domestic demand. Lower inequality and policies aimed at less priority for asset purchases and private lending (houses!) may help these policies.

References

Coppola, F. (2015) *The insane Eurocrats. Coppola Comment.* 13 September. http://www.coppolacomment.com/2015/09/the-insane-eurocrats.html Retrieved 14 September 2015.

ECB (2013) "Output, demand and the labor market." *Monthly Bulletin* April 2015 pp 47-49. https://www.ecb.europa.eu/pub/pdf/other/mb201304_focus05.en.pdf Retrieved 20 September 2015.

Eurostat (2015) *Labor Force Survey 2014.* http://ec.europa.eu/eurostat/documents/2995521/6800423/3-27042015-AP-EN.pdf/08a0ac51-c63d-44d0-ad29-248127fd01c3 Retrieved 16 September 2015.

Friedman, M. (1967) "The case for abolishing the draft – and substituting for it an all volunteer army." *New York Times Magazine* 114-119. 14 May.

Hendry, D. and G. E. Mizon (2014) "Why DSGE models crash during crises." *Vox-eu* 18 June. http://www.voxeu.org/article/why-standard-macro-models-fail-crises. Retrieved 14 September 2015.

Henshall, D. (2015) *Labor market flows*. Office for National Statistics. May 2015. http://www.ons.gov.uk/ons/dcp171766_403357.pdf Retrieved 15 September 2015.

Knibbe, M. (2013) "A Eurozone NAIRU-fallacy of composition?" *World Economics Association newsletter* 3-6 December 2013 p. 8.
http://www.worldeconomicsassociation.org/files/newsletters/Issue3-6.pdf   Retrieved 17 September 2015.

Knibbe, M. (2015) "Labor market flows and the musical chairs economy." *Real world economics blog* 15 October 2015. https://rwer.wordpress.com/2015/10/24/labour-market-flows-and-the-musical-chairs-economy/ Retrieved 4 February 2016.

Milanovic, B. (2015) "For whom the wall fell? A balance sheet of the transition to capitalism." *The Globalist* http://www.theglobalist.com/for-whom-the-wall-fell-a-balance-sheet-of-the-transition-to-capitalism/ Retrieved 18 September 2015.

Mitchell, W. and J. Muysken (2009) "Full employment abandoned: shifting sands and policy failures." *Working paper 08-01*, Center of Full Employment and Equity.

Pissarides, C.A. (2007) "Unemployment and hours of work: the North Atlantic experience revisited." *International Economic Review* 48-1 pp. 1-36.

Tong, L. (2015) NAIRU *Estimation of 28 EU-member States*. Master's Thesis Submitted to Prof. Dr. Wolfgang K. Härdle and Prof. Dr. Weining Wang, Ladislaus von Bortkiewicz Chair of Statistics. C.A.S.E. - Centre for Applied Statistics and Economics. Berlin: Humboldt-Universitätzu.

Villa P. (1995) "Chômage et salaries en France sur longue période." *Economie et Statistique* 282, 1995. pp. 47-64.
http://www.persee.fr/web/revues/home/prescript/article/estat_0336-1454_1995_num_282_1_5953 Retrieved 28 August 2015.

Conclusions

Victor A. Beker and Beniamino Moro

The hard core of the Conference was devoted to discuss the perspectives of the euro. In this respect, there were three kinds of conclusions. The first one belongs to those (Marelli and Signorelli; Vleeschhouwer and Koning; Duarte and de Melo Modenesi) who think that the EMU is an imperfect but viable project. The second one to those (Sapir; Lima; Papadimitriou, Nukiforos and Zezza) who think that it has no viability and that the sooner it is dismantled the better. Finally, there is a third group of papers (Ferlito; Knibbe) that do not assume a clear position on this argument, but they analyze some side-effects of the crisis.

Among the first group the main conclusions that emerged are:

i. Radical reforms are needed to implement governance in the EU institutions – in particular to guarantee a viable monetary union and favor real convergence of its economies – as well as changes in the current macroeconomic policies;
ii. Macroeconomic stabilization and macroeconomic imbalances can be improved by a supranational government. The only, but certainly not insignificant, obstacle seems to be that politicians and voters may not be willing to transfer their authority to that government;
iii. The path for a sustained growth recovery in the Euro area goes through unconventional monetary policies, complemented by a coordinated fiscal policy, flexible and counter-cyclical in periods of economic downturns, coupled with adequate institutional reforms that foster credit markets, encourage private and public investments in the long term and reduce regional asymmetries. Additionally, a more robust and integrated financial supervisory framework (not only on banking but also on capital, insurance and pension markets) would contribute to reduce negative spillovers from financial volatility episodes, break the sovereign-bank "doom loop" and bring more financial stability to the zone.

The European crisis

Among the second group, the main conclusions are:

i. Europe is still decades away from a federalist future, and may be it would never be reached. So, it is time now to dismantle the EMU, and if possible to do it in a cooperative way;

ii. The idea of parallel currencies or parallel banking systems could be useful as transitional tools toward a general dismantling of the Eurozone, but certainly they are not stable solutions. A parallel currency issued by state-members will make local fiscal policy possible;

iii. Parallel currencies could also play a role in the context of a post-Euro situation, where the Euro itself could resurrect as a parallel currency for trade with non-zone countries.

The third group of papers concentrates on the mechanism that trigger a financial crisis (Ferlito) and on its consequences on the labor market (Knibbe).

The Organizers of the Conference and Editors of this e-book, Victor A. Beker and Beniamino Moro, share the first group main conclusions. In fact, we must not forget that most EU countries wanted the euro as a fundamental step of a process that in the long run should lead to greater and more significant political unity of Europe, and for that reason the euro was considered irreversible since its beginning.

This was decided because of both political as well economic reasons. Political reasons call back the impellent necessity for European countries not to repeat the tremendous disaster of two world wars combated in Europe in the past century. And, as long as the economic reasons are called for, let say what would happen if the euro were to disappear, which was already a matter of speculation in the recent European Great Crisis. A clear answer to that question was given by the president of the ECB, Mario Draghi, who in an interview to *Die Zeit* (15 January 2015) answered as follows: "If all countries were to start devaluing, prices would no longer be stable. Would the countries where complaints about reforms and fiscal consolidation are the loudest be better off exiting the euro area? They would still have to continue with their reforms! You cannot simply keep on devaluing a currency forever. It would simply lead to higher prices."

Conclusions

In light of all this, how can we redesign the Eurozone? In this regard, there is no other alternative than to strongly increase coordination of macroeconomic policy among EMU countries. Ultimately, such coordination should bring about the completion of the banking union and the start of a real fiscal union. This in turn requires a real political union, following the principle of "no taxation without representation". In the short run, what we need is monetary and fiscal expansion at the EU level. The ECB has started its quantitative easing programme, and that is for the better. However, we still need fiscal policy to be managed, or at least coordinated, at the EU level.

Anyway, the resilience of the Eurozone in the long-run depends on the continuing process of political unification, which must proceed hand in hand with the creation of a fiscal union. Such a political unification is needed, as pointed out by Paul De Grauwe, because the Eurozone has dramatically weakened the power and legitimacy of member States' governments, and left a vacuum in their place instead of creating a supranational government. This would imply the creation of a supranational fiscal risk sharing mechanism that could insure European countries against very severe downturns like the recent Great Crisis.

The European crisis

About the editors and authors

Victor A. Beker is Professor of Economics at the University of Belgrano and the University of Buenos Aires, Argentina. He has been Director of the Economics Department at the University of Belgrano and of the Economics Programme at the University of Buenos Aires. He got several prizes for his works in Economics. Former Associate Editor of the Journal of Economic Behavior and Organization. Author of several Economics books and papers. He is co-author of *Modern Financial Crises*, Springer, 2016.

Beniamino Moro is Professor of Economics, University of Cagliari (Italy). He has been Dean of the Faculty of Economics and Director of the Department of Economics at the same university. He was a member of the Presidential board of the Italian Economic Society. He is the author of several Economics books and co-author of *Modern Financial Crises*, Springer, 2016. He also published several articles on the recent Great Crisis and the European debt and banking crises.

Enrico Marelli is Full Professor of Economic Policy (since 1997) at the University of Brescia (Italy). He has been the Deputy Dean at the Faculty of Economics of the same University (2002–07). From 2012 until 2015 he was the local co-ordinator of the research project "The Political Economy of Youth Unemployment" (within the EU 7th Framework Programme, Marie Curie Actions "People", International Research Staff Exchange Scheme – Project IRSES GA-2010-269134), in co-operation with the Universities of Naples-Parthenope, Perugia, Brunel (London) and the Higher School of Economics (Moscow). He was awarded the best paper prize 2013 of the *European Journal of Development Research* (with M. Signorelli and M.T. Choudhry) for the paper "The Impact of the Financial Crises on Female Labour": http://www.palgrave-journals.com/ejdr/ejdr_best_paper_prize.html.

Marcello Signorelli is Associate Professor (with eligibility to Full Professor) of Economic Policy, Department of Economics, University of Perugia (Italy). Member of the Academic Senate of the University of Perugia. Executive Committee member of the "*Italian Association for the Study of Comparative Economic Systems*". Advisory Board Member (past-President) of the

"*European Association for Comparative Economic Studies*". He has been President of the *European Association for Comparative Economic Studies* during the period 2010-2012. Between 2012 and 2015 he has been the local coordinator of the research project: "*The Political Economy of Youth Unemployment*" (within the EU 7th Framework Programme, Marie Curie Actions "People", International Research Staff Exchange Scheme – Project IRSES GA-2010-269134), in co-operation with the Universities of Brescia, Naples-Parthenope, Brunel (London) and the Higher School of Economics (Moscow). Since 2012 he is Member of the Research Project "Mixture and Latent Variable Models for Causal Inference and Analysis of Socio-Economic Data" (FIRB 2012 – "Futuro in Ricerca" – MIUR, Italian Government).

Tara Koning (1992) has obtained a master's degree in Economics and Business degree with a specialisation in Policy Economics from Erasmus School of Economics, located in Rotterdam. While pursuing this degree, she has worked as a teaching assistant, teaching courses in applied statistics, and teaching middle school children introductory courses in economics. At the same time, she has pursued a bachelor's degree in Dutch law. She is currently working for the department of Econometrics and the department of Applied Economics of the Erasmus School of Economics, coordinating courses in applied statistics and econometrics.

Tom Vleeschhouwer (1993) has obtained a master's degree in Economics and Business degree with a specialisation in Policy Economics from Erasmus School of Economics, located in Rotterdam. While pursuing this degree, he has worked as a teaching assistant, teaching courses in mathematics and applied statistics. At the same time, he has pursued a bachelor's degree in Dutch law. He is currently working for the department of Private International Law of the Erasmus School of Law.

Jacques Sapir is professor of economics at EHESS-Paris and Director of the CEMI Research Centre at EHESS. He is also the director of IRSES-FMSH. Since 2004 he is associate professor at the *Moskovskaya Shkola Ekonomiki* (MSE-MGU). A specialist of Soviet Union and after 1992 of Russia at first, he worked for the CEMI-EHESS and the National Foundation for Defence Studies (French government). He has published several books

About the editors and authors

on the Soviet/Russian economy but also on economics and geo-strategy. Specializing since 1988 on financial and economic crisis (with an emphasis on banking and financial systems) and was particularly involved in the forecasting of the Russian financial crash of August 1998. From 1991 he led a CEMI research group set-up in coordination with the Russian Institute of Economic Forecasting (INP-RAN). Since fall 2007, he has delivered several lectures and presentations on this topic in front of selected audiences including Russian, Ukrainian, Venezuelan, South-African and Korean decision-makers. He published several papers in academic journals as well as several books on the EMU crisis. He is a well-known French blogger, his blog having more than 250.000 connections a month: http://russeurope.hypotheses.org

Cristiano Boaventura Duarte is an Economist, Ph.D. in progress since 2015, Institute of Economics, Federal University of Rio de Janeiro (UFRJ) and Analyst of the Central Bank of Brazil (BCB) since 2010. Between 2006 and 2010 he worked as an Economist for the Gas & Power Department of Petrobras. Between 2005 and 2006 he was Analyst at the Labor Statistics Department of the Brazilian Institute of Geography and Statistics (IBGE).

André de Melo Modenesi is Associate Professor at the Institute of Economics of the Federal University of Rio de Janeiro (UFRJ) since 2009 and researcher of the Scientific and Technological Development Council (CNPq). He has been Director of the Brazilian Keynesian Association (AKB) between 2012 and 2014. Researcher at the Institute for Applied Economic Research (IPEA) between 2007 and 2009 and between 2012 and 2013. Professor at the Fluminense Federal University (UFF) between 2001 and 2003.

Dimitri B. Papadimitriou is president of the Levy Economics Institute of Bard College, Annandale-on-Hudson, New York, and Executive VP and Jerome Levy Professor of Economics of Bard College. Author and co-author of many papers in academic journals, edited volumes and Levy Institute publications. He is contributor and editor of 13 books.

Michalis Nikiforos is a research scholar at the Levy Economics Institute of Bard College, Annandale-on-Hudson, New York. His research interests include macroeconomic theory and policy, distribution of income, the theory of economic fluctuations, political economy, and economics of Monetary Union. He has published papers in several peer reviewed-journals and he has co-authored many policy reports on the prospects of the U.S. and European economies.

Gennaro Zezza is Associate professor in Economics at the University of Cassino, Italy, and a research scholar at the Levy Economics Institute of Bard College, Annandale-on-Hudson, New York. His main interest is on macroeconomic modeling. Author or co-author of papers in academic journals, edited volumes, and most model-based analysis of the U.S. and the Greek economy at the Levy Institute.

Gerson P. Lima is Doctor in Economic Theory by the University of Paris X (1992). Before assuming the academic position he was a leading real world economist at some private companies and public institutions until leaving the Civil Office of the President. After the doctorate degree he became Titular Professor of macroeconomics (graduation and post-graduation) at the Federal University of Paraná, where academic related activities included serving the Economics Teaching Committee of the Federal Government, the National Association of Post-graduate Courses in Economics, and the Regional Professional Economists Council as vice-President. Retired from the Federal University of Paraná, he published some more papers. His major contribution to economic theory and teaching, the textbook *Economics, Money and Political Power* (in Portuguese), is successfully used to teach real world Economics to non-economics students at private colleges.

Carmelo Ferlito is Adjunct Faculty Member at the INTI International College Subang (Subang Jaya, Malaysia), where he teaches *History of Economic Thought* and *Microeconomic Theory and Policy* for the University of Wollongong Programme. He is also Senior Fellow at the Institute for Democracy and Economic Affairs (IDEAS), a pro free-market think tank based in Kuala Lumpur, Malaysia. He obtained his M.Sc. in Economics in 2003 at the University of Verona (Italy), where he obtained also his Ph.D. in Economic History in 2007. From 2004 to 2009 he cooperated as teaching assistant with the chairs of Economic History at the University of Verona and of History of Economic Thought at the Salento University and University of

About the editors and authors

Macerata (Italy). In 2011 he moved to Malaysia where he became a member of the Malaysian Economic Association, the Southern Economic Association, the Ludwig von Mises Institute and the Society for the Development of Austrian Economics. His research activity is mainly oriented to develop a new version of the Austrian Theory of Business Cycle and of the Austrian Theory of Capital, with a special focus on the role of expectations and the application of the hermeneutical approach to economics, following the example of Ludwig M. Lachmann. Carmelo Ferlito's latest book is *Phoenix Economics. From Crisis to Renascence* (Nova Publishers, New York 2013). In total he published five books and more than thirty papers on different academic journals. The full list of his publication is available here: https://newinti.academia.edu/CarmeloFerlito.

Merijn Knibbe is an economic historian. His present work focuses on the relation between the concepts used in economic models and those used by economic statisticians and on capital markets in early modern Friesland (sixteenth century). He lives in Leeuwarden, The Netherlands.

CPSIA information can be obtained
at www.ICGtesting.com
Printed in the USA
BVOW10s0551140916
462053BV00017B/17/P